BALLAD
OF THE
BULLET

Forrest Stuart

BALLAD
OF THE
BULLET

*Gangs, Drill Music, and the
Power of Online Infamy*

PRINCETON UNIVERSITY PRESS

PRINCETON AND OXFORD

Published by Princeton University Press

41 William Street, Princeton, New Jersey 08540

6 Oxford Street, Woodstock, Oxfordshire OX20 1TR

press.princeton.edu

First paperback printing, 2021

Paperback ISBN 978-0-691-20649-3

Cloth ISBN 978-0-691-19443-1

ISBN (e-book) 978-0-691-20008-8

The Library of Congress has catalogued the cloth edition as follows:

Names: Stuart, Forrest, author.

Title: Ballad of the bullet : gangs, drill music, and the power of online infamy / Forrest Stuart.

Description: Princeton : Princeton University Press, [2020] | Includes bibliographical references and index.

Identifiers: LCCN 2019036488 (print) | LCCN 2019036489 (ebook) | ISBN 9780691194431 | ISBN 9780691200088 (ebook)

Subjects: LCSH: Gangs—Illinois—Chicago. | Violence—Illinois—Chicago. | Social media—Illinois—Chicago. | Technology and youth—Social aspects. | Urban poor—Illinois—Chicago.

Classification: LCC HV6439.U7 C387 2020 (print) | LCC HV6439.U7 (ebook) | DDC 364.106/60977311—dc23

LC record available at https://lccn.loc.gov/2019036488

LC ebook record available at https://lccn.loc.gov/2019036489

British Library Cataloging-in-Publication Data is available

Editorial: Meagan Levinson, Jacqueline Delaney

Production Editorial: Terri O'Prey

Text Design: Leslie Flis

Jacket/Cover Design: Karl Spurzem

Production: Erin Suydam

Publicity: Maria Whelan, Kathryn Stevens

Copyeditor: Madeleine Adams

Cover photograph: *The Washington Post* / Getty Images

This book has been composed in Sabon LT Std and Gotham Narrow

Printed in the United States of America

Contents

■ ■ ■

Preface

■ ■ ■

On a warm September evening in 2012, eighteen-year-old Joseph Coleman rode a bike down a tree-lined street on Chicago's South Side. A nondescript Ford sedan slowly approached. Without warning, someone inside the car fired seven shots at the young man, striking him as he tried to flee. Pronounced dead at a nearby hospital, Coleman had become the latest victim in the city's infamous gang violence.

I first heard about Coleman's death two years later, during conversations with Chicago teenagers. At the time, I was directing an after-school program designed to help South Side youth cope with neighborhood violence. Coleman's murder was just one of the local shootings they shared with me. The more I dug into the details, however, the more I knew something was different. As I would learn, the attack on Coleman had escalated on social media, across platforms like YouTube, Twitter, and Instagram. Over several months, Coleman—an aspiring rapper known as "Lil JoJo"—had been embroiled in an online, musical war of words with a rival gang. He sparked hostilities when he uploaded a homemade music video to YouTube. The grainy footage features the teen and a dozen shirtless friends holding a small arsenal of pistols and machine guns, taunting their rivals. Then, Coleman uploaded a second video. This one showed him driving through rival gang territory, taunting his enemies through the open window of a passing car. As the death threats poured in, Coleman brazenly advertised his physical location on Twitter, daring his enemies to come find him and make good on their word. Four hours later, he was dead. His rivals used social media to celebrate the killing, kicking off more rounds of retaliatory shootings that continue to this day.

Even more surprising than the role of social media in Coleman's death were local teens' responses to it. They were simultaneously terrified and enthralled. In one moment, they worried about getting trapped in the crossfire of this new brand of gang warfare. But in the next moment, they devoured any and every piece of related digital content. Teens huddled around their phones, debating which gang was "really" the most violent. They kept a running "score," tallying who had buried the most bodies. I noticed a morbid similarity between their giddy discussions of gang violence and their debates about favorite professional basketball players. But instead of comparing stat lines and three-point percentages, they discussed gunplay and homicide.

These teens are far from unique in their obsession. As the details surrounding Coleman's murder went public, audiences across Chicago, the United States, and the globe flocked to social media to witness the still-raging rivalry for themselves.[1] The half dozen videos bearing Coleman's name drew tens of millions of views, "likes," and comments. Practically overnight, dozens of websites and blogs sprang up to chronicle online feuds and forecast the next street-corner battle. Hoping to claim some of that attention for themselves, scores of Chicago youth—particularly gang-associated teens—began emulating Coleman's online content.[2] Consider this: Of the estimated 45 gang factions in the six square miles surrounding Coleman's Englewood neighborhood, a staggering 31 of them—roughly 69 percent—had uploaded one of these inflammatory music videos to YouTube by 2016.[3] This means that for every two blocks there is at least one group of teens creating violent, gang-related content. The race to attract clicks didn't stay confined to Chicago for very long. Media outlets in New York, Los Angeles, London, Paris, and other global hubs report similar trends.[4] Some of these cities have responded by launching "social media policing units," arresting young people based (sometimes solely) on their social media activity.[5] National intelligence agencies, including the FBI, are developing artificial intelligence (AI) and digital surveillance tools to aggressively investigate and incarcerate them.

As I watched these audiences variously consume, celebrate, and decry this online content, I couldn't help but ask: How had this all begun? Who were these young men, and why were they so willing to risk death and arrest for something as fleeting as a YouTube video or Instagram photo? Why did their online behavior so captivate the public? And how was it affecting social life in their surrounding communities?

In 2014, I set out to find answers. I started interviewing young people in my after-school program, and in communities across the South Side. As enlightening as these initial conversations were about the dynamics of teenage consumption, it was a frustratingly partial picture. After hundreds of conversations, I still didn't know much at all about the whys and hows of production. I still hadn't spoken to a single one of the young men who were creating such startling content. This would all change one afternoon, during a fortuitous interview with a young man named Ryan, who had been enrolled in my program. Ryan disclosed that his nineteen-year-old brother, known on the street as Zebo, was a member of a gang faction responsible for filming and uploading some of Chicago's most watched

music videos. They called themselves CBE, short for Corner Boys Entertainment, or simply the Corner Boys.[6] The thirty or so young men controlled a roughly four-block territory located a couple of miles away in
the Taylor Park neighborhood. Over the span of just two years, the Corner Boys had attracted millions of views and tens of thousands of social
media followers from around the world. I was already familiar with CBE's
online content; their videos were a constant topic of conversation in my
after-school program. I knew that if I truly wanted to get my head around
this issue, I had to go to the source. I had to talk to the Corner Boys.

I asked Ryan to broker a meeting.

Three months later, I sat in the living room of one of the Corner Boys'
central figures—a dreadlocked, fast-talking nineteen-year-old named AJ.
For nearly four hours, we discussed a range of topics—from AJ's initial
decision to upload violent content to how it had transformed his daily
life. He introduced me to other key members of CBE, encouraging them
to talk about their own experiences with social media, gang life, and violence. I met Dominik, a stoic teen who likes to flash the latest street wear
trends on his Instagram account. I spoke with Adam, known in the neighborhood for his quick wit and controversial Twitter profile. I sat down
with Xavier, the most well known of the Corner Boys. The lanky twenty-
year-old was quick to show off his recent YouTube music video, which
had surpassed two million views. After the introductions, AJ encouraged
me to stick around for a few more hours to watch them record their newest music video. As they wrapped up for the evening, he invited me to come
back the next day.

And so began my relationship with the Corner Boys. Over the next two
years, I spent virtually every day with these young men, shadowing them
throughout their daily lives.[7] Each morning, I made the half-hour drive
from my home near downtown to Taylor Park. We'd spend hours watching music videos, discussing gang rivalries, shooting dice, and generally
hanging out until late in the evening, sometimes past sunrise. The time I
had devoted to the Corner Boys' younger siblings and family members in
after-school programs opened the door to their world. But remaining there,
for as long as I did, required real give-and-take. These young men were
providing access and information as a kind of favor to me. And they
vaguely wanted something in return.

Following that first day in AJ's apartment, several of them asked me to
drive them to early morning court hearings. Others approached me for
rides to work, to see family, and visit probation officers. Without cars and
licenses, and fearing attacks on public transportation, they had few safe

options for moving around the city. That was, until I showed up. I soon became their go-to option—a role I was happy to play. They had invited me in and entrusted me with their stories; I wanted to give back however I could. I started responding to calls at all hours of the day and night, from various young men desperate to get across town. I drove them to see grandmothers, girlfriends, and sons. I accompanied them to funerals, baby showers, and birthday parties. And as their online popularity gained momentum, we packed into my car for road trips across the United States— to cities like Indianapolis, St. Louis, and Atlanta—where they met up with online collaborators, fans, and lovers. Back in Taylor Park, we'd spend hours in my parked car, listening to music and watching online videos as we escaped the sticky summer heat and chilling winter winds. Before I knew it, my passenger seat had become something of a confessional—a place where they shared hopes and fears and dreams that they otherwise hid from the public eye. I used an audio recorder and notetaking application on my phone to preserve their words.[8]

The more entwined I became in the Corner Boys' lives, the more deeply I came to care for them. The more I cared for them, the more tension I felt between my professional and personal responsibilities. As a researcher, I was trying to understand the Corner Boys, not change them. But as a violence prevention worker, and as someone increasingly invested in their well-being, it felt irresponsible to sit idly by when they engaged in harmful and self-destructive acts. I eventually found a middle (if not entirely satisfactory) path forward. When I heard about or witnessed problematic behaviors, I refrained from judgment and paternalism. Instead I listened closely, probing their underlying feelings and rationales, allowing them to be the authorities about their own lives. Sometimes I created distractions and alternatives. One summer, I made a standing offer to pick them up and get them out of the neighborhood whenever their rivals attempted a drive-by shooting. I provided lunch, dinner, and other diversions for as long as it took for the neighborhood to cool off, returning only after their talk of retaliation had died down. As I watched online audiences applaud the Corner Boys' violent personas and encourage ever riskier behaviors, I committed to serve as a counterweight. I actively celebrated their noncriminal identities and accomplishments that they withheld from social media—a newborn son, a month of sobriety, a high grade on a school assignment. I also leveraged my social networks to find them jobs, re-enroll them in school, and help them recover from addictions, access healthcare, and fulfill family obligations. I even supported some of their efforts to abandon their violent online personas by uploading more nonviolent content. I tapped my own background in audio production and arts pro-gramming to support alternative modes of creative expression.

Across all of these moments, I found the answers I was looking for, and far more that I hadn't anticipated. The pages that follow recount what I learned. For generations, society has denied young black men a seat at the table, disregarding their voices while demonizing their mere existence. They've been labeled urban predators and menaces to society. But now, thanks to the proliferation of social media, these young people have found a new way to be seen and heard, if only by twisting these age-old stereo-types to suit their own needs. In Taylor Park and across the globe, gang-associated youth are exploiting digital platforms to commodify urban vio-lence and cash in on the public's long-standing fascination with ghetto poverty. In the process, they're forging a new, if often dangerous, path-way toward upward mobility, self-worth, and social support. And as they jockey for online infamy, they're reshaping everyday life in their commu-nities, forcing us to reconsider many of our taken-for-granted ideas about gangs, violence, and urban disadvantage.

It's easy to jump to conclusions when we hear stories about teens like Joseph Coleman, or when we watch videos from groups like the Corner Boys. Unfortunately, most of those conclusions are wrong. Yes, these young men brazenly celebrate crime and violence, but they're doing it for rea-sons we don't often consider. Behind their online bravado is a desperate attempt to build a better future for themselves, to feel loved, to be seen as someone special. In that respect, they're flocking to social media for some of the same reasons as everyone else. They're just doing it under drasti-cally different conditions—conditions that should provoke our conster-nation more than these young people do. Their online behaviors are in-separable from an offline world scarred by immense structural violence. Like all youth, they're just trying to live their lives within the possibilities and limits of the world we've created for them.

BALLAD
OF THE
BULLET

Introduction

■ ■ ■

It was about 5 AM when I left my apartment in Chicago's South Loop neighborhood. I merged onto the Dan Ryan Expressway and pointed my car south. The summer sunrise loomed just below the horizon to the east, so the roads were still clear. The highway took me past familiar landmarks—the ominous Cook County criminal courthouse, the modern architecture of the Illinois Institute of Technology, the dark silhouette of the White Sox stadium. After a short drive, I exited the highway and pulled onto the quiet streets of Taylor Park—one of the city's struggling black neighborhoods.

A generation ago, this area would have been buzzing with activity, even at this hour. Residents clad in work attire would be making their way to the train platform and shopping district. They'd likely wrinkle their noses at the acrid clouds from awakening smokestacks. Today, those sights and smells are distant memories. Once the sun rises, the only thing that will fill the air are the white plumes of cottonwood seeds, unleashed by the overgrown trees that are reclaiming the neighborhood, one abandoned lot at a time.

I turned onto one of Taylor Park's side streets, stopping in front of a collection of dull brick apartment buildings—home to dozens of the neighborhood's poorest residents. I spotted a familiar young man sitting alone on the curb, clad in his weathered black hoodie and faded jeans. I knew I'd find Junior here. After his mother kicked him out of her home, he had been sleeping in one of the apartment stairwells. If Junior noticed me, he didn't show it. As usual, his eyes were glued to the cracked screen of his iPhone. In these early morning hours, it cast a dull blue light on his dreadlocks, framing his sharp but boyish features. A couple of dozen facial hairs curled around his chin—a hopeful attempt at growing a beard. Junior was eighteen years old but looked much closer to fifteen. Born with a serious heart condition, he was small for his age, weighing 130 pounds at most. But it would be a mistake to underestimate him on account of his size. Until recently, Junior had been one of the most feared stick-up kids in the neighborhood. What he lacked in physical presence, he made up for in his record of robberies. His arms, though thin, were covered in scratchy tattoos. Some paid tribute to his gang faction—the Corner Boys. Others memorialized the friends he'd lost to gun violence and gang warfare.

Like so many other young South Siders, Junior had recently devoted himself to a new passion—recording homemade music videos and uploading them to social media platforms such as YouTube and Facebook. In these uploads, Junior and his fellow Corner Boys boast of violent crimes, taunt rivals, and brag about drug profits. It's been a lucrative formula. In the previous few months, Junior's online notoriety had skyrocketed. As his content traveled the globe, he began receiving messages from viewers and fans hoping to follow his lead and build their own online fame. Some invited him to collaborate, even offering to pay him to make appearances in their music videos and Instagram photos. This, in fact, was why the two of us were up before sunrise today. A couple of weeks earlier, Junior had received a Facebook message from an adoring fan in Los Angeles, who offered to fly Junior there to meet with him. He asked Junior to help him increase his own online following and launch his own online career. If all went according to plan, they'd record music videos together and plaster their photos all over social media. To seal the deal, the fan sent Junior an eight-hundred-dollar down payment and bought him a roundtrip flight to LAX.

When Junior invited me to tag along, I immediately bought myself a ticket. I even volunteered to drive us to the airport. When we arrived at Midway, I saw a side of Junior that few others ever see. He grinned with childlike wonder as we checked in for our flight, passed through security, and boarded the plane. His stoic demeanor gave way to a wide-eyed awe. I couldn't help smiling too. It was a day of firsts: his first time in an airport, his first time on a plane, one of his first times ever stepping foot outside Chicago. As I watched him take his seat, fumble with the seatbelt, and upload a final selfie photo to Instagram, I was struck by the weight of what I was witnessing. Here was one of the most disadvantaged youth, from one of the most distressed communities, enjoying a level of celebrity that few people—regardless of background—will ever experience. By most accounts, the future looks bleak for someone like Junior. Yet, from the stairwells of a low-income apartment building, this homeless, unemployed, gang-associated young man had managed to build a global brand, bringing him new levels of income and admiration.

Junior isn't alone. In places like Taylor Park, viable options in both the formal and informal economies are steadily drying up. But in the void, young residents like the Corner Boys have developed new, creative, *online* strategies for making ends meet. Specifically, they've learned to exploit the unique affordances provided by digital social media to capitalize on a burgeoning market for urban gang violence (or, more accurately, a market for the *representation* of urban gang violence). They're doing so through the creation and dissemination of what has become known as "drill music." Drill music—which, in slang terms, translates to "shooting music"—is an emerging genre of hyperviolent, hyperlocal, DIY-style gangsta rap that claims to document street life and violent criminality.[1] Through music videos and other social media uploads, these "drill rappers"—often referred to simply as "drillers"—compete on a global stage to prove that they're more ruthless, more delinquent, and more authentic than their competitors.[2] In a perverse system of benefits, the victors receive a range of spoils, including cash, housing, guns, sex, and, for a select few, a ticket out of poverty. The rest, however, can end up behind bars, seriously injured, or dead. Known for little else but their stigma, these young men have found an innovative way to package and sell it, all in the hope of escaping their desperate conditions.

WELCOME TO THE ONLINE ATTENTION ECONOMY

Drill's sudden appearance and spread across the internet caught most of the world by surprise. But it's only surprising if we look at it in a vacuum. When we consider it in the context of broader social, economic, and technological shifts, the production and dissemination of hyperviolent content becomes remarkably legible. Predictable even. It's what happens when the digital economy and urban poverty collide.[3]

Nowadays, it's something of a cliché to say that technology—particularly digital social media—is transforming society. In 2018, two-thirds of American adults had Facebook accounts and nearly 95 percent of young people used YouTube.[4] By the year 2027, an estimated 1 in 3 American adults will transition to online platforms to support themselves financially.[5] What was once a technological fantasy has become a major source of entertainment, socialization, and employment. Unsurprisingly, social media platforms and related services now dominate the global economy. As recently as 2006, Exxon Mobile and General Electric were the world's largest companies, sitting atop a list of traditional manufacturing, transportation, and financial firms. A decade later, tech companies had completely taken over this list. By 2017, Apple, Alphabet (Google's parent company), Microsoft, Amazon, and Facebook ranked (in that order) as the five largest companies in the world.[6]

In the wake of the Great Recession, many commentators still consider the tech industry as one of the lone bright spots in an otherwise disappointing and unstable economy.[7] They applaud a range of online platforms for appearing to offer *all* people—whether rich, poor, black, or white—a new model for attaining financial and personal success within a precarious and competitive job market. More than anything else, social media are heralded for providing the public with the tools to become more entrepreneurial and "self-made."[8] This is perhaps most pronounced in the creative industries, where social media have massively democratized the means of cultural production. Once monopolized by traditional media corporations and their gatekeepers, the power to create, disseminate, and profit from original content has been transferred into the hands of everyday people. Today, freelance journalists use Twitter to disseminate op-eds and political commentary. Aspiring fashion designers show off their latest creations on Instagram. Independent musicians use YouTube to debut original songs and videos. The list of amateur cultural producers grows by the day.

But with so many people engaging social media in this way, how does someone go about distinguishing their own self-brand from everyone else trying to do the same? How do they make their own content more visible and attractive than their competitors? Consider the difficulty of standing out on a platform like YouTube. In a single year, YouTube's 1.3 billion users—roughly one-third of the earth's internet users—uploaded 210 billion hours of video to the platform.[9] That's the equivalent of four hundred hours of content uploaded *every minute*. Although digital content is virtually endless, the time and energy necessary to consume it is finite. This asymmetry has given rise to what is loosely referred to as the "online attention economy"—a competitive field where cultural producers vie for the eyes and ears of audiences.[10] In today's social media age, attention has become a scarce, valuable, and quantifiable resource. Each social media platform offers its own metrics for keeping track of the winners and losers: Twitter and Instagram have "followers," YouTube has "views," Facebook has "friends." The higher these numbers, the more attention someone commands. The more attention they command, the greater their potential returns.

Open up a recent issue of *Vanity Fair*, *People*, or any other popular magazine and you'll find detailed articles about the attention economy's latest champion. The updated version of the American bootstraps story goes like this: Some otherwise "ordinary" person followed their passion, displayed their talents on social media, and amassed enough of a following to catch the attention of investors, tastemakers, and other industry gatekeepers, who paved the way to fame and fortune. The best-known examples have occurred in the world of music. Justin Bieber, the Chain-smokers, Carly Rae Jepsen, and Ed Sheeran—these are just a few of the chart-topping household names who built their careers on the backs of viral YouTube uploads. Like most companies operating in today's creative industries, record labels don't have the financial stability to take chances on unknown and untested artists anymore. With profit margins growing slimmer, they have to make much safer bets about what audiences want. By waiting to sign artists until they've built a sufficient online reputation, record execs capitalize on existing fan bases and brand recognition.[11]

As more industries use social media to "crowdsource" talent scouting, development, and marketing, aspiring creatives scramble to amass online popularity, or "micro-celebrity," among a large following.[12] The social media researcher Terri Senft originally coined the term to describe "a new style of online performance in which people employ webcams, video, audio, blogs, and social media networking sites to 'amp up' their popularity among readers, viewers, and those to whom they are linked online."[13] This typically involves "viewing friends or followers as a fan base; acknowledging popularity as a goal; managing the fan base using a variety of affinitive techniques; and constructing an image of self that can be easily consumed by others."[14] Despite popular tales of overnight stardom, cultivating micro-celebrity is no simple task. It demands a significant investment of time, energy, and other resources. Although the means of cultural production are now more open than ever, some people are better equipped to exploit them than others. As the communication scholar Brooke Erin Duffy importantly reminds us, "those who have been especially successful at channeling their passion projects into lucrative social media careers come from a position of relative privilege—by virtue of economic and/or social capital."[15] The most successful micro-celebrities benefit from financial investments from family and friends, social ties to industry powerbrokers, access to the latest technology, and the economic stability to forgo paid employment to concentrate on content creation.

The persistent unevenness in this supposedly open and democratized space raises important questions: How do people with less economic and social capital build micro-celebrity? How do they create and cultivate a self-brand that is compelling enough to stand out in the attention economy?

Perhaps the most influential study of cultural production by disadvantaged groups was written long before the arrival of social media. In *The Rules of Art*, the sociologist Pierre Bourdieu studied competition between nineteenth-century Parisian novelists, not online micro-celebrities. But his insights are still instructive.[16] Bourdieu discovered that novelists from lower-class backgrounds were forced to adopt alternative strategies to better compete against their more privileged bourgeois counterparts.[17] One of the most powerful strategies was to produce novels that exoticized their own already stigmatized group—a genre Bourdieu refers to as "autodestructive homages." Lacking the conventional resources for building profitable reputations, they peddled exaggerated stereotypes and parodies that aroused the voyeuristic desires of consumers. They effectively commodified their stigma, converting negative stereotypes—as backward, savage, and provincial people—into a new form of capital that they exchanged for financial success.

This strategy is even more seductive in the social media age. Amid the onslaught of banner ads, spam marketing, and disingenuous "click bait," consumers are increasingly on the hunt for cultural products that are both alluring and authentic.[18] As the cultural sociologist David Grazian notes, "the increased global commodification of popular culture creates an even stronger desire among many consumers for that which seems *un*commercial and therefore less affected by the strong hand of the marketplace."[19] Whether we're talking about music, food, or tourism, pursuit of the genuine article provides consumers with the opportunity to experience something that feels raw, unadulterated, and "real."[20] Today's cultural producers scramble to meet this demand by proving that they're more authentic in their online persona than their competitors are. For those with limited resources, this means finding new and innovative ways to demonstrate that they *truly* embody the negative stereotypes of their stigmatized social group.

Drillers epitomize this process. They use social media to create and disseminate morally charged caricatures of themselves as "black superpredators" in the hope of going viral, building micro-celebrity, and generating levels of financial success that would otherwise be impossible.[21] Among other things, this entails demonstrating an expertise with guns, displaying unwavering support from fellow gang members, flaunting close connections to well-known homicide victims, and challenging rivals. Having realized the age-old adage that "violence sells," drillers saturate their online content with the evidence necessary to authenticate the violent criminality that they proclaim in their music.[22] In the drill world, the young men perceived as most authentic are labeled as "real," "with the shits," or "in the field." If there is a dominant message running through virtually every drill song, video, and related content, it's an appeal to superior authenticity: I really do these violent deeds. I really use these guns. I really sell these drugs. My rivals, however, do none of this.

It's important to note that displaying violence online doesn't necessarily require engaging in offline violence; it merely requires a convincing performance. As I came to learn in my time with the Corner Boys, a good number of those perceived as the most authentically violent actually live lives that look nothing of the sort. Some of those known worldwide as homicidal drug lords reside in neighborhoods where such roles are no longer possible. At the same time, this gap between online performance and offline behavior has become the newest battleground between gang-associated youth. One of the most effective ways to build micro-celebrity is to publicly challenge the authenticity of more popular drillers. Art becomes reality when these disputes spill into the streets.

WHAT THE DRILL WORLD CAN TEACH US ABOUT POVERTY, INEQUALITY, AND VIOLENCE IN THE SOCIAL MEDIA AGE

Although drillers comprise only a small portion of neighborhood residents, their actions—both online and off—increasingly set the tone for local life. Today, it's impossible to understand the conditions in urban poor communities without considering the role and influence of digital cultural production. But once we do, we start to see just how antiquated many of our taken-for-granted ideas about urban poverty, inequality, and violence have become.

In the late twentieth century, the sociologist William Julius Wilson revolutionized public thinking about urban poverty. In *The Truly Disadvantaged* and *When Work Disappears*, Wilson refuted the conservative ideology that blamed poverty on residents' cultural failings and moral deficits.[23] He pointed to Chicago's South Side, directing attention to the deindustrialization, unemployment, and "social isolation" that separated black residents from the institutions, people, and opportunities in "mainstream society."[24] Wilson's research exposed the important connection between urban poverty and the decline of American manufacturing, the offshoring of blue-collar jobs, the steady erosion of organized labor, and other structural disruptions. Wilson provided a blueprint for renewed anti-poverty programs, calling on public leaders to build new and stronger connections between poor residents and the world beyond their isolated communities.

Three decades later, the economic currents that once swept factory jobs from Chicago's South Side to the global South have returned, this time in the form of digital platforms and communication technologies, rife with new profit models, market relations, and modes of interaction. In turn, urban poor residents are seizing the opportunity to do what web developers, entrepreneurs, and savvy business school graduates have been doing since the early years of social media—that is, to leverage their personal biographies and unique skill sets to become tomorrow's hottest internet sensation. In the process, these residents are challenging the antiquated definition of the ghetto as an unproductive, isolated place. Thanks to the proliferation of social media, these communities have become sites of intense cultural production. As a recent University of Chicago study found, black teens create more online content than any other racial group.[25] More than 10 percent of black teens upload music, videos, and other media on a daily basis, compared to a mere 5 percent of whites. As they generate and disseminate this content, they become increasingly embedded in social networks that extend well beyond their immediate neighborhood boundaries. As drillers' experiences reveal, however, poor black residents derive few, if any, of the benefits Wilson predicted. Instead, these cross-racial and cross-class interactions are often highly exploitative, and often end up exacerbating the worst conditions of urban poverty.

This irony suggests the need to reconsider the broader relationship between technology and inequality. In policy circles, it's increasingly common to talk of a digital divide separating Americans along race, class, and geographic lines.[26] Without access to fast and reliable internet technology, the story goes, the poor get poorer while the rich get tech jobs. Philanthropic organizations, local governments, and other techno-optimists spent the past decade or so clamoring to outfit classrooms and community centers with computers and tablets, as though the mere presence of technology would automatically improve socioeconomic outcomes. But as recent reports suggest, the digital divide may not be as wide as we once imagined. In fact, new data show that poor black youth are *more* glued to their smartphones, tablets, and social media accounts than their more privileged peers.[27] And yet, socioeconomic inequalities persist at historic levels.

Rather than think solely in terms of a digital divide, it's time to focus on what I've come to call *digital disadvantage*. If the digital divide refers to the quantitative disparities in *access* to technology, digital disadvantage refers to the qualitative differences in the *uses* and *consequences* of technology. When we study digital disadvantage, we ask how different people, with contrasting levels of privilege, fatefully engage with the same technology in their daily lives. This requires lengthy, detailed observations as they create, share, and otherwise engage with digital content. It also means paying close attention to how this engagement spills into seemingly unrelated social spheres like work, family, and community relations. Once we start thinking in terms of digital disadvantage, we stop treating technology as a panacea. We're forced to recognize that every new gadget, app, or online platform always "touches down" in a heavily stratified society, in ways that reinforce and even intensify long-standing inequities.

Drillers provide a unique (if admittedly extreme) window into three key realms of digital disadvantage.[28] First, these young men reveal how someone's position in the broader social, economic, and moral hierarchy necessarily structures their orientation to, and engagement with, any given technology. Drillers' production practices are, at the end of the day, a creative response to extreme poverty. Unlike aspiring micro-celebrities from more privileged backgrounds, these young men are unlikely to treat digital production as a mere hobby. For them, it's one of the few viable options for upward mobility and self-worth. Second, and directly related, drillers illustrate how someone's position on the socioeconomic ladder necessarily shapes the stakes of their technological engagements. Given their precarious conditions, they feel both the positive and negative consequences of their digital production far more profoundly than their more privileged counterparts do. For young men coming of age in impoverished and violent neighborhoods, micro-celebrity yields valuable resources for daily survival. A well-crafted online reputation can spell the difference between going hungry and securing a hot meal, between homelessness and a warm bed, and between abandonment and care. Yet, these benefits come with steep costs that include prison time and elevated risk of victimization. Third, drillers show how long-standing inequalities shape the ways outside parties read and react to different users of technology. Young men on the South Side certainly aren't the only Americans uploading photos full of firearms and lethal weaponry. Amid the heated gun control debate, white residents from across the country are uploading photo after photo of themselves brandishing pistols, shotguns, and assault rifles. Some even threaten extreme violence against politicians and fellow citizens. And yet, their online activities seldom produce much alarm. Their uploads are usually brushed off as "just for show," or even celebrated as a brave defense of gun rights. Meanwhile, young black men's photos with firearms and song lyrics about violence are treated as direct, unambiguous evidence of their offline behaviors and true identities.[29] Their Facebook posts land them in gang databases. Their rap verses show up in court as proof of violent tendencies. In short, the way our broader society treats a person's online displays of violence (or displays of just about anything, for that matter) is largely determined by preexisting stereotypes and power relations.

Finally, drillers offer a much-needed opportunity to understand urban gang violence in our social media age. This was one of my initial motivations when I heard about Joseph Coleman's murder. What role do digital media play in today's gang violence? More specifically, are they making our streets more dangerous? According to the vast majority of police and city leaders, platforms like Twitter, Facebook, and YouTube are propelling new, even more deadly gang feuds. In 2016, amid an unexpected (though temporary) upswing in homicides, the Chicago Police Department, Mayor's Office, and Crime Commission all blamed social media.[30] "It creates instantaneous conflict," declared the Crime Commission vice president Andrew Henning.[31] "We have deaths taking place, murders taking place, instantaneous[ly] after a video is posted." Journalists and academics overwhelmingly agree with Henning's position, treating social media platforms as merely an additional high-stakes breeding ground for gang wars.[32] "Conflicts between rival crews," write the sociologists Marta-Marika Urbanik and Kevin Haggerty, "have been *supplemented* and *exacerbated* by social media. New animosities emerge quickly and take on added seriousness."[33]

This narrative is as seductive as it is common. Unfortunately, it suffers from two major flaws. First, it's not based on much empirical evidence, if any. Systematic and reliable data on the causal relationship between social media and violent crime simply don't exist.[34] The Chicago Police Department—the agency responsible for collecting details on every violent crime in the city—isn't able to identify the suspect in a staggering 95 percent of shootings.[35] If they don't even know *who* pulled the trigger, how can they claim to know *why* they did it? How can they possibly assume the offender was responding to something posted online, and not acting on some other motive? Second, the popular narrative withers in the light of broader crime patterns. Even a cursory look at U.S. crime statistics shows that violence actually *decreased* to historic lows during the exact period when gang-associated youth *increased* their social media use.[36] In fact, over the past four decades, America experienced the greatest crime *reduction* in history.[37] Violent crime fell by half, from its peak rate of 758 per 100,000 in the 1990s to 369 per 100,000 in 2018.[38]

Don't get me wrong. I'm not denying the troubling relationship between social media and gang violence. As the Corner Boys taught me, however, the link between the two is far more complex, and far less inevitable, than most people imagine. It's certainly true that more gang violence is related to social media today than two decades ago. But this may only be due to the fact that social media didn't exist two decades ago. What's more, when gang-associated youth started picking up smartphones and posting antagonistic content, they did so in a particular historical moment, in response to very specific changes underway in urban poor communities.

The first thing to understand is that the gang conflicts supposedly amplified by social media simply don't occur in the number and intensity that they once did. In the 1980s and 1990s, street corners were the sites of deadly turf wars between large, heavily armed "corporate" gangs that fought for control over the crack market. When these markets eroded in the late 1990s, it caused these organizations to fracture and break apart. They simultaneously lost their customer base, shed their core economic purpose, and fell under the hammer of new police and prison policies.[39] "The open-air drug markets that were responsible for some of the most visible violence in the 1980s were forcibly shut down," writes the sociologist Patrick Sharkey.[40] "Street corners all over the country were no longer the sites of lethal gun battles to capture or retain prime real estate for the drug trade." The rapid disintegration of the crack economy and corporate gangs means that today's youth possess fewer of the *reasons* and *resources* that once drove violence. There are fewer gang hierarchies to climb. Fewer drug markets to fight over. Fewer guns available to do the fighting.[41] In short, and contrary to the popular imagination, the violent conflicts endemic to yesterday's street wars haven't been transposed to digital platforms.

Rather, the introduction of social media altered the very *meanings* and *functions* of gang violence. In the past, violence was primarily a tool for ensuring the success of the gangs' chief commodity—crack cocaine. As the means of cultural production digitize and democratize, gang violence has become a premier commodity in and of itself. Rather than use violence to control drug corners, today's gang-associated youth use online *displays* of violence to attract views, clicks, and online attention. But it's not long after a young man starts posturing on social media that rivals, and sometimes even strangers, start pressing him to prove his authenticity. Publicly humiliating a well-known driller is one of the most powerful strategies for building a reputation. Sometimes this entails physical attacks. More often, in the vast majority of cases, it unfolds via taunts and insults that stay confined to social media. In either case, the young man's public persona is put to the test. Is he really the hardest man on the block? Does he really use those guns in his photos? He faces a choice—either find a way to affirmatively answer these questions or risk being labeled an imposter. It's here that we find the mechanism linking social media and physical violence. The likelihood of future violence is primarily a function of the amount and depth of counterevidence required to refute a given challenge.

Offline confrontations are far more likely if these rebuttals bring feuding parties into shared physical space, or if the dispute damages (or threatens to damage) important social ties.

Unfortunately, it's impossible to calculate the exact percentage of total violence that's rooted in these online challenges. Again, the data simply don't exist yet. What I *can* say, however, is that participation in drill and its related digital practices greatly increases a young man's risk of exposure to violence. The bigger his name in the drill world, the larger the target on his back. The more he and his peers perform toughness on social media, the more they're expected to validate their authenticity. The larger their micro-celebrity, the steeper the costs if they refuse or fail to respond.[42] At the same time, we shouldn't treat violence as an automatic, predetermined outcome. Young men are as creative in avoiding physical showdowns as they are in displaying virtual toughness. Online, they deflect and de-escalate through witty ripostes and well-timed counters. Offline, they surround themselves with loyal defenders, constrict their mobility, and restructure their days to reduce the odds of assault. Of course, these efforts never reduce those odds to zero. And some of these strategies produce their own negative consequences, inhibiting success in other social spheres like work and education. It's hard for a young man to get to his job or school when the bus travels through neighborhoods full of people hoping to catch him while he's at his most vulnerable.

Taken together, these insights about digital production, social stratification, and gang violence suggest that it's time to start paying far more attention to *culture* when we talk about urban poverty and violence.[43] By culture, I mean art, music, and other symbolic modes of expression. For too long, we've focused narrowly on the material factors driving urban disadvantage. Whether it's social isolation amid the deindustrializing job market, a digital divide in the technology market, or gang disputes over the crack market, we've placed economic concerns at the very center of our thinking.[44] But seemingly "immaterial" objects like online videos and social media uploads matter, too. Sometimes even more so. Drillers' pursuit of online infamy shapes a host of outcomes that stretch well beyond their own lives and peer networks. As they traffic in sensational images of the ghetto, they actively reify the symbolic boundaries—the stereotypes and stigmas—that separate their communities from so-called normal, morally upstanding ones. When they're pressed to defend their online reputations in the streets, they end up reproducing the objective conditions—the shootings, arrests, and homicides—that set their communities apart and fuel the stereotypes they'll traffic in tomorrow.[45]

WHAT COMES NEXT?

In the pages that follow, I draw on my time alongside the Corner Boys to explain why, how, and with what consequences young people in disadvantaged neighborhoods are using digital social media to commodify violence and urban poverty. Chapter 1 puts the rise of drill, drillers, and their digital production practices into much-needed historical context. Chicago's South Side has undergone pronounced changes over the past couple of decades. With the erosion of the once-booming crack market and the fracturing of the associated gang structure, young men have come to feel alienated from previous modes of economic survival. After watching a handful of neighbors and classmates gain fame and fortune on the back of violent social media content, young men like the Corner Boys are making the transition from the drug economy to the online attention economy.

Chapter 2 details how drillers create, upload, and disseminate their digital products. Running counter to talk of a digital divide, these young men exhibit serious ingenuity in bending social media to their needs. Over time, they've learned to manipulate search engine algorithms and exploit big data analytics to attract ever more clicks and views. Given their limited resources, however, they're often forced to rely on the assistance of "support personnel," who are often located across the city, across the country, and across the globe. As it turns out, some of those people most responsible for producing popular images of Chicago's deadly streets have spent little, if any, time there. By exploring digital production practices, we begin to see that distant, non-gang-associated, and ostensibly "upstanding" citizens not only benefit from the commodification of ghetto stigma but are also implicated in its negative consequences.

Chapter 3 moves even deeper into drillers' production practices and daily lives, examining how they use social media platforms to validate their authenticity and build micro-celebrity. Leveraging the unique affordances of Instagram, Twitter, and Facebook, drillers upload hyperbolic displays of violence to corroborate the violent claims they make in their music videos. Once again, they depend on outside help in creating and disseminating this content. This often consists of bloggers and citizen journalists who host drill content on monetized websites and YouTube channels. Drillers also rely on friends and fellow gang members. In fact, the quest for micro-celebrity has become so central to neighborhood life that it has become one of the most powerful engines of group cohesion and discipline among gang-associated peers.

Chapter 4 explores the range of rewards drillers reap from building micro-celebrity, or "clout," as it's known on the streets of Chicago. Whereas most accounts dismiss micro-celebrity as providing few "real-world" returns, for those at the bottom of the social, economic, and moral hierarchy, it translates into significant benefits. What more privileged social media users might marginalize as "hope labor," drillers celebrate as one of the most practicable, stable, and dignifying options available. They typically refuse to give up these rewards without a fight.

Chapter 5 reveals the negative, sometimes lethal, costs of micro-celebrity. The shooting death of a Taylor Park teen provides a window into the various ways violent online content follows young people into offline spaces and contaminates social interactions. Drillers face a tragic irony: The more attention their social media uploads attract, the harder it is to avoid street violence, gang life, and the criminal justice system. On one side, they face competitors hoping to "steal" their clout. On the other side, they face police, prosecutors, and judges who rely on online content to arrest, convict, and sentence them.

Chapter 6 shifts the focus to drillers' audiences. I present some of the Corner Boys' ongoing relationships with wealthy, white, and noncriminal consumers who live outside of Taylor Park. I report on the Corner Boys' relationships with a well-to-do Beverly Hills man looking for street cred, a white law school student in search of transgressive sexual encounters, and a black pastor hoping to attract more young people into his aging congregation. Thanks to social media, individuals like these can now experience the ghetto with the simple click of a mouse. As with other forms of digital consumption, they can even have the ghetto (or, more accurately, the stereotypical ghetto denizen) delivered right to their doorstep, enjoying customized thrills from the comfort of home. As they do, they encourage these young men to continue their micro-celebrity practices while undermining the positive influence of mainstream social ties.

Chapter 7 brings the story full circle, examining the consumption practices of local South Side teens. For these youngsters, drillers and their content play a highly contradictory role. On the one hand, drill music makes life precarious. Merely listening to music videos, or clicking on social media uploads, exposes local teens to new dangers. On the other hand, drill music provides them with new and unexpected resources for socializing with peers, sidestepping street violence, and even charting positive courses of action.

The conclusion reflects on the broader lessons I learned during my time with the Corner Boys. I offer a number of interventions (both big and small) for addressing digital disadvantage in the lives of marginalized groups. Through compassionate programs and policies, digital technologies provide new opportunities to harness creativity and channel it for good.

Before continuing, I need to offer a few final caveats, along with a plea for readers' patience. First, I've organized these chapters thematically, not chronologically. I've chosen to anchor focus on the successive stages of digital production and consumption rather than my own serendipitous path of discovery. Traveling back and forth on the timeline means offering enough background for the discussion at hand, and returning at various points to fill in necessary details. I've interspersed mention of my own position and role across these moments. Readers interested in a more systematic discussion of these topics may wish to read the author's note before proceeding.

Second, when I offer evidence for my claims, I privilege the richness of interactions and episodes over reductionist, bite-sized quotations. If we're serious about understanding these young people, we need to acknowledge a fuller range of dilemmas and decisions they face in their daily lives. It means writing about them as complex individuals who occupy a number of simultaneous and competing social roles. At times, the narrative will appear to veer far from the world of tweets and status messages, taking us into living rooms and high school hallways. But we'll emerge with a far more accurate account of how social life flows online and off, across seemingly unrelated moments and identities.

Third, like the highly gendered nature of the drill world itself, this book focuses primarily on the lives and perspectives of young men. During my time on the South Side, I didn't meet a single woman engaged in this form of digital production. Although there were several young women in Taylor Park who were "down" with the Corner Boys, none were considered official members. As I read through early versions of the book, I realized that many of the interactions I discussed between young men and women—particularly those surrounding drill's sexualized rewards—were antagonistic and exploitative. This certainly doesn't reflect the spectrum of the relationships I witnessed. Where possible, I've devoted additional space to capture this complexity, toeing the difficult line between parsimony and fullness.

1
...

From the Drug Economy to the Attention Economy

Like many teens growing up in urban poor neighborhoods, Xavier spent his high school years dreaming of playing Division 1 college basketball and entering the NBA draft. Blessed with an early growth spurt and a natural talent on the court, he spent evenings at a nearby park, practicing his free throws. If he worked hard enough, he always told himself, basketball would be his way out of Taylor Park. He planned to use his first professional paycheck to move his mother and younger brother out of the neighborhood once and for all. The three of them liked to fantasize together about the lavish details of their future house in the Chicago suburbs.

But as Xavier's senior year wound to a close, the college scholarship offers never arrived. He was heartbroken, but eventually graduated. With his lifelong dream shattered, Xavier was desperate to find another way to make good (and fast) money. Like some of his classmates and neighbors, Xavier decided to try his hand at drug dealing. He immediately sought help from the neighborhood's "big homies"—men in their thirties and forties who, throughout the 1980s and 1990s, dominated the local drug economy as members of Taylor Park's Black Counts gang. Much to Xavier's continued disappointment, however, the big homies wanted nothing to do with him. They refused to bring him into their business.

"Shit's fucked up, bro," Xavier complained as we sat across from each other at one of our favorite greasy spoon diners on the South Side. "Shit's *all* fucked up."

Xavier kept his eyes down as he spoke. His shoulder-length dreadlocks hid his quietly watering eyes. He was depressed. Very depressed. Again. Over the past year, as I had become close to the soft-spoken twenty-year-old, I had seen him repeatedly sink into periods of dejection, slipping from the highest of highs to the deepest of lows in a matter of hours. When Xavier was feeling especially down, he had a habit of disappearing for a day or two, holing up in his room, self-medicating with a mixture of PCP (Angel Dust) and weed. I worried about him. I did my best to intervene when I noticed his mood starting to sink.

That day, hoping to distract Xavier from his usual coping mechanisms, I treated him to lunch. It had been a difficult week, leaving Xavier broke, hungry, and frustrated. His cell phone had been shut off. His mom was hounding him to start contributing to the household financially.

"You know the most messed-up part?" he asked me after a few minutes of tense silence. He stuttered a bit as he spoke—a side effect of his most recent PCP binge. "It ain't used to be like this. Back in the day, if I was out here fucked up [broke], the big homies woulda hooked me up. They woulda gave me a corner and a pack [of drugs to sell]. And if I did good, they woulda let me run the whole block, push more weight. It really ain't like that no more, though. They see me out here tryna' make some kind of paper [money]. They see me. But they don't do shit." Xavier chewed on a mouthful of fries. "They ain't rockin' with *none* of us no more. We on our own, bro. We on our own."

With its mix of nostalgia and dejection, Xavier's rant captures a new dilemma facing those coming of age in urban poverty, and helps to explain the recent turn to the online attention economy. Of course, it's never been easy for undereducated and unskilled youth to make ends meet, much less to achieve the upward mobility necessary to climb out of poverty. Throughout the late twentieth century, these youngsters turned in staggering numbers to the drug game, joining the ranks of gangs that monopolized the underground economy.[1] When crack cocaine became widely available in the 1980s, street gangs "corporatized," redirecting their energy and organizational structure toward drug distribution.[2] As one of the most attractive and reliable options available, young men could count on enlisting as "foot soldiers," peddling small quantities of crack on a consignment basis on one of the street corners controlled by their local gang. Evocatively described by the historian Mike Davis as a "crypto-Keynesian youth employment program," these drug-selling gangs became a community institution, providing young black men with useful skills, access to consumer goods, and self-worth otherwise denied by their racial and class background.[3]

Times, however, have changed.

Beginning in the 1990s, the crack economy and corporatized gangs simultaneously eroded. Crack's grip on the urban landscape loosened as U.S. drug markets diversified with other substances such as heroin, prescription opiates, PCP, and designer synthetic drugs like MDMA (Ecstasy), ketamine, and GHB.[4] Gangs' previous hierarchical, franchise structure—a model developed for the specificities of crack dealing—suddenly grew unprofitable. At the same time, federal and local law enforcement agencies used the Racketeer Influenced and Corrupt Organizations (RICO) Act to arrest high-ranking gang leaders and unravel their hierarchies.[5] Neighborhood youth like Xavier and the Corner Boys have found themselves locked out of the underground job market once available to their fathers. Although their eventual turn to the online attention economy is new, they're following a long-standing pattern in the history of America's urban poor communities. Facing one period of economic dislocation after another, young men have always found creative, if controversial, ways to pursue their dreams. Disappointed by local adults who appear "out of touch" with the reality faced by the younger generation, they find new role models to follow. This process unfolded most famously in the mid- and late twentieth century, amid the wreckage of deindustrialization, when the drug corner replaced the shop floor.

THE GOOD OL' DAYS

Rick and I stood chatting on his back stoop at nine o'clock on a dew-soaked morning. A cigarette hung loosely between his lips. He shuffled about in his house slippers and calf-length white socks. The younger of his two daughters busied herself terrorizing their small terrier, who squirmed as she held it over the lip of their above-ground pool. Rick's other daughter emerged from the house, grinning ear to ear, carefully hugging a large plastic bowl filled to the brim with breakfast cereal. On the eve of his fortieth birthday, Rick's frayed cornrow braids, round belly, and startling domesticity belied the fact that just fifteen years earlier, he and his Black Counts associates had held a tight grip on daily life in Taylor Park. Throughout the crack epidemic, Rick had steadily worked his way up in the organization, eventually saving up enough money to move out of Taylor Park and into this three-bedroom, two-story, single-family house in a quiet middle-class neighborhood. Every morning, Rick waves his wife off to work, drops his daughters off at school, and heads back to his old stomping grounds. There, he meets up with his childhood friends Lewis and Lil Mark—two similarly balding, bellied, veteran Black Counts. Working as independent, or "freelance," dealers outside of their old corporate gang structure, they stay on the move, pacing the neighborhood streets selling weed and baby bottles filled with "lean"—a prescription cough suppressant containing a euphoric mix of codeine and promethazine.

Rick describes his twenty-plus-year career in "pharmaceutical sales" as beginning somewhat unexpectedly, perhaps even reluctantly.

"Growing up, I was gonna work in the mill, like my pop." Rick was referring to the collection of rolling steel mills that billowed over Chicago's South Side for more than a century. Collectively, the Wisconsin Steel mill, U.S. Steel mill, Republic Steel mill, and a collection of smaller mills made up the region's largest employer, furnishing the steel for the nation's railroads and downtown skylines. These towering industrial plants provided black Chicagoans, like Rick's father, with decent-paying, unionized jobs. By 1970, the United Steelworkers of America (USWA) counted 130,000 members in the Chicago region, most of whom were black or Mexican.[6] But these numbers, like the mills, wouldn't last. Beginning in the 1980s, the mills were hard pressed to compete with foreign firms. They started laying off workers. Before the end of the 1990s, U.S. Steel's South Works, the last mill standing, closed its doors for good. The crumbling carcass of the old ore wall still stands today, casting a long shadow over the city's largest vacant lot. The effects were immediately felt, even miles away, in neighborhoods like Taylor Park.

"By the time I was about sixteen," Rick told me, "they had all just stopped. That was the beginning of the end right there. Everything went downhill. Pop was out of work. Hell, *everyone* was out of work. Once those mills closed, everything else closed too. All the mom and pops. And all the people who could get the hell out, they got the hell out."

The closing of the South Side's mills was a microcosm of the larger trends of economic restructuring that ravaged black communities across Chicago, the rustbelt, and America more generally. In 1950, the employment rate in the South Side's "black belt" mirrored the city average.[7] But then a number of political and economic factors—including the relaxation of trade restrictions, stagflation, and other jolts to the world market—encouraged the flight of U.S. manufacturing to cheap-labor locations in the developing world.[8] More than ten million jobs were lost nationally due to closures or decreased production demand between 1979 and 1985 alone.[9] By 1980, Chicago's manufacturing base had been cut in half.[10] Because black residents were overrepresented in the manufacturing sector, they were disproportionately dislocated. By 1980, the number of working residents in the black belt had fallen by a staggering 77 percent, leaving nearly three out of four persons older than sixteen jobless.[11] The departure of big plants triggered a domino effect, leading to the subsequent demise of small stores, banks, and other businesses that relied on the wages paid by large employers.[12] With few employment options in cash-strapped neighborhoods, the black belt hemorrhaged close to half its population over the second half of the twentieth century.[13]

Amid deindustrialization, the U.S. economy simultaneously "reindustrialized" through the steady expansion of the service sector and jobs related to the finance, insurance, and real estate (FIRE) industries.[14] During the 1980s, for the first time in U.S. history, the service sector surpassed manufacturing as the largest single division of the domestic economy. Between 1972 and 1988, 40 percent of all new jobs were in the service sector.[15] New jobs increasingly reflected a bipolar distribution. On one end of the spectrum were high-paying, high-skill positions that demanded high levels of education. By the late 1980s, the volume of jobs requiring some college training rose by 44 percent; jobs mandating a four-year university degree grew by 56 percent.[16] Lacking sufficient education and white-collar skills, many black residents found themselves channeled to the other end of the spectrum. These are low-paying, low-skill, and "dead-end" jobs—dishwashers, cashiers, bus boys—that offer little opportunity for meaningful advancement.

Large-scale economic shifts dramatically transformed interpersonal relations and neighborhood culture. Writing in the early 1990s, the sociologist Elijah Anderson documented that long-standing ties had begun to fray between neighborhood youth and "old heads"—middle-aged men of stable means and employment who socialized youngsters into their responsibilities regarding work, family, and the law.[17] As meaningful employment grew scarcer, and as young people recognized their limited and subordinate place in the emerging service economy, the old head lost his prestige and authority. "The youth," Anderson observed, "mock and patronize the old heads . . . for not understanding the 'way the world really works.'"[18] They turned instead to the flashy and seductive trail blazed by what Anderson called the "new old heads"—men in their twenties and thirties squarely employed in burgeoning drug-selling gangs. "On the local street corners," Anderson wrote, the new old head "attempts to impress people through displays of material success like expensive clothes and fancy cars. Eagerly awaiting his message are the unemployed black men, demoralized by what they see as a hopeless financial situation and inclined to emulate his style and values."[19]

As if reading directly from Anderson's account, Rick reminisced with a longing grin. "We saw our uncles and our cousins out there gettin' that paper. They had the girls and the expensive cars, and all. We hadn't never really ever seen nobody from *our* hood ballin' out before, so we wanted to be just like them." Rick followed in the footsteps of his older siblings and formally joined the Black Counts gang at age sixteen. "They were runnin' *everything* back then," he continued, "so they took us under their wing. They hooked us up with a hustle." That "hustle" was a job selling crack cocaine alongside a half dozen of his friends as part of a corner crew along one of Taylor Park's busier thoroughfares. Although the pay wasn't especially high—foot soldiers' wages reportedly hovered between six and eleven dollars in untaxed cash per hour—it was certainly better than the minimum wage Rick and his buddies could expect from the menial service jobs available in the formal sector.[20] Street dealing also offered better employee support and "benefits." This included bonuses during special holidays, and bail money and lawyer fees in emergencies.[21] The few who were lucky enough to avoid arrest and death were rewarded with a swift climb through the organization's ranks and into local leadership, where they could pull in as much as one hundred thousand dollars per year.[22] According to Rick, by the time he was in his early twenties, he had risen to a mid-level position overseeing multiple Black Counts corner crews.[23]

Rick cherished his officer role, and not just for the compensation it provided. It elevated his social standing in the surrounding community. Although corporatized gangs were responsible for introducing narcotics and violence into their local neighborhoods, they were also able to provide (and placate) residents with vital monetary resources and in-kind services, including transportation, manual labor, security, and recreational programming like basketball tournaments and picnics. As the public face of the gang, officers served as guardians, mediators, and mentors.[24] Whenever I spoke with Taylor Park's big homies about their life histories, they launched into romantic Robin Hood tales, describing how they used drug profits to improve the community and help raise the neighborhood's wide-eyed youth, stepping in where the government and economy had failed.

Rick's smile widened as he reminisced about the mid-1990s. "We was just shorties before, and now *we* was the ones runnin' the block. We was on top of the world. We show up and *everybody* knew who we was. You need some money for diapers? We got you. Light bill? Got you. Shorties [children] need some food. We on it."

Romantic tales of the good ol' days still dominate local Taylor Park lore. Today's teens, like Xavier, were barely kindergarten-age during the Black Counts' pinnacle years. Yet, Xavier's generation claims to remember what it felt like in Taylor Park at the time. "It was like this," Xavier explained during our lunch at the diner. "He [the big homie] would pull up and if there's twenty kids out there, he's gonna put all twenty to the front of the ice cream truck and buy them ice cream. If there's twenty kids out there and he's eating pizza, he's gonna order another one so every kid gets a slice. He don't care who kids they are or nothin'." Xavier had composed himself a bit in the course of eating his double cheeseburger and fries. "That's why people loved him. He was like the mayor of the whole neighborhood. Like, the king. If you had a problem you go to him. If you're fighting with your neighbor, he was the judge. All the bitches loved him, and all the niggas wanted to *be* him!"

Given the combination of cash and respect that buoyed the big homies of yesterday, it's not hard to see why multiple generations in Taylor Park set their hearts on pursuing this path. Yet Xavier, Rick, and others would soon come to learn that this elevated economic and social role in the community was quickly being rendered obsolete. The introduction of RICO enforcement and the beheading of corporate gangs transformed such leadership opportunities, and their associated rewards, from coveted assets to dangerous liabilities. This new prosecutorial strategy worked its way up the gang's hierarchy by cutting deals with low-level gang members and other community residents, offering them pleas and lighter sentences in return for incriminating evidence against their superiors.[25] Although much of the city greeted this new enforcement effort with great fanfare, it had the unexpected effect of destabilizing the previous social order by sowing significant tension between the remaining big homies and the youngsters they once employed. Whereas men like Rick once coveted leadership roles, they now actively avoid taking young men under their wings.[26] According to Rick and his associates, the incentive to "turn snitch" has given rise to a new mantra among neighborhood youth when they find themselves in handcuffs: "Why do ten when you can tell on a friend."

Rick learned this lesson the hard way. Five years before our morning chat at his house, he had gone against his better judgment. He tried to expand his drug business. Despite breaking from the corporate model in the early 2000s and operating in a small, mobile selling crew with his close friends, Rick decided to employ three teenage "delivery boys" from the neighborhood. He had received an unexpected discount on a large quantity of cocaine and needed extra manpower to help him unload it. They could help him with overnight distribution while he returned home to spend time with his family. One such evening, however, the police arrested one of the delivery boys with Rick's product. In return for a plea to a lesser charge, the young man helped the police arrest Rick in an undercover sting, resulting in a three-and-a-half-year prison sentence.

For Taylor Park's big homies, repeated stories of betrayal do more than just prevent them from incorporating younger gang members. Perceiving a rampant decline of loyalty and honor, older members take steps to actively *separate* themselves, both physically and socially, from the younger generation.

"To be honest, I'm scared of them," Lil Mark said as he, Rick, and I leaned against a car watching several of the Corner Boys playing dice in a nearby alley. "They're too hardheaded nowadays," he complained. "Back in the day, when I was a shorty, the niggas that was older than me, they brought me in. They took me to their house. They hooked me up with a hustle. They fed me, let me watch TV. They had me learning my [Black Counts] literature: Go to school, go vote, take care of your family, take care of your hygiene. I'm older now and I just don't want to do that kind of shit. I don't even want them near me." Lil Mark's words dripped with resentment. "That was one of the reasons the shorties [neighborhood youth] really fell out with us," he continued. "Because we wouldn't put the money behind them. But we don't want to put the money behind them because if we do that, then we're responsible for them. And I can't be responsible for them because I'm scared of them. I don't know what they're gonna do when twelve [the police] rolls through."

Throughout my time in Taylor Park, I encountered plenty of evidence of the big homies' fears. When Rick invited me to spend the morning with him at his family home, he made me promise to keep the location of his house a secret from the young men in CBE. He feared that they might turn him over to the police if they ever got pinched, or maybe rob him when they were particularly hard up for cash.

"The problem with this generation," Rick complained, "is that they don't know what loyalty is anymore. You see, back in the day, the idea of breaking into my house wouldn't have even crossed their minds. But this generation is making up their own rules. Rules they don't even follow themselves."

As little as a decade ago, the corporate gang was able to keep teenage rebelliousness in check through an explicit ultimatum: Fall in line, obey your elders, and respect the laws of the larger organization, or else forfeit the financial opportunities distributed by the gang. It was a difficult offer to refuse, resulting in a stream of influence that flowed downward. Today, in contrast, with the big homies both unwilling and unable to hold the carrot of economic advancement over the heads of youngsters, the older generation feels as though they're at the mercy of their younger cousins, nephews, and neighbors.

LOCKED OUT

From the perspective of today's youth, the big homies' fears seem less like a reversal of power and more like willful abandonment. Xavier and the rest of CBE have grown resentful. They feel that they've been left to fend for themselves. Across the United States, the number of people living in concentrated poverty—neighborhoods where 40 percent or more of residents live at or below the poverty line—has dramatically increased, nearly doubling from 7.3 million people in 2000 to 13.8 million in 2013.[27] By 2010, nearly half of Taylor Park residents were living below the poverty line; roughly one in five was unemployed.[28] These numbers are even more startling once we consider how durable they are across multiple generations. An estimated 70 percent of black families that begin in concentrated poverty will remain there for the duration of their lives.[29]

Although none of the Corner Boys have seen these statistics, they recognize that their chances of climbing out of poverty are slim. Consider the story of Dominik, one of CBE's drillers. He recalled spending his childhood eagerly awaiting his induction into the Black Counts and the associated economic opportunities. Hard up for cash and having recently fathered a child with his longtime girlfriend, Dominik was fond of talking about the child-rearing expectations placed on fathers in neighborhoods like his. He recalled some of his earliest memories of family gatherings, where his older brothers, cousins, and uncles playfully taught him the intricate Black Counts handshakes and tested him on the edicts laid out in the official gang literature. Reflecting a sense of inevitability, Dominik explained that he "just kinda fell in line." Becoming a Count was something all the men in his family "just did." Like the rest of the Corner Boys, Dominik's Black Counts family members proudly initiated, or "blessed," him, into the gang at age thirteen. Like several of his peers, he immediately received a tattoo bearing the word BLESSED to commemorate the occasion.

The weeks following their blessings brought the new initiates praise and affection from their new fictive uncles. But this did little to improve their economic fortunes. Several of the Corner Boys recalled approaching the Black Counts big homies, just weeks or months after their initiation, to formally join up with their economic franchises. Much to these young men's dismay, the big homies never fully brought them into the fold.

As Dominik complained, "That Count shit didn't change nothin', really. I mighta' got a pack [of drugs] thrown my way now and then, but really we was out on our own." The message from the older Counts was clear to local teens: Given the new prosecution strategies, they'd occasionally provide them small quantities of product to sell, sometimes free of charge or at discounted prices, but they would *not* be bringing them into their own narcotics operations.

I learned quite a bit about this arrangement from another one of the Corner Boys' drillers—eighteen-year-old Junior. He recounted that shortly after his initiation, one of the big homies "fronted" Junior what he described as a "fist-sized" amount of crack cocaine to sell on his own as a kind of welcome gift.[30] The older man wouldn't assist him with the street sales, but he agreed to allow Junior to keep the profits. Although initially excited about the opportunity for quick returns, Junior soon learned how difficult it is to conduct street sales without the help of an established organizational structure.

The Difficulties of "Freelancing"

For those unfamiliar with the logistics of the drug economy, dealing can appear to be a quick and easy way of making money. My time with the Corner Boys disabused me of this idea. It didn't take long to notice that these young men were abysmal drug dealers. In fact, they struggled to turn any profit at all.

"With crack, you got to be on top of your shit," Junior explained one afternoon as we sat lounging in my parked car behind an apartment building. He shook his head, seemingly embarrassed about his own youthful naïveté. "If people don't be knowing your product, then you gotta give them free bags and testers. But then you gotta keep track of who got the free shit and who need to pay. You need like an accountant and someone to keep track of the money and the customers and the drugs. I didn't have none of that, so I ended up losing all the money *and the drugs*. So I just said fuck it."

Junior's experience is surprisingly common in Taylor Park. Young residents quickly learned that the former gang structure played an important functional role, providing practical advantages denied to those dealing outside of their organization. According to the sociologist Felix Padilla, drug-selling gangs' forceful control of neighborhood turf provided their teen dealers with important benefits.[31] Rick, for example, began his career inheriting a loyal customer base that was already familiar with the gang's product. The gang's organizational structure also socialized him into profitable sales techniques and customer management. As Padilla notes, "The act of dealing entails much more than simply standing on the corner or middle of the street block and disposing of available drugs. . . . Youngsters learn to deal by interacting and observing those who have worked in the occupation for some time. Would-be dealers simply hang out and observe the various techniques employed by veteran dealers."[32] A final advantage held by corporatized gangs was the availability of start-up capital. Given their size and ties to larger drug distribution networks, they were able to purchase far larger quantities of product at wholesale prices, increasing their profit margins at the retail stage.

I witnessed the importance of these benefits as the Corner Boys continually struck out as independent drug dealers. In fact, they often ended their days with *less* money in their pockets than when they started. For instance, following Junior's failed stint in the crack market, he turned to selling weed. After borrowing $150 from an ex-girlfriend, he purchased a half-ounce of a strain of highly potent marijuana known as "loud." He saw the plan as incredibly straightforward: After "bagging up" the half-ounce into forty individual bags, or "nickels," that retailed for $5 each, he would gross $200, netting him a $50 profit once all the bags were sold. Junior expected to sell out his inventory within two or three days. If he could resist the constant temptation to dip into his bags for his own personal consumption, he could make around $25 per day. He knew it wasn't much; barely enough to live on. But if he could string together a few profitable months, he could start buying larger quantities at a more competitive price, enlarging his eventual retail profits. If he could squirrel away enough to purchase a full ounce of loud at $250, perhaps pooling his money with one of his friends, he could net around $150 once it was all sold.

But when Junior hit the streets with his pockets full of small cellophane baggies, his lack of start-up capital turned out to be just the start of his troubles. He was walking into a highly competitive, largely unregulated market. With no local gang structure to restrain youthful entrepreneurialism by divvying up the neighborhood into dedicated selling spots, Junior was forced to reduce his prices—sometimes to as low as $3 per nickel bag— just to attract customers. Even when he was able to convince buyers to pay full price, there was always the threat of another aspiring dealer interrupting the sale and offering a better deal. I spent an afternoon watching Junior and AJ race one another around the neighborhood, trying to solicit potential customers before the other arrived to undercut the asking price.

Facing such stiff competition in public space, Junior shifted his strategy indoors. His new plan was to sell primarily to his friends, extended family, and fellow members of CBE. He assumed their relationships and potential loyalty would help him maintain sales. Although this new customer base agreed to buy almost exclusively from Junior, they did so with the expectation of discounts. He was back to selling nickel bags for less than $5. When he resisted, they wore him down by reminding him of various favors they had done for him in the past—letting him crash on their couches, arranging for relatives to drive him to court, or cutting *him* discounts on weed when he was broke.

Things would only get worse for Junior. His sales abruptly ended when someone stole his inventory. Out of fear that he might be stopped by the police while carrying around his nickel bags, Junior convinced a friend to let him keep the stash locked in a mailbox. But when Junior returned to "re-up" his supply, he found the mailbox wide open and empty. Apparently, someone in the neighborhood, perhaps one of his own friends, had gotten word of his hiding place and pried it open with a crowbar. At the end of the day, Junior recouped only half of his initial costs, leaving him around $75 in the red. During my two years with the Corner Boys, I watched most of them repeat this same process with similarly disappointing results.

Alternatives to "Freelancing"

Lacking the organizational structure and drug market benefits granted by yesterday's corporate gangs, and finding today's drug trade too difficult, Junior, Xavier, and their group of friends turned to "staining"—the local term for robbery and burglary.[33] After school let out each day, they changed out of their public-school uniforms and set out in search of easy targets, or "stains." It was on one of these afternoons that the group's first collective identity emerged, independent of the Black Counts. The young men jokingly started referring to themselves as the "the Cinder Block." It's a reference to the ubiquitous cinder blocks that they gathered from Taylor Park's abandoned lots and homes, which they used to smash the windows of parked cars. Staining proved more lucrative, but brought serious heat from the police.[34] The Cinder Block's increasing contact with the criminal justice system culminated one evening, when Junior and one of his buddies borrowed a pistol from an older sibling. They used it to rob an elderly man at gunpoint as he withdrew cash from an ATM. A squad car intercepted Junior before he could make it back to his apartment. He had the foresight to toss the gun as the officers gave chase, and avoided an illegal firearm possession charge. The elderly man identified Junior as the perpetrator, earning the teen a short jail sentence and probation.

Fearing a similar outcome, the less daring members of the group resigned themselves to what they all saw as the option of very last resort—a job in the low-wage service industry. Throughout my time with these young men, we occasionally filled out applications for entry-level positions in fast-food restaurants, grocery stores, and other hospitality-centered businesses. Several national and local chains have a reputation for hiring black teens with little to no employment history. Yet, even when these young men managed to get through the application process, survive the interview, and lock down reliable transportation to and from their first few shifts, they confronted a world of workplace conditions and interactions that can be even less forgiving, and certainly less inviting, than the street corner. It's not long before they start looking for reasons to avoid waking up and putting on their uniform.

"I Can't Be Workin' Like That"

As much as these young men openly disparaged work in the low-wage service economy, AJ recalled that he was excited on the morning of his first day of work. With the help of a family friend, he landed a job at Chicago-Midway International Airport, restocking the sodas, snacks, and magazines in the various stores lining the terminal walkways. The commute was a bear—more than an hour on public transportation, plus another half hour spent moving through security lines and metal detectors. Yet, something about the hassle of it all seemed to contribute to AJ's sense of accomplishment and adult responsibility. Within less than a month, however, AJ had begun skipping his shifts and eventually stopped showing up altogether. The two of us sat discussing his short stint at Midway. I asked him to explain why his earlier, optimistic outlook had turned so bitter.

"I can't be workin' like that," he said with a tone of disgust.

"Come on," I reasoned. "It couldn't have been *that* bad."

AJ looked at me with disappointment. "Would you work there? Hell naw you wouldn't. So why should I have to?"

"Because you need the money?"

"Not *that bad* I don't," AJ replied. He launched into a detailed explanation of his dissatisfaction, describing his typical work conditions and the escalating conflicts with his supervisor. "It's like this, bro. All day, you load up this cart in the back, and then you gotta go, like, take it to the little shops. Then you unload all the stuff. Then you go back and load up the cart again. Then you unload it. Then you load it again. *That's all you do!* Over and over and over and over. Every day it's the same thing. They don't even let you listen to music or nothin' while you're workin'. And if you talk to anybody you get in trouble. You can't even *look* at your phone." AJ grew even more agitated as he spoke. He held his phone out in front of him. "My boss, he tried to take it dead out of my hand! I shoulda knocked this nigga out. He thinks he can talk to me like I'm some kind of bitch. Out here in the streets, niggas get smoked [shot] for that!"

Beyond highlighting the mind-numbing boredom and subservience of the available employment options, AJ's experiences shine a light on a deeper cultural clash.[35] In the words of the anthropologist Philippe Bourgois, young men like AJ confront workplaces where "middle-class Anglo modes of interaction prevail with a vengeance."[36] The tough swagger and cool pose honed on the streets of Taylor Park are wildly out of sync with the humility and obedience demanded in customer service and support roles.[37] Workplaces provide little time or opportunity to find common ground with expendable workers. Youngsters from disadvantaged neighborhoods have difficulty interacting with, or even looking at, coworkers, bosses, and customers without inadvertently intimidating them.[38] And when these people aren't intimidated by street culture, they ridicule it, shaking their heads at sagging pants, dreadlocks, and mumbled slang.

AJ punctuated this point. "I ain't lettin' niggas talk to me like that," he said with a scowl. "I had to get up outta there before I did something to this nigga and caught a case [got arrested]."

For these young men, this cultural mismatch is exacerbated by the instability marking their nonwork lives. Shawn, another Taylor Park resident and peripheral member of CBE, is a prime example. Shawn's gregarious personality, quick wit, and high-pitched laugh had earned him a reputation as a class clown in high school. After graduation, his charisma helped him land a minimum-wage job at a busy Panera restaurant in the downtown Loop. He spent his shifts mopping floors, stocking display cases, and hawking pastries and coffee to professionals from nearby highrises. Unlike AJ, Shawn's interactions with supervisors and customers were rarely antagonistic. In fact, they were typically friendly, perhaps even fulfilling.

"They loved me up there," Shawn said proudly as we chatted about his formal employment history. "I was always crackin' 'em up, doin' some stupid shit. I mess with 'em. I make all the white ladies smile in the morning when they goin' to work."

But Shawn's favorable workplace interactions weren't enough to save his job. He told me his boss fired him after four months. Shawn had begun clocking out too early from his shift, showing up late, and, on a couple of occasions, not showing up at all.

"It wasn't my fault," Shawn complained as he recounted the ordeal. Once, when Shawn's little brother got sick at school, Shawn had to race out of work to pick him up. Another time, Shawn had to wait at home for a repairman to arrive to fix a broken window—his family dared not leave their apartment unattended for fear of burglary. Not long after that, he overslept his alarm after he stayed up most of the night comforting his youngest brother following a late-night shooting down the street. Shawn's mother, who was also working long hours for little pay, leaned heavily on Shawn—the oldest of four sons—to help raise his siblings. It seemed that there was always some small, unanticipated emergency that pulled Shawn away from work. These kinds of familial obligations are a normal part of life for young people growing up in resource-depleted neighborhoods.[39] Unfortunately, low-wage service jobs have little patience for the erratic and unpredictable home lives of the urban poor. Hearing how Shawn solved one minor crisis after another, I was amazed that he was able to hold down his job as long as he did.

During my time in the neighborhood, young residents continually shared war stories from both the legal and illegal economies. They recapped their disappointing pleas to the big homies to incorporate them into drug operations; they recounted the boredom of jail time; they recited their bosses' paternalistic lectures about punctuality and work ethic. At every turn, they felt as though the world was pitted against them. And then, beginning around 2011, they felt their luck start to change. On the small, rectangular screens of their smartphones, they caught glimpses of new role models—young men in neighborhoods just like theirs, who had found a way to use their troubled biographies to climb out of their neighborhoods and into the mainstream spotlight.

THE ALLURE OF THE ATTENTION ECONOMY

As we did on most summer afternoons, AJ and I sat in my parked car, blasting the air conditioning. And like most afternoons, we chatted about his hope of stardom through his drill music videos. With a thin black auxiliary cord trailing into my car stereo, he held up his iPhone to show me a clip on YouTube.

"This is it, bro," he said in a serious tone. He pointed to the screen, pushing the play button. "This is the video that started it all. *This* is what started the drill movement, I say. This is what got niggas out here tryna' *really* do something with this rap shit."

I immediately recognized it. It was the music video for a song called "I Don't Like," by Chicago's most notorious driller, Keith Cozart, known to most of the world as "Chief Keef." Looking at the video's YouTube page, it's easy to see what AJ means. It's one of the most watched drill videos ever made. On YouTube alone, it has amassed roughly ninety million views.[40] That's equivalent to the populations of California, Texas, and Florida *combined*. It's a truly impressive feat, particularly once you consider that it was accomplished by a sixteen-year-old living in one of Chicago's most maligned neighborhoods. But to fully grasp the significance of the video—to understand why it holds such revered status—we have to look beyond these numbers. Through its shaky, homemade footage and slightly off-time vocals, Cozart's music video has come to represent a new, hopeful pathway out of poverty. Given the other options available to South Side youth, it's a formula that feels attainable and realistic. They're about the same age as Cozart, they grew up in the same area, and they attended the same schools. When young men like AJ look at Cozart, they see themselves.

The Rise of Chief Keef

When "I Don't Like" hit the internet in 2012, Cozart was on the cusp of a meteoric, if unconventional, rise to international celebrity—a rise that began, quite literally, from his grandmother's living room.[41] A year earlier, at just fifteen years old, Cozart and his friends in the Englewood, Grand Crossing, and Washington Park neighborhoods began making drill songs and music videos, posting them to YouTube. They too had grown up with dreams of rising up the ranks of the local corporate gang. Similarly forced to make it without the big homies' help, they splintered off into their own faction, referring to themselves alternatively as GBE (short for Glory Boyz Entertainment) or Lamron 300 (the name of their street spelled backward, along with a reference to the blockbuster movie about Spartan warriors). As a hybrid gang faction/music group, GBE attracted a small following in the local neighborhood and nearby school yards, though not much beyond that. The Glory Boyz started attracting a larger fanbase after a series of Cozart's well-publicized run-ins with the law. In 2011, Cozart was arrested and charged with felony drug distribution. Only a few months later, he was arrested for assault with a firearm on police officers. He had pointed a pistol at two cops outside of his home; they opened fire on him as he fled through an abandoned lot. A judge placed him under house arrest, which forced him and GBE to record songs and videos indoors, using his graffiti-scrawled bedroom and dimly lit kitchen as a backdrop.[42]

"I Don't Like" was recorded during this period. In today's world of crime-obsessed entertainment culture, "I Don't Like" appeared to offer a rare, unbridled glimpse into a social world that both terrifies and fascinates the American public.[43] The video opens with Cozart and seven or so other Glory Boyz sitting on folding chairs in a sparse living room. The shot cuts to someone counting a stack of cash. Pan to close-up, slow-motion shots of a young man exhaling a thick cloud of weed smoke. Cozart, now shirtless, paces in front of his crew, some of whom prominently display their prison-style facial tattoos for the camera. The beat builds. Quick "machine-gun" bursts of hi-hats and snare drums pierce epic orchestral strings and foreboding bells. Thirty seconds into the song, the scene begins to shake with bone-rattling kick drums that make Cozart's gathering feel overwhelming and inescapable. The group is on their feet now, bouncing up and down, their dreadlocks bouncing along with them. Cozart drapes his arms over another one of the lean and shirtless teens. He begins his rap. The highly repetitive lyrics brag of ongoing crimes and the moral code that Cozart and his gang claim to live by, as well as the consequences for anyone who fails to obey the unwritten rules of the street.

The chorus begins by listing the behaviors and people that the Glory Boyz do not tolerate:

A fuck nigga, that's that shit I don't like.
A snitch nigga, that's that shit I don't like.
. . .
I done got indicted sellin' all white.
But I won't never snitch none in my life.
. . .
I'm killin' these niggas, shit they don't like.
Broski got the 30, he ain't tryna' fight.

Mere months after uploading the video, Cozart had become an internet phenomenon. "I Don't Like" climbed to number seventy-three on the Billboard Top 100 chart, earning Cozart attention, praise, and invitations to perform on tour with popular recording artists who hoped to boost their own internet following. A number of mainstream music icons—

including multiple Grammy Award–winner Kanye West—went so far as to create their own remixes of Cozart's songs and featured him on forthcoming albums. As if the dream couldn't get any more surreal, in June 2012, Cozart signed a six-million-dollar recording contract with Interscope Records—the label associated with such legendary names as Tupac Shakur, Madonna, and Elton John. Keef also reportedly reached a publishing agreement with the longtime producer and music mogul Dr. Dre to establish a GBE record label, movie rights, and a line of luxury audio headphones called "Beats by Keef."[44]

The public marveled at Cozart's success in breaking the age-old rules of artistic ascent while proving the effectiveness of new, social-media-driven forms of self-branding and production. "The defining document of hip-hop's current evolutionary state isn't a song, or a music video, or a concert," wrote the *New York Times*'s Jon Caramanica in 2012. "Years from now, cultural archaeologists will do much better to look back over the Twitter account of the 17-year-old rapper Chief Keef, who's been exploding . . . one short burst of text at a time."[45]

Caramanica and others pointed to two key aspects of Cozart's "raw burst of change." First, he largely bypassed the conventional gatekeepers that once monopolized access to the entertainment industry.[46] In the past, catching the attention of label executives and fans required more than just talent; it demanded dogged self-promotion through the mostly *physical* distribution of mixtapes and demo CDs. Standing on busy downtown street corners for hours at a time, rappers tried to grab the attention of passersby—"Hey, you like hip-hop?"—before shoving a CD marked with their contact information into their hands. The hope was that this stranger would take the time to listen to the CD, enjoy what they heard, and perhaps even pass the CD along to an agent or manager in their social network, who would then share the music with label heads. The artist might receive a small (often highly exploitative) record deal to produce a few songs, or even an album, on a kind of trial basis. If he was able to grab the attention of radio stations and attract a fan base, the label might extend his contract.[47]

By embracing *online* distribution, Cozart leaped over most of these steps, cutting out the middlemen.[48] He didn't need to beg managers and tastemakers to give him a shot. If anything, he inverted this relationship, causing record labels to court *him*. Already in command of the eyes and ears of millions of millennials by the time his name graced the lips of mainstream media, Cozart offered record companies a large and growing consumer base that they could easily capitalize on, becoming the poster child for a new model: Generate enough YouTube views, Twitter followers, and other measures of popularity, and businesses like Interscope, and moguls like Dr. Dre will come knocking at the door and pluck you from the 'hood.[49]

Importantly, Cozart built his brand squarely on the back of a gang-associated, violent public persona. It seemed that the more his name was associated with crime, the bigger his popularity and earning potential became. For example, Cozart's industry buzz only intensified when he appeared in court on suspicion of his involvement in the murder of Joseph Coleman (discussed in the preface). After Coleman's death, Cozart mocked him on Twitter, posting a series of celebratory tweets:

> Its Sad Cuz Dat Nigga Jojo Wanted To Be Jus Like Us #LMAO
> HahahahahhahahahahahahahaahhAAHAHAHAHA #RichNiggaShit
> He died damn Thought he was team no lackin

Cozart's popularity grew with each subsequent run-in with the law, which included arrests and jail time for drug possession, illegal gun possession, probation violations, and failure to pay child support.[50] Instagram shut down his account for posting a photo of himself having sex. Parents of Chicago public school students circulated petitions to ban his music from proms and other school-sanctioned events. The City of Chicago banned Cozart from performing within city limits. The badder he was, the more attention he grabbed. In the end, Cozart's public indiscretions assisted him in overcoming one of the most enduring tasks faced by urban musicians, particularly hip-hop artists and gangsta rappers—namely, the quest to prove authenticity.[51] Each news report, mug shot, and concerned statement by public officials served to assure audiences that Cozart genuinely embraced the oppositional identity, gang membership, and delinquent behaviors that he bragged about in his lyrics. It appeared that his larger-than-life persona wasn't just a performance for the cameras.

But Cozart's formula for building authenticity wasn't just innovative; it was also replicable. In the subsequent months, a handful of other teenage drillers similarly vaulted from the South Side to the mainstream. Several came out of Keef's infamous Parkway Gardens housing project—a location the *Chicago Sun-Times* once called "the most dangerous block in Chicago."[52] By reminding audiences of this distinction, Tavares "Lil Reese" Taylor, one of the young men prominently featured in Keef's "I Don't Like" music video, along with another young man, known as "Lil Durk," signed record deals with Def Jam Recordings. One of their friends and neighbors, producing videos under the name "600 Breezy," signed a contract with Empire Records. Even those who have yet to ink major recording deals have managed to grab the international spotlight. Four miles to the east of Parkway Gardens, in a part of the South Shore neighborhood known as "Terror Town," a group of Keef-inspired teens formed a gang/drill group called NLMB (short for "No Limit Muskegon Boyz" and "Never Leave My Brother"). One of their members, who goes by the moniker "Lil Bibby," was featured in *Vibe, XXL,* and *Billboard* after his song hit number forty-six on the Billboard charts. Another member of NLMB, known as "G Herbo," has appeared in videos alongside a range of mainstream hip-hop and R&B artists. Meanwhile, another driller, "Montana of 300," parlayed his YouTube popularity into an acting role on the primetime Fox television show *Empire*. The entertainment industry, it seems, simply can't get enough of these young men and their street authenticity.

"If Keef Can Do It, Why Can't We?"

For young men like the Corner Boys, drillers like Chief Keef and Lil Durk weren't untouchable celebrities that existed "out there," on the pages of gossip magazines and music blogs. Rather, they were cousins, classmates, and neighbors. Before attaining their celebrity status, drill's earliest pioneers lived lives that were indistinguishable from those of most youngsters in their communities. As the Corner Boys watched these drillers' profiles grow, they dissected their self-branding strategies and began emulating their behavior. If Chief Keef and Lil Durk could do it, they asked themselves, why can't we?

This mixture of inspiration and aspiration was on full display as AJ and I sat in my car, once again, watching YouTube videos on our phones. At one point, AJ recalled witnessing one of these early drillers' rise to fame. The two had attended high school together, and were well acquainted long before either of them ever had dreams of musical stardom.

"Before this," AJ began, pointing to the video on the screen, "he was just, like, a regular nigga. Just comin' to school like everybody. Ain't no big deal. Then he dropped his videos and started goin' crazy." AJ recounted the young man's sudden surge in lunchroom popularity, particularly among girls. "Everybody was on his dick," he continued, a bit more crudely. His voice jumped an octave in excitement. "He was gettin' with *mad* girls. These girls was, like, the *baddest* in the whole school! And they was just throwin' it at him! I ain't never seen nothin' like that, bro!"

"You do good with the ladies," I reminded him. "I'm sure you did just fine."

"Back then? Not like *that* I didn't," AJ argued. "I'm tellin' you, bro. This nigga coulda got *any* girl up in that whole school. All he had to do was go up to her and that's it. He just got it like that! Those videos put him in his glow [made him look good]. And I'm over here looking at him, like, damn bro, I'm tryna' get like *that*."

"*That's* why you started rapping?" I asked with a bit of disbelief. "To get more *girls*?"

"Hell ya, bro! You woulda done the *same thing*, and you know it." Thinking back to my own awkward and insecure high school years, I couldn't help but chuckle a little. "See, bro," AJ said, laughing along with me. "You was in high school once. You know how it is."

"I guess," I quickly replied, before deflecting the conversation back to him. "So what happened when *you* started?" I asked.

"Then they was giving *me* love, too," AJ replied with a smile. "Not like what he had, but he was famous already. I was just starting. I did alright though. I got mine."

I was taken aback as AJ described this source of motivation. It was strikingly mundane—he was trying to impress girls. Following our conversation, I made a point to ask the rest of the Corner Boys about their initial impulses. Several described how they had watched, in envy, as budding drillers at their various schools had rocketed up the campus hierarchy, winning the hearts of the most desirable young women. Seen in this light, drillers don't look so different from young men all over the country who, for generations, have picked up guitars and started garage bands to score dates and impress classmates. Decades of research on teens shows that many of their most consequential behaviors—everything from drug use to sexual practices to suicide—can be traced to the social pressures and status competitions they face in school.[53] It's difficult to think of a more consistent and powerful motivator in the lives of young people, regardless of race, class, or location.

Amid their jealousy of classmates, the Corner Boys developed a fair amount of optimism regarding their *own* chances of attaining celebrity. For young men like AJ, jump-starting a career in drill seemed straightforward and accessible. The Corner Boys don't see Cozart and other successful drillers as virtuosos with God-given talents and natural skills, but rather as innovative and shrewd self-marketers who found ways to satisfy the world's demand for ghetto bad man tales.

"The crazy part," AJ explained about the prominent driller at his school, "is that he wasn't even the best rapper that went there [to the school]. Not even. Some of these niggas had real bars [lyrical rapping skills and techniques].[54] I think he just, like, knew *what* to talk about. These other niggas was quick on their feet with their rhymes and stuff, but they wasn't giving people what they want. He was different."

"What do you mean, different?" I asked.

"Like, he got on there [on YouTube] talkin' 'bout that Chiraq gang-bangin' shit," AJ said. "Everybody's lookin' at Chicago like, 'Damn, these niggas is crazy.' They see the capital murder rate, they hear about Chiraq, they hear about all the drillin' and the drill music. Keef got a record deal off that Chiraq shit! So that got us sayin', 'Why can't we?' That's when we *really* got to work making music. We figured if we gave people what they want, we could get rich off this drill shit."

By the time I met him, AJ and his peers already had a large digital footprint—music videos and Instagram uploads with millions of views, followers, likes, and comments. It hadn't always been this way. In one conversation after another, they traced their popularity back to its humblest roots. When the Corner Boys first began their efforts to emulate their drill idols like Chief Keef, their biggest concern was simply finding a way to record and upload content. Lacking consistent access to audio and video recording equipment, they were left to create videos using limited, unreliable, and time-consuming tools. In the earliest stage, around 2012, they used their camera phones and inexpensive point-and-shoot cameras to make short videos of one another freestyle rapping. They'd take turns standing against the brick façade of a nearby apartment building, a stereo blaring from a few feet away, making up improvised rhymes.[55] One of the more tech-savvy Corner Boys—a stocky, dreadlocked teen named Gio—edited the footage using a free video production program that he had downloaded to his family's shared laptop. Despite his gradually improving skills, it was a long and arduous process. It often took Gio two to three weeks to edit a single, three-minute, low-resolution video, and upload it to his personal YouTube channel. More than a few video projects simply went unfinished, defeated by computer crashes, corrupted data files, and other technical difficulties.

Production improved when one of AJ's neighbors, a soft-spoken twenty-year-old named Meezy, acquired a top-of-the-line Sony DSLR camera through his job stocking shelves at a big-box electronics store. With his Coke-bottle glasses and slight social awkwardness, Meezy had spent much of his adolescent years on the periphery of Taylor Park's teen culture. When he wasn't working, Meezy spent time practicing his video editing skills, hoping to someday attend art school and become a professional cinematographer. Walking through the neighborhood with his camera slung around his neck, he attracted the attention of the Corner Boys, who pestered him to begin recording and editing their music videos. Meezy leaned into this new role as the neighborhood's resident videographer. He even created his own YouTube channel—called "Meezy Visuals"—where he uploaded all of his recordings, including the Corner Boys' content. Along the way, Meezy took Gio under his wing as his apprentice and production assistant, teaching him how to use more advanced programs and equipment.

When the Corner Boys weren't making music videos, they were watching music videos. And when they weren't doing that, they were scrolling through the tweets, Instagram photos, and other content produced by the most successful drillers. Their drive to imitate Chief Keef and other pioneers hadn't faded by the time I entered their lives. If anything, it had intensified. As we pored over the most popular online content, they were quick to point out the communal, teamlike quality of both digital production and the stardom that results. There was a common formula to this new avenue for upward mobility: When people like Chief Keef gain fame and fortune, they share the spoils with lifelong friends and fellow gang members—the young men bouncing to the beat in the background of their videos. CBE's fascination with the success of Lil Durk provides a fitting example. When Lil Durk went on a national concert tour in the fall of 2015, he posted a four-part "day in the life" documentary.[56] With Durk's music pumping in the background, the videos portray the driller accompanied by a half dozen others affiliated with the 600 OTF faction of the Black Disciples gang. In scene after scene, they flirt with attractive women fans and flash handfuls of cash. In five months on YouTube, these videos averaged roughly ten thousand views per month. At least a few dozen of these views were coming from Taylor Park, where the Corner Boys and I watched them over and over.

Outside AJ's apartment building one afternoon, a group of us stood hunched over an iPhone, dissecting Durk's garish displays. This was the kind of micro-celebrity status that the Corner Boys so badly wanted. Junior, who had practically memorized the dialogue in the videos, spoke to several of the young men huddled around us.

"Look at this nigga," Junior told the group. "Durk's got it like that. He's so rich, bro. He's fuckin' *on*! Look. They're in that nice ass hotel just coolin' out. Drinkin' lean. Ain't nobody fuckin' with them. Nobody tryin' a come through blowin' [committing drive-by shootings]. They *outta* this shit."

Stevie, one of Junior's childhood friends, continued the narration, but drew special attention to the four young men who accompanied Durk in his hotel room. "You see how he got his boys with him? That's his niggas right there." Stevie counted them off. "One, two, three. . . ." Stevie even knew some of them by name after following them on Instagram.

"We gon' be right there," Junior said, responding to Stevie's comment. "Just watch. I'm bringing you with me. You comin' too. All my real niggas is coming with me."

"See," Stevie continued, pointing to Durk on the screen. "That's Junior right there." He pointed to a member of Durk's entourage. "And that's me right there." He raised his head and addressed Junior with a smile. "We gon' be on like that. Right, my boy?"

"Like this," Junior responded, directing our attention back to the iPhone rather than answering Stevie outright. The video showed Lil Durk and his posse walking through a Walmart buying toiletries and last-minute items to stock their tour bus. Off screen, a woman approaches Durk's group and asks who the "star" is. Without breaking stride, Durk offers a concise response: "All of us." Junior nudged Stevie and repeated Durk's statement with a slow emphasis. "You hear that, bro? All of us."

For drillers and their peers, these kinds of videos serve as more than just inspiration; they also play a pedagogical role. As Junior's final comment captures, the march toward micro-celebrity carries an unspoken social pact: If local drillers can manage to reach their lofty goals and move out of poverty, they'll bring their "real niggas" along with them.[57]

"Going Legal"

Young men also gravitate toward the attention economy because they perceive it as carrying a relatively lower risk of arrest, incarceration, and death than drug dealing, robbery, and other illegal pursuits. In fact, quite a few CBE members first began displaying and representing violent criminality on the internet as part of their efforts to reduce their involvement in such behavior in their offline lives. They saw digital production as a means to *escape* street life.

I might have missed this counterintuitive motivation if I hadn't developed such a close bond with Junior at a time when he was desperately trying to, in his words, "go legal." Our friendship began several months after my initial introduction to the Corner Boys, when Junior was released from jail following his arrest for armed robbery. Although the other Corner Boys had grown comfortable with my presence in their neighborhood, and despite their vouching for my trustworthiness to Junior when he returned to the neighborhood, he maintained a skeptical distance as he sized me up. This all changed one evening, as the two of us unexpectedly found ourselves deep in conversation. We were trying to pass the time as a dozen of his fellow Corner Boys gathered in a South Side warehouse that one of their friends had converted into a makeshift music studio. Junior and I sat on a broken-down leather couch as AJ, Xavier, Dominik, and a couple of others took turns in the homemade recording booth. He resigned himself to chatting with me. I tried to ease his wariness by sharing a few sodas and a family-sized bag of nacho-flavored Doritos I had picked up on the way.

Slowly, Junior opened up. He began filling me in on his long-standing legal and financial troubles. Like far too many of his peers, Junior had been caught up in the criminal justice system from the time he hit puberty. As a juvenile, he cycled in and out of detention centers for various criminal charges and probation violations. Each arrest caused serious disruptions and delays to his progress in school—he had already fallen two grade levels behind. These entanglements also strained his relationship with his mother, Tasha, who was doing her best to care for Junior and his three siblings on her own. Now, after his most recent arrest, he was feeling more rudderless than ever. As with each previous release from custody, he returned to Taylor Park desperate for cash and direction.

Lacking the funds to purchase a new phone, Junior had been pestering everyone all evening to let him borrow theirs to send text messages, post Instagram photos, and update his Facebook news feed. I handed him mine. I quickly grabbed it back after watching him lick the nacho cheese dust off his hands and then touch the screen with his wet fingers. After wiping it down, I volunteered to transcribe his text messages and status updates for him. As I tapped away at the keyboard, I learned even more about Junior's recent difficulties. When he was released from custody, Tasha had prohibited him from entering her home or interacting with his younger siblings. Working long hours in the city's parking enforcement office, she was afraid of his influence on her household and worried that the police, or even his recent robbery victims, might come looking for him. With few other options, Junior had been spending nights sleeping in the stairwells of Taylor Park apartment buildings, dozing in the back seat of his friend's Pontiac sedan, or "pulling a two-four," which entailed staying awake all night simply walking the streets of Taylor Park. I noticed that Junior had been wearing the same pair of jeans and t-shirt for the past week. His clothes were covered in food stains and reeked of teen body odor.

In just a few hours, Junior was due in court for a morning probation hearing. Through me and my phone, he pleaded with his mother to give him a ride to the courthouse on her way to work. She refused. I read her text messages out loud as they streamed in. "She says she's 'Fed up with your shit,'" I relayed in a low voice, keeping our conversation as private as possible. "She says she's 'Done with you.' She says you can 'Take care of yourself.'"

I realized that I was watching Junior's mother disown him, via text message. I felt him slump even further into the couch as I read her words aloud. I pretended not to notice the tears that began to well in his eyes. We sat in silence for a few minutes.

"I can't be sittin' in jail no more," he finally said. The resilience in his voice caught me off guard. "I just need a *legal* way to make some money. I can't be fuckin' around no more. I'm out here fuckin' up niggas lives." His words were soaked in guilt. "My mama ain't havin' it no more, bro. You seen what she said. She ain't fuckin' with me no more. I'm out here on my own now."

"What are you gonna do?" I asked.

Junior replied without hesitation. "I'm gonna start rappin'." He pointed across the room to the other Corner Boys who were engrossed in their phones, quickly typing up song lyrics before stepping up to take their respective turns at the microphone. "I look up to them," Junior continued. "They're like my big brothers. If I keep working on this music shit, they gon' put me on. No more of this stainin' shit. You heard my mama!"

Freshly motivated, Junior pushed himself off the couch and strode over to the others. He looked back to me with determination in his eyes.

"Watch," he instructed. "I'm gonna show my mama she wrong about me."

Junior spent the next hour pestering the other Corner Boys to let him try his hand at rapping. I sensed some pity on their part, and they eventually caved to his pleas. They let him record his very own song—a short, two-verse tune boasting about his recent arrest and incarceration. It took him all of five minutes to type the lyrics on my phone. Motivated by the late night in the warehouse, Junior found a way to record four new songs over the next month and prepared to make music videos. With his free time devoted to making music, he told me that he planned to give up his stick-up career. I believed him. Rather than join friends in their search for victims to rob, he retreated to the apartment stairwells, or to the passenger seat of my car, where he spent hours writing songs about robberies instead.

■■■

Back at the diner, Xavier's mood slowly improved. Belly full, sipping on his third refill of sugary lemonade, he stared quietly out the window. He started the meal reminiscing about the past; he ended it looking to the future.

"I'm finna make a new video," he said confidently, planning his next move. "It's about to rack views [generate attention on YouTube]. If I could drop [upload] one of them, I'll be a'ight [alright]. These fans is thirsty. They *need* my videos, bro." With noticeable conviction, he capped off our earlier conversation about the big homies. "Fuck 'em. I'm finna do this shit on my own."

I was relieved when I heard the positivity in Xavier's voice. In contrast to his earlier depression, he was suddenly invigorated by the prospect of digging himself out of his predicament *without* help from the neighborhood's Black Counts elders. He was determined do it *his* way, on *his* terms, by creating and uploading music videos to social media.

Xavier isn't alone. Every year, more and more teens turn to digital cultural production as a strategy for upward mobility. The more time I spent alongside them, the more I realized how thoroughly academics, the media, and the public have underestimated, or completely ignored, just how forcefully these young people are seizing the opportunities offered by the attention economy.[58] This blind spot is a testament to just how hegemonic the notion of a digital divide has become. Even today, some of the best "experts" on urban poverty are surprised to hear that impoverished South Side teens have access to cell phones and social media at all. They're even more shocked to learn that these youngsters have harnessed these tools as a new pathway out of poverty.

When I began sharing this discovery with wider audiences, I heard one question perhaps more than any other—a question about the feasibility of this "long-shot" goal. Once, after presenting some of these stories to a room of university donors, a middle-aged white gentleman—the father of a University of Chicago student—immediately raised his hand. With a cynical scoff, he pointed out what he referred to as "irrational behaviors" on the part of AJ, Xavier, and the rest of the Corner Boys.

"Come on," he said smugly, "deep down, these kids don't *really* think they're going to get rich and famous from this stuff, do they?"

"Is it really *so* outlandish?" I asked in return.

I went on to put their digital dreams in context. These young people aren't naïve. Far from it. They know full well that only a handful of drillers will ever reach the micro-celebrity necessary for real and meaningful upward mobility. But for them, this slim success rate is still better than the odds offered by their other options. They've watched as their most determined neighbors failed to get ahead via conventional means. They've witnessed uncles and cousins toil for years without promotions in low-skill, minimum-wage jobs. They've watched older brothers and sisters pour energy into school assignments that are designed more to increase standardized test scores than prepare them for higher education. We shouldn't lose sight of the fact that a mere 8 percent of students in Chicago's notoriously under-resourced school system go on to attain a four-year college degree—a credential demanded of anyone hoping to enter the white-collar world.[59]

Considering statistics like these, is the turn to the attention economy really that irrational?

For these young men, if anyone is naïve, it's their neighbors who still buy in to the conventional mythology. Besides, of all their options, the attention economy is the only one that treats their background as an asset rather than a deficit. Why should they continue trying to appease demeaning teachers and scornful bosses when swarms of social media fans not only accept their biographies but *celebrate* them?

I was reminded of this point whenever I spoke with the Corner Boys about their backup plans.

"What are you gonna do if this drill stuff doesn't work out?" I once asked Xavier.

"I ain't got nothing else, bro," he answered. "I *gotta* make it. I ain't even tryna' think about 'What if.'"

Of course, it's one thing to *aspire* to create impactful uploads, and another thing to actually do it. To understand how drillers create content that is enticing enough to attract millions of viewers, we have to dive into the nuts and bolts of their digital production practices.

2

∎∎∎

Algorithms, Analytics, and AK-47s

The music industry is changing. Gone are the days when distribution followed the same supply chains as other commodities—when record labels delivered "master" versions of songs to printing presses, assembly lines molded plastic into cassettes and CDs, and cross-country trucking lines delivered new albums to brick-and-mortar stores every Tuesday morning. Thanks to streaming media services and social media platforms, today's cultural producers can deliver content directly to their audiences. The path from conception to global consumption is now a matter of minutes, not months. In turn, today's consumers enjoy immediate access to a virtually endless universe of online content. Want to watch the newest drill music video? Simply enter the title in YouTube's search engine. Want to save and rewatch it on the walk to school? Just click a button to add it to your personal playlist. Want to pass it along to friends? Hit "share" to embed it in a text or email message.

Hoping to seize on these new consumption habits, aspiring drillers upload a steady stream of music videos to YouTube. But much to their frustration, most of their content will never grace consumers' screens. The truth is, the vast majority of videos receive very little sustained attention. They might attract a couple hundred views from friends and family, but they'll quickly be buried under the avalanche of new daily uploads. Some videos will fare relatively better, tallying up a few thousand views before slowly fading from memory. A very small portion will go viral. They'll amass millions of views as consumers play and share them throughout their day. They'll spark new slang terms, maybe even a dance craze or two. They'll send audiences in search of other related content, leading them to drillers' Twitter, Instagram, and Facebook profiles. There, they'll learn biographical information, keep up with daily activities, and perhaps strike up a friendship. Maybe even a romance. For the young men making drill-related content, this is the ultimate goal—maximum exposure and connectivity. This is how Chief Keef punched his ticket to stardom, up and out of poverty.

How do they do it? How do these young men increase the odds that their own songs and videos will cut through the noise of the internet? How do they ensure that their content will outlast their competitors in the on-line attention economy?

The answers can be found in drillers' digital production practices, in the ways they distinguish their own uploads from those languishing in obscurity. Their strategies grow directly out of their disadvantaged starting place. They enter the attention economy with far fewer resources. Just think of household brands like Nike and Starbucks. These companies can afford to pay millions of dollars to social media platforms to ensure that users will see their content first. Drillers have no such luxury. In turn, they've developed and refined alternative methods for steering online audiences in their direction. First, they grab attention by manipulating the selection algorithms that control the content circulating on social media platforms. Second, they hold that attention by saturating their content with provocative (if usually exaggerated) images of street violence and gang life.

I spent considerable time watching these young men wrestle with algorithms and magnify violent criminality. It wasn't long, however, before my gaze shifted beyond those standing at the center of the frame. Although people like Chief Keef and the Corner Boys have become the human face of drill—and of urban gang violence more generally—they don't operate on their own. What's too easily lost in the public fascination and media panic is that drillers' over-the-top displays of gangsterism depend on a vast network of backstage collaborators. In sociological terms, every drill song and video is the collective product of what the sociologist Howard Becker famously referred to as an "art world."[1] An art world consists of all the contributors, or "support personnel," necessary for a cultural commodity to occur as it does. This includes everyone who conceives of a work, provides equipment and material, engages in the performance, and consumes the final product. Thinking in terms of the broader "drill world" helps us see that although drillers are the most visible player in the production process, they aren't the lone gravitational center.[2] In fact, as the public fascination with drill continues to grow, more and more people (beyond drillers) are becoming invested in, and benefiting from, violent depictions of urban America.

STEP #1: GRAB ATTENTION

Like that of young people across the world, media consumption among South Side teens takes on a competitive edge. Every day, they race their friends and classmates to discover the newest and best drill music videos.

As teens share their newest finds with their peers, they gain bragging rights and status. Running an after-school program, I saw my fair share of this content. I recall one particular afternoon, when the debut of one of the Corner Boys' music videos completely overtook one of our weekly creative writing sessions. Following an opening brainstorming exercise, we split the teens up into small groups to work on short stories. As was common, several young men broke out their headphones and opened up the YouTube mobile application on their smartphones. Although I worried that they might be distracted from the task at hand, I bit my tongue. To my pleasant surprise, each of them got down to work, shimmying quietly to their music as they wrote in their notebooks and tapped away at computer keyboards. Unfortunately, their focus didn't last long.

"Damn!" I heard from the table behind me. I turned around to see three young men huddled tightly around a phone screen. "This joint raw as hell," one of them remarked.

The owner of the phone, Matthew, sat at the center of the group, enjoying the attention. He shot me a guilty smile as I approached. As one of the savvier teens in the program, Matthew preempted me from scolding them and setting them back to task. "Check it out, Forrest," he said with a sly grin. "CBE just dropped a new video. It's so cold." I couldn't help but chuckle a little at his tactic. I had been asking the teens about their thoughts on the Corner Boys over the past few weeks. Matthew knew I would be curious to discuss the new release. I took the bait, leaning over his shoulder to watch the video, which was titled "Murdering Murderville." The song was an insulting reference to one of the Corner Boys' rivals, the Murderville Almighty Knights, a gang faction located a few blocks from Taylor Park.

"This *just* dropped like two days ago," another one of the teens said, proudly pointing to the upload date displayed in the video's description box.

"How did you find it?" I asked.

"It just popped up," Matthew said with an innocent shrug. He explained how it had appeared on his personalized YouTube homepage just moments earlier.

It wasn't long before word of the video spread to the other teens in the room. By the end of the week, the song's melody was a ubiquitous presence in the halls of the community center. Teens recited the lyrics and discussed the large pistol that CBE brazenly featured in multiple scenes. The video spread from there, picking up tens of thousands of views in a few short months. At the time, I assumed that the viral quality of "Murdering

Murderville" had been mostly a matter of luck. The Corner Boys' new content had merely managed to show up in the right consumers' hands at the right time.

Once I began spending time with the creators of the video, however, I learned that luck had very little to do with it. The fact that CBE's video had "popped up" in Matthew's YouTube application was no coincidence. Rather, it was the result of hard-learned lessons and intentional strategies on the part of the Corner Boys, who had discovered ways to exploit the algorithms engineered some two thousand miles away at Google's headquarters.

Learning to Manipulate Algorithms

By allowing everyday people to generate and distribute their own content, digital technologies have radically democratized the field of cultural production. This is not to say, however, that this field is now flat, open, or free of gatekeepers. Today's producers confront new barriers, none having a greater impact than the AI programs employed by virtually all social media platforms.[3] Facebook, Google, and Twitter all use complex filtering algorithms that sift through the deluge of online information to deliver personalized content to individual users. By collecting and analyzing data on users' previous online activities—what we watch, listen to, and interact with—these programs quickly learn our tastes and interests, and then tailor content accordingly. These algorithms are designed to ensure psychological gratification, which leads to more clicks, more screen time, and thereby more chances to see and interact with paid advertisements.[4]

As the most dominant platform in the drill world, it's worth reviewing YouTube's algorithmic filtering system, referred to as the "suggested video algorithm."[5] First, the algorithm notes the title, description, and "tags" for whatever video a user is currently watching.[6] This is referred to as the "seed video." Second, the algorithm compiles a list of "associated videos" that contain similar words in their titles, descriptions, and tags. For example, if the seed video contains the words *Corner Boys* or *CBE AJ* in its title, the algorithm will search through YouTube's billions of videos for other titles that contain these same terms. Next, the algorithm ranks the associated videos according to the individual user's previous YouTube activity. Which other videos did they recently watch? Which videos did they "like" by pressing the "thumbs up" button? This allows YouTube to better anticipate which content a given user will most likely want to watch next.[7] Finally, after compiling and rank ordering the associated videos, the algorithm presents a list of recommended videos in the "Up Next" sidebar on the right side of the YouTube interface. Once the seed video ends, YouTube automatically plays the top recommended video.

This automated curation process wields immense control over the content that reaches viewers' screens. In fact, YouTube's suggested video algorithm is responsible for a reported 70 percent of all time spent on the platform.[8] I witnessed its power to shape consumption practices among South Side teens virtually every day in my after-school program. When groups of young people gathered to do homework, socialize, or play basketball, they'd open up the YouTube application and cue up their favorite music video. When it ended, they'd pull up another one. But, as typically happens with teens, their attention almost always drifted to other matters. This is when the YouTube selection algorithm took over, automatically playing associated videos, one after another. After only a few minutes, YouTube had taken full control. For many teens I spoke with, this automated process is precisely why they love the application so much. As we saw with Matthew, the platform consistently introduces them to new music videos that closely match their existing tastes and viewing habits. As one teen told me, "It's like it always knows what kind of stuff I want."

Although teens like Matthew enjoy this process, algorithms like YouTube's have come under intense scrutiny in recent years, and for good reason.[9] By automatically sorting, classifying, and ranking content to better satisfy users, these programs can quickly pigeonhole users into specific niches.[10] Algorithmically curated content streams grow increasingly narrow, biased, and tilted toward users' existing tastes and opinions, much like an echo chamber. Once an algorithm sufficiently "learns" a user's preferences, it's far less likely to present different, unrelated, or contradictory content.[11] It's perhaps no surprise, then, that an entire industry has emerged in response to this dilemma. Sometimes called search engine optimization (SEO) or news feed optimization, specialized firms offer programs and expertise for manipulating algorithms in ways that penetrate content streams and boost clients' visibility.[12] For a steep fee, Facebook, Twitter, and other platforms also provide companies the opportunity to insert their "sponsored" content into users' content streams.

For all those who can't afford to purchase SEO services and sponsored search results, algorithmically curated content streams are major obstacles to being seen and heard.[13] Facing this threat of invisibility, drillers have learned to create content in ways that make it more "algorithm friendly." To be clear, very few of them are able to articulate the nuts and bolts of YouTube's selection algorithm. I never once heard one of the Corner Boys utter the word *algorithm*. Yet, they don't need an in-depth, technical understanding of the platform's artificial intelligence to successfully manipulate it.[14] All it takes is a general recognition that particular actions tend to increase viewership. Over the course of their initial foray into digital content creation, the Corner Boys slowly, if serendipitously, learned to overcome this barrier.

It was only after the Corner Boys had uploaded a dozen or so videos that they even began noticing the patterns in online traffic. Some videos attracted exponentially more views than others. They started obsessing over these statistics.[15] View counts were typically the first topic of debate when they gathered each morning on stoops and sidewalks. Whose videos were "doing numbers"? Whose videos had received the biggest "bump" overnight? It wasn't long before these questions brought them into the world of data analytics.

Keeping a close watch over his YouTube channel, Meezy was the first to discover the algorithmic logic driving YouTube viewing patterns. He recounted his revelation one afternoon as we sat chatting outside his apartment.

"It's all about how many *other* videos you got," the Corner Boys' resident videographer relayed to me. Meezy used my tablet to scroll through his YouTube channel. He showed me the different view counts for his music videos.

Meezy described how every new video upload had a kind of multiplier effect. He noticed that each time he uploaded an additional music video on behalf of a driller, the view counts on all of that driller's *previous* videos suddenly increased. He detailed this process for me by logging into the administrative "back end" of his YouTube channel. There, he clicked a tab labeled "Analytics." It produced an assortment of color-coded charts, maps, and statistics provided by YouTube to all its channel owners. Meezy pointed to the different data on the screen, rattling off the total number of views for each video, the length of time viewers spent watching each video, the geographic locations of viewers, and how these trends were changing over time. With noticeable excitement, Meezy showed me his most coveted set of statistics. He clicked on a tab that read "Traffic Source." It provided a detailed description of how, exactly, viewers had found their way to each of his videos.

"This is the trick," Meezy said, half laughing, as though letting me in on a well-kept secret. "I remember when I first found this. I clicked on it by accident. I started seeing where they [viewers] was comin' from." He pointed to several columns on a table of information. "Look," he instructed, "it says it right here. They're comin' from my *other* videos. The fans, they watch one of my videos, then they watch another, and another. That's why you need lots of videos, 'cause they help each other."

Consider the Traffic Source report for one of Junior's music videos, called "Haters." It was one of his newest uploads, but in just a few weeks it had attracted roughly thirty-eight thousand views. According to YouTube's analytics, the majority of viewers (almost half) had arrived at Junior's video because the AI program had designated it as a "suggested video."[16] In other words, viewers had been watching a related video, as designated by YouTube's algorithm, when the platform suggested that the user would also be interested in watching "Haters."[17]

"Every video you got is like money in the bank," Junior told me when I asked him about this pattern. "It's like they say, you gotta *have* money to *make* money. These videos is the same." He drew my attention to one of his most popular music videos to provide an example. "Once I started getting love off my other videos, then everything I dropped just started smackin' [generating views]. The fans was on there [on YouTube] like, 'What else he got?' 'When the new joint gonna drop?' That got 'em ready. They're thirsty now. Now it don't even really matter what I do, they gon' watch it. That's why you see me tryna' drop new shit like every couple weeks!"

Once the Corner Boys realized the multiplier effect of their existing videos, they restructured their production practices. Speed and efficiency became the top priorities as they raced to upload new content as quickly as possible. They anticipated that if they saturated YouTube with enough videos bearing their individual and collective names, they could improve the chances that YouTube's selection algorithm would recommend their videos to their current fans and followers. In other words, they proactively created a content stream made up exclusively of CBE content. The data analytics pages on Meezy's YouTube channel indicate that the Corner Boys have been mostly successful in their efforts. But algorithmically curated content streams are a double-edged sword. For every viewer they've locked into CBE's recommended video stream, there are thousands of potential viewers who are locked *out*. If a driller truly intends to expand his audience, he has to find ways of inserting himself into *others'* recommended streams. For this, he needs outside help. It's time to call in support personnel.

"Features," "Video Men," and "Diss Tracks"

One of the most common methods for penetrating other drillers' content streams is to invite them to make a guest appearance, or "feature," in a song or music video. By placing both young men's names in the title, description, and tags of a single music video, these collaborations effectively "reroute" the YouTube selection algorithm. For example, not long after our late-night conversation in the recording studio, Junior recruited a better-known driller from the far South Side, who goes by the moniker "Lil Hype," to provide a feature. By making a video bearing both of their names, Junior increased his chances of reaching Lil Hype's existing audience. Whenever anyone watches one of Lil Hype's videos, they're likely to encounter the video of Lil Hype and Junior together. If they click on it, the algorithm is likely to recommend one of Junior's solo videos. And from there, it's likely to recommend one of the other Corner Boys' videos. In just a few steps, the collaboration with Lil Hype has created a bridge between two otherwise insular streams.[18] Of course, the inverse is also true. Lil Hype can count on YouTube to reroute CBE's viewers to *his* content.

When two drillers command similar levels of popularity, they approach features as mutually beneficial. When they don't, things get more complicated. In the attention economy's competition for clicks, drillers are wary of boosting others' viewership without increasing their own. This puts relatively unknown young men at a real disadvantage. They're forced to sweeten the deal by offering monetary incentives, typically referred to as "feature money." As one of CBE's original and most popular drillers, Xavier typically charges six hundred dollars to write and record an "eight-bar verse"—roughly thirty seconds' worth of rapping. Throughout my time with the Corner Boys, Xavier completed a feature every one to three months. At the height of Junior's eventual popularity, he charged an aspiring rapper eight hundred dollars to collaborate. When hopeful collaborators lack the necessary cash, they offer nonmonetary forms of compensation. This includes gift cards, cell phones, and firearms, as well as more mundane items like home electronics and even food.

Of course, this all assumes that well-known drillers will be responsive, available, and amenable to collaboration. When they aren't, novices resort to other techniques to penetrate content streams. If they have the money, they can hire one of the city's high-profile videographers, or "video men," to come to their neighborhood, record a music video, and upload it to the videographer's YouTube channel. As they were making a name for themselves, the Corner Boys obsessed over one particular channel, operated by a thirty-something Chicago native named Duan Gaines. Known widely throughout the drill world as "D. Gaines," he is responsible for recording and uploading the videos of such homegrown heroes as Chief Keef and Lil Durk, who successfully rode this content to internet stardom and multi-million-dollar record deals. AJ often insisted that if he could just find a way to convince D. Gaines to record and upload one of his videos, he could exponentially increase his viewership. He'd be able to take another step on the road to becoming the next Chief Keef.

AJ had reason to be confident in his assessment. First, by creating a video bearing the names of both AJ *and* D. Gaines, he would increase his odds of entering the suggested video stream tied to *every other* video D. Gaines has made. This includes dozens of Chief Keef videos that continue to attract millions of viewers every year. Second, enlisting well-known videographers allows drillers to tap into the videographer's YouTube subscribers, or "subs." Whenever D. Gaines uploads a new video to his channel, YouTube alerts his nearly half million subs via an automated notification system, providing them with a direct link to the music video. It's a powerful tool for grabbing the attention of new audiences.

Given videographers' ability to cast a bright spotlight on drillers' content, they ask significant prices for their services. Operating out of his cramped bedroom, Meezy charged clients between one hundred and three hundred dollars to record, edit, and upload music videos to his YouTube channel. Music videos typically require about five to ten hours of work, meaning that even Meezy—one of the relatively lesser-known videographers in the city—can bring in as much as sixty dollars an hour. Meezy would have gladly left his day job stocking shelves, but his paid videography gigs were too sporadic and unreliable to replace his consistent minimum-wage earnings. This was compounded by the fact that the Corner Boys and other neighborhood clients continually badgered him to provide his services for free or at a significantly discounted "friends and family" rate. He might have had more power to deny their appeals if he were able to build a wider client list. But without a car or other means of reliable and safe transportation, and lacking much free time outside of school, work, and familial responsibilities, he had difficulty recruiting and working with any drillers beyond Taylor Park. To make matters worse, as the Corner Boys' popularity grew, Meezy's previous negotiating power steadily dwindled. Whereas the Corner Boys once pestered him to record and upload their videos, he increasingly finds himself begging *them* for opportunities. For Meezy, it's difficult to compete against people like D.

Gaines, who tend to be older, more financially stable, geographically mobile, and capable of disseminating content to a far wider audience.

I met one such videographer when he traveled to Taylor Park to film a music video for Xavier. Terrance—known throughout the drill world as "Canon-T"—is an unassuming thirty-five-year-old resident of Chicago's middle-class Bronzeville neighborhood. After short periods living away from Chicago, including several semesters at Howard University, Terrance now shares an apartment with his girlfriend and infant son. Along with a bit of financial support from his family and an occasional part-time job, Terrance's videography services and YouTube channel are his primary sources of income. He hopes to save up enough money to attend one of Chicago's downtown art schools, which would put him closer to his life-long goal of shooting television commercials for a living. When I first met Terrance, his YouTube channel already commanded fifty thousand subscribers (more than five times as many as Meezy's), boasted more than twenty million total views, and hosted a diverse range of content from drillers across the Midwest. Given the high demand for his videography services, Terrance regularly charges as much as five hundred dollars for his services. While Meezy's work remains confined to the area surrounding his own neighborhood, Terrance drives to his clients' homes to record videos in their neighborhoods. He also drives his clients around Chicago to film additional scenes portraying a diverse array of backgrounds. Similar to collaborations between drillers, videographers provide discounts to Chicago's more popular names in the hope that they will drive additional traffic to their channel.

For those drillers who are particularly cash strapped and can't afford a premier videographer, there is one last option for penetrating others' algorithmically curated streams. It's less expensive but carries higher risks. It involves creating what are commonly known as "diss tracks." These are songs and music videos that explicitly insult, or "diss," more popular drillers. Like features, diss tracks allow drillers to manipulate video selection algorithms. By creating titles containing their own name alongside the name of a more prominent figure, they immediately build a bridge between two otherwise insulated content streams. Diss tracks also allow upstart drillers to pique the voyeuristic curiosity of unfamiliar viewers. These young men know that when audiences encounter a diss track on YouTube, they'll be tempted to investigate the story behind the potential feud, which will lead them to view the creators' other content and social media activity.

Junior was one of the first to clue me in to this logic. The two of us had been lounging against the hood of my car watching YouTube videos on my tablet. He reflected on one of his new videos. Although it had attracted a few thousand views in its first months online, its daily view count had plateaued and then fallen off. He spent the afternoon stewing about the analytics.

"These fans really ain't messin' with me at all," he complained.

"Well," I began, hoping to pull him out of his sour mood. "You just started. Nobody really knows you yet."

"True," he agreed. "Nobody really know my name." He stood in contemplation for a few seconds before I saw his eyes go wide. "That's it!" he yelled, hit by inspiration. "I know what I'm finna do. I'm finna get real disrespectful. That's how these other niggas got on [became popular]. Imma diss *everybody*. These fans gon' definitely know my name after that!"

Junior immediately began brainstorming his new approach. Having spent his teenage years primarily as a consumer of drill music videos, Junior knew full well the influence that diss tracks have on viewers. Now, as he transitioned into the role of driller, he intended to use them to his advantage.

"Look at this," he ordered, grabbing my tablet. He quickly typed a name into YouTube's search engine. He pulled up a series of videos made by a well-known South Side driller who goes by the name "Lil Jay."

Junior looked back toward me. "Even you heard of *this* nigga, right?"

"Yeah, I've seen a few of his videos."

"But did you know," Junior continued, "that he got on [became popular] because he was out there dissin'?"

"Really?"

"Hell yeah. That's what put him on! 'Cause he got on there dissin' *Keef*." Junior pointed at the screen. "Look."

I pulled closer to the tablet as Junior scrolled through a series of Lil Jay's music videos. Several prominently featured the word "diss" in their title. Junior clicked on each one, insisting that I read each title and description out loud. We proceeded like this through the chronology of Lil Jay's uploads. It began in 2012, just as Chief Keef was gaining national recognition. Lil Jay began releasing diss tracks that aimed explicitly at Chief Keef. One of Lil Jay's very first uploads is titled "Chief Keef Diss CRITICAL (LIL Jay & FBG Duck)." In it, Lil Jay and his collaborator, "FBG Duck," openly belittle one of Keef's closest friends, a young man named Odee Perry, who had been gunned down the year before. At one point in the music video, Lil Jay aggressively raps:

I'm Lil Jay, you already know.
Sending shots at your homies, screaming fuck Odee.
Shout out number three, yeah I said it first.
Fuck Chief Keef, you ain't puttin' in work.

Amid new and elevated levels of attention, Lil Jay continued uploading diss tracks. In October 2012, Chief Keef—who sometimes goes by the
nickname *Sosa*—released a song called "Love Sosa." A month later, Lil Jay
uploaded a music video titled "Lil Jay #00 Fuck Sosa." He followed this
with a music video titled "KING Lil Jay Take You Out Your Glory Chief
Keef Diss." The title has a doubly disrespectful meaning. On the streets of
Chicago, to take someone "out of their glory" is slang for murdering them.
This is combined with the fact that Chief Keef's group refers to themselves
as Glory Boyz Entertainment. Over the next three years, Lil Jay would go
on to record and upload four more diss tracks aimed directly at Chief Keef
and his friends. Three of these videos have eclipsed two million views.

As Junior went on to explain, this strategy catapulted Lil Jay onto the
public stage alongside Chief Keef. In fact, these videos were how Junior
first discovered Lil Jay.

"I remember when I first saw that 'Fuck Sosa' video," Junior recalled.
"I was watchin' Keef's videos all the time. You know I love me some Sosa.
But then I saw Lil Jay on there [in the recommended videos panel] comin'
steady with them disses. I was like, 'Who is this nigga dissin' Keef?' So
then I went and checked him out. I spent the whole day steady watchin'
Jay's videos. Me and everybody else is tryna' see who he is. Jay even got
Keef's fans watchin' him. That's when he started stealin' Keef's fans. They
mess with Jay now."

I couldn't help but notice a disapproving tone as Junior recounted Lil
Jay's string of diss tracks. "It sounds like *you're* not a fan," I said.

"Hell naw," Junior replied. "Fuck Lil Jay."

Initially I assumed that Junior might have disapproved of Lil Jay's
attention-grabbing tactics. "Do you feel like he cheated?" I asked. "Like
he got all those views the cheap way?"

"Naw," Junior replied, quickly rejecting my theory. "Ain't no cheatin',
bro. Niggas gotta do what they gotta do. You get on any way you can,
you know what I'm sayin'?"

"So then why don't you like Lil Jay?" I asked.

Junior's reply was as immediate as it was concise. "'Cause he a lame."

"What do you mean?"

"Look at his video, bro!" Junior pulled up the YouTube application once more. "Look for yourself. This nigga ain't really in the field [authentically engaged in violent hustling]." Junior scrolled through Lil Jay's video, pointing out moments of disbelief. "Jay ain't ever got no pole [gun]," Junior remarked at one point. "His boys look foo as hell," he said, critiquing a scene where Lil Jay is surrounded by several other teens. He turned to see if I agreed with him. "Even you could see that, right?"

"I guess. I don't know."

"Well *I* could tell," Junior said. "That's why you ain't never seen me messin' with his music. I ain't messin' with no computer gangsters."

I had heard this term over and over during my time with CBE. A "computer gangster" is a young man who, via music videos and related social media activity, falsely claims to be involved in street violence and gang life. Junior's disapproval captures the next dilemma that drillers face in their efforts to dominate the attention economy. Though features, video men, and diss tracks are highly effective in manipulating selection algorithms and grabbing viewers' initial attention, they don't ensure lasting engagement. For that, these young men have devised techniques for confirming authenticity and putting to rest any assumption that they might be a computer gangster.

STEP #2: HOLD ATTENTION

Amassing a million YouTube views doesn't happen overnight. Drillers have to entice audiences to repeatedly watch their video, add it to their personal playlists, and share it with friends and classmates who will do the same. An unrivaled method for increasing a video's staying power is to overdramatize representations of violence, gangs, and crime. Long before I ever met the Corner Boys, I saw the gravitational pull that the most provocative content exerted on teen consumers in South Side community centers. The more extreme the video, the more these wide-eyed youth loved it. The bigger the guns, the thicker the drug baggies, the darker the mood, the longer the video's shelf life. I'm certainly not the first to make this observation. Social scientists have been writing about the public obsession with hyperviolent musical content for decades.[19] In her ethnographic research on middle-class black youth growing up in 1990s Chicago, the sociologist Mary Pattillo revealed that even the highest-achieving, church-going teens derive transgressive pleasure from consuming gangsta rap songs, videos, and associated media.[20] These thrills are even more accessible in today's digital age as consumers flock to platforms like YouTube to enjoy a seemingly endless stream of ghetto bad man tales.[21]

In one of our after-school programs, one drill music video commanded more sustained attention than any other. It was called "Computers Remix," made by a prominent South Side driller who goes by the nickname "Tay 600." I heard about the video long before I ever saw it. For at least a month, teens discussed and debated the automatic submachine guns, or "choppas," that Tay 600 and his crew brazenly display throughout the video. They argued over the type of gun ("Is it a MAC-10 or an Uzi?") and the size of the magazine ("Is it a 30- or 50-round clip?"). I once walked into the community center to see three young men reenacting the video, mimicking the ways that Tay 600 holds the large gun as he postures for the camera. The group of teens were especially fond of two particular lines from the song, where Tay 600 raps about shooting a rival in the face:

Just don't approach me, or we shootin' like a basket.
And now he gone, ain't got no face, it's a closed casket.

Given the basketball metaphor, these youngsters liked to sing the lyrics on the basketball court, whenever they drained a difficult shot.

A year or so later, once I started spending time with the Corner Boys, I marveled at how open they were about their intention to evoke these exact responses, strategically crafting sensationalized images of their communities and themselves. I recall speaking with Junior one late afternoon, scrolling through the Corner Boys' music videos on YouTube. Noting each video's relative numbers of views, Junior launched into an explanation as to why some of these videos continued garnering attention long after their upload dates.

"It's all about that *gang* shit," Junior instructed me. "White people, Mexicans, bitches—all those people that don't *live* the life, they love *hearing* about the life." He walked me through a hypothetical situation to make sure I understood. "Like, say there's this boy. He had everything he wanted. He never had to struggle. Never had to tote a gun. Never had to rob nobody. Never had to stretch [shoot at] a nigga, never had to do none of that. He hear a nigga rappin' 'bout it, and that's *exciting* to him. He gets a kind of emotion off that." I immediately thought of the teens in our after-school programs, and their excitement while watching drill videos. "Then you got the street nigga who done some of that shit," Junior continued. "He's listenin' 'cause he feel like he can relate. He been through some shit you rappin' 'bout. At the end of the day, *everybody* really just listenin' based off their *feelings*."

Ensuring continual views requires drillers to arouse intense emotional responses among their audiences. Whether piquing the voyeuristic or appealing to familiarity with "the struggle," Junior is ultimately describing an aesthetic project—one that hinges on creating online content that *sounds* and *looks* a particular way. Like manipulating selection algorithms, creating stirring representations of violent street life depends heavily on the services provided by support personnel. This has given rise to a somewhat unexpected arrangement in which many of the individuals who are the most necessary for portraying street life actually have very little personal experience with it. In fact, some of the people most responsible for cementing the infamous reputation of "Chiraq" have never actually set foot in the city. The varied influences of outsiders—as an imagined audience and as coproducers—are central to each phase of the production process, from creating beats to recording vocals to filming and uploading music videos.

The Sound of the Streets

The basic building block of every drill video and song is its beat—the combination of drum patterns and instrumental melodies that give the genre its distinctive sound. Sonically, drill beats are most akin to the music styles emerging from the American South over the past decade and a half, often referred to as "trap." Southern musicians eschewed the long-established "West Coast" practice of sampling the feel-good hooks, harmonies, and bass lines of classic funk and R&B songs—think James Brown and Earth, Wind, and Fire. In their place, both trap and drill embrace dissonant minor keys played on electronic synthesizers—think *Jaws*, *Psycho*, and suspenseful horror movies. The booming Roland 808 drum machine provides the percussive punch. The kick drums, snares, and hi-hats are often layered in rapid sequences that simulate the sound of an automatic machine gun.

Beats provide drillers with one of their first opportunities to "hook" their audiences and stir emotions. But which beats are most effective? Which percussive arrangements, harmonies, and sonic compositions make one beat better than another?

I began asking the Corner Boys these questions not long after we met. Despite the importance of beats to their long-term success, they had incredible difficulty articulating what, precisely, makes an ideal beat. In one conversation after another, they struggled to offer anything more than vague and brief answers. Despite their online popularity, at the end of the day, the Corner Boys are novice, self-taught musicians. Without formal training, they lack the technical vocabularies necessary to answer my questions. But just because they lack the precise words to describe the sonic elements of beats doesn't mean that they don't have systematic criteria for evaluating quality and potential virality. Indeed, rather than assess a particular beat in terms of its technical composition, they judge it according to the kinds of images, emotions, and experiences it conjures. AJ helped me to understand this one afternoon as he pushed back against my questions about technical jargon.

"It ain't something you could really describe like that," AJ told me. "You just know it when you hear it."

"But what are you *hearing* when you '*hear it*'?" I asked.

"You hear what's goin' on out here," AJ said. "The perfect beats sound like what the streets sound like."

"Ok," I replied. "So then what *do* the streets sound like?"

"You know what these streets sound like!" He gave me a displeased look but ultimately humored my question. "You've seen it. Niggas slidin' through [committing drive-by shootings]. Niggas gettin' shot. Babies dyin'. Everybody snakin' [betraying one another]. The opps [rivals]. Twelve [the police]. The hypes [addicts]. Even your own mans [friends]."

"So, like, dangerous. Chaotic."

"Yeah," AJ agreed. He was picking up momentum now, and dove even further into his explanation. "It's like when you out there posted on the block [standing on the corner]. You ain't know if you dyin' today. You ain't know if this nigga walkin' up to you is tryna' blow [shoot at you]. That's what I'm sayin' the beats be soundin' like. Like the streets. It gets real out here, bro. You might gotta up that pole [pull a gun] on 'em. That's why they call it drill music. 'Cause it makes you wanna go do some drills [shoot at enemies]. It puts you in that mode. Geeked up. It's kill or be killed."

AJ's statement is revealing. Although his explanation doesn't include a single detail on the technical attributes making a beat ideal, he provides a wealth of information about the embodied responses that it evokes. According to AJ, the best beats simulate the experience of moving through neighborhoods saturated with violence. They arouse a sense of paranoia and suspicion, as if life-threatening dangers—rivals, addicts, the police, duplicitous friends—loom around every corner. At the same time, these beats put listeners in a state of hypervigilance that someone "posted on the block" might rely on to face down and eliminate potential threats.

Given the importance of emotive beats for holding audience attention, I initially expected drillers to devote considerable time and energy to producing them. This isn't the case, however. In fact, not one of the drill-ers I met had ever created a beat themselves. Instead, they outsource the task. If we think about it, their reliance on others isn't too surprising. Even today, as powerful music production software has become cheaper and more accessible than ever, producing beats tends to require a level of privilege that most drillers simply don't have. At a minimum, it takes access to a fast, reliable computer with sufficient memory to run large programs and store hundreds of audio files. It's also helpful to own a keyboard or drum machine. Skill-wise, producing beats requires a proficiency with audio production software and at least some minimal knowledge of music theory. It means knowing the difference, for example, between 3/4 and 4/4 time signatures, and the effects this difference has on the mood and pacing of a song. It means knowing the difference between a C-major and a C-minor chord, the location of these notes on a keyboard, and their relative positions within varying chord progressions.

A far more efficient method for securing beats is to simply search content-sharing platforms like YouTube and SoundCloud. There, one can quickly find hundreds of thousands of beats available for free download. Hoping to emulate the sounds of their role model, the Corner Boys usu-ally just type the words "chief keef type beat" into these platforms' inter-nal search engines. This produces a virtually endless catalog of beats that have been uploaded by aspiring music producers, themselves hoping to be discovered by popular drillers. If someone uses one of these beats in a music video, and if that video goes viral, and if the rapper was respectful enough to credit the beat, these producers can build a reputation and in-crease future demand for their products. If the demand grows high enough, the producer can start charging a fee for exclusive and custom beats.

Outsourcing beats to more qualified (and more socioeconomically priv-ileged) producers means that many of those who conjure what it sounds like to be "posted on the block" and "drilling on opps" have likely never done either. Rather, they work from their own assumptions about Chi-cago's South Side, derived mostly from the public imagination. This was nowhere more apparent than in the case of one of the drill world's most successful producers, a twenty-two-year-old white college student named Mark Hoffman. In just two years, Hoffman became one of the most sought-after drill producers, responsible for the beats in at least fifty songs and music videos. As a testament to the power of digital communication technology, he's managed to do so from his family home just outside of Frankfurt, Germany. I got to know Hoffman through AJ. Despite collab-orating on a half dozen songs, their ongoing collaboration began somewhat coincidentally. AJ stumbled on Hoffman's name while watching a new music video uploaded by one of AJ's drill idols. After AJ made contact via email, Hoffman began sending AJ his newest beats. One of these led to AJ's most popular music video to date.

When I spoke with Hoffman via Skype, I learned that his initial exposure to the drill world mirrored that of many in America, with exposure to Chief Keef and Lil Durk in 2012. In that year, the coach of Hoffman's soccer team—an American expatriate—introduced him and his teammates to a series of drill music videos. According to Hoffman, he and his friends were "blown away" by the genre's imagery. They were particularly fascinated with the talk of gang violence.

"I think the music, it's like, crazy," Hoffman told me. "I think it's really awesome. I think they got a sound that nobody else got, but, like, the violence. The violence is crazy. It's scary." Although he has never visited the United States, Hoffman holds strong impressions about the inescapability of street violence, which makes Chicago seem far more exciting than his own hometown. "A lot of kids over here would be afraid to walk over there," he continued. "Like, they would get shot like instantly for walking down the street. But I really love it. I don't know. Like, they [drillers] are always talking about violence in the music." Titillated by these stories of gunplay, Hoffman and his friends started following, and sometimes messaging, South Side drillers. Hoffman even joined Twitter—a platform that is relatively unpopular in much of Europe—for the express purpose of keeping tabs on drillers' feuds. "I follow all those artists," Hoffman informed me, "so I can keep updated on what they're saying. I'll see their beefs [rivalries] too."

Like other consumers who write their own "fan fiction" stories to connect more deeply with the characters and plotlines of their favorite television shows, Hoffman decided to try his hand at making beats.[22] A quality beat, he reasoned, would allow him to form personal relationships with Chicago drillers. Every day for several months, Hoffman rushed home from school to devote his evenings to learning music production on his home computer. As he consulted online blogs and how-to videos, his skills developed more quickly than even he expected. He soon began sending his beats via email and direct Instagram and Twitter message to his most beloved drillers, including the Corner Boys. As the quality of his beats improved, drillers started replying to his messages, asking for exclusive permission to use his beats in their newest songs and videos. One of those replies came from AJ, kicking off their ongoing international collaboration.

Through exchanges with AJ and other young Chicagoans, Hoffman gained a better sense of drillers' needs. He developed a knack for doing precisely what drillers *hadn't* been able to do for themselves: using expensive equipment and music know-how to translate the images and emotions of street life into evocative soundscapes.

"What does drill *sound* like?" I asked Hoffman at one point in our conversation.

Unlike the Corner Boys, Hoffman didn't fumble for words. His response was far more technical. "It's just minor keys, all the time," he replied, highlighting the importance of creating the foreboding mood. "It's just like *dark* to me," he added. "All the time." Hoffman went on to describe the importance of using what he described as "military sound snare drums." These are percussion patterns that intentionally resemble gunshots and the tense march into battle.

Producers like Hoffman have a financial incentive to create the most evocative beats possible. It's a lucrative business. Producers usually charge somewhere between ten dollars and three hundred dollars per beat. One producer I met, a twenty-five-year-old Atlanta resident named Chris, reported making nearly three thousand dollars in a single week.

Some producers have even begun using their reputation in the drill world to break into other, more mainstream and profitable musical genres. For Hoffman, producing beats for Chicago drillers elevates his desirability among German clientele, including local rappers and other pop acts. As Hoffman confessed, "People in Germany, they think I'm awesome because I produce for people in the States. Because they kind of look up to all of them. So, like, producing for AJ, that helps me a lot." He chuckled a bit as he spoke. "Yeah, it gives me a lot of cred in Germany." Producers' reputations grow alongside the global popularity of Chicago drill music. As the fascination with Chicago street life increases, so do their profits.

Streets Talking

Acquiring a provocative beat is critical for holding attention. But it's only the first stage in a lengthy production process. Let's assume that a driller is able to find a "perfect beat" and pay the producer for exclusive use. When he receives the audio file in his email inbox, he faces a new, equally pressing dilemma: He has to find a way to "engineer" the song; he must somehow download the audio file to a computer, record his own vocals over the top of the melody, fix any lingering audio problems, and save the results as a complete song. If he wasn't able to produce the initial beat himself, it's unlikely that he has the necessary equipment or skills to complete the remaining tasks. It's an obstacle that leads drillers to enlist the next set of support personnel—a group sometimes referred to as "hood engineers."

Much like the producers of drill beats, hood engineers tend to be older, more educated, and more economically stable than drillers. During my time with the Corner Boys, they maintained a close working relationship with one particular engineer—a forty-something Chicago native named Antoine. Around 2012, Antoine recognized a growing demand for his formal training in audio production and engineering. The bigger Chief Keef's popularity grew, the more *other* Chicago youth hoped to follow suit. Like Keef, they needed someone to record their vocals. Antoine was happy to fulfill this demand. When I met him, Antoine was leasing a small music recording studio in one of the multiuse, redeveloped warehouse spaces on the Near South Side of the city, where he charged aspiring drillers sixty-five dollars per hour for his services.

As soon as a client arrives at Antoine's studio, he downloads their beats into professional (and pricey) audio production software called Pro Tools.[23] He ushers his client into a small, closet-sized room that serves as a semi-soundproof recording booth. There, drillers spend the next twenty minutes or so rapping into the microphone, reading lyrics off their phones. Antoine sits at his computer in a different room, adjusting the audio levels. After spending a few more minutes completing the "mix down," he emails the finalized song back to the client, who hands over his payment. It didn't take Antoine long to streamline this method, soon completing the entire process in just forty-five minutes per song. Word of his quick turnaround time spread across the city. Demand for his services grew so large that he had to hire and train two additional employees. Together, they work in shifts to keep the studio running practically twenty-four hours per day. When we first met, Antoine told me that his business was bringing in around five thousand to eight thousand dollars in cash per month.[24]

Recording sessions are often stressful events, carrying a palpable sense of urgency. Every studio session I've ever attended has had at least one small argument. Shoving matches, even between best friends and collaborators, aren't uncommon. These conflicts usually erupt when someone feels as though others are interfering with their ability to make the most use of their expensive studio time. This usually happens when a fellow driller spends too long recording his vocals. By using too many takes to get through his various rhymes and verses, he cuts into others' opportunities in the recording booth. Slowdowns also occur when engineers struggle to complete a mix-down efficiently enough, whether because of computer malfunctions or perfectionism. Having gone to great lengths to borrow, pool, and otherwise scrape up the cash necessary to hire these support personnel, drillers try to produce as many songs as possible in a single sitting. This desire to work quickly structures how they approach their craft, particularly how they write and record lyrics. An unmistakable rule permeates every studio session: Produce the most extreme lyrical content, and do so as fast as possible.

The dual goals of speed and sensationalism were on full display one summer evening when I accompanied Xavier, AJ, Dominik, and Junior to Antoine's warehouse studio. The four had combined their cash to buy three hours of Antoine's services. Moments after walking in the door, Xavier, who had contributed the most money to the collective pot, immediately walked into the recording booth. Less than two minutes later, he was rapping his song into the microphone. Meanwhile, AJ, Dominik, and Junior each sat silently in different corners of the room, quickly typing lyrics into their phones. I watched them occasionally stare up at the ceiling, deep in thought, searching for rhyming words. I immediately realized how unprepared the three of them were. They had spent so much time and energy over the past few days raising funds, coordinating with Antoine, and sorting out transportation that none of them, except for Xavier, had written *any* rap lyrics. And now they had to come up with something. Junior, who had the least experience writing lyrics, was struggling. He looked up from his phone every few minutes to solicit the others' help in completing his half-baked couplets. I took note of the words he was hoping to find rhymes for, as they would become the dominant themes organizing his song. The first three were squarely tied to violent murder. *Pole*, *mop*, and *nina*—all slang terms for gun. Between slightly annoyed looks, AJ and Dominik offered Junior rhyming words that maintained Junior's running theme.

Ten minutes later, Junior began writing the second verse of his tune. He looked up from his phone with a confounded expression. "What rhymes with gang?" he asked the room.

"Bang," AJ replied without hesitation.

"Stain," Dominik said, offering the slang term for a robbery victim.

"Brain," AJ offered.

The two provided a few more rhyming words before diving back into their own songwriting. This was a routine practice; I had watched every one of the Corner Boys crowdsource their lyrics like this at one time or another.

"Gratitude," Junior thanked, furiously typing these options into his phone. A few minutes later, his verse was complete. He used almost all of their suggestions to construct a short verse, which he proudly read out loud to AJ and Dominik. The lyrics depicted the three of them sneaking up on a robbery victim, putting a gun to his head, pulling the trigger, and blowing his brains out.

An hour and a half later, it was Junior's turn in the recording booth. It was time to record his freshly written lyrics. He put on the oversized head-phones and pulled close to the microphone. After the familiar cue from Antoine, Junior launched into his first verse. It was only a few seconds before he began fumbling through his hastily written lines. Despite several fits and starts, he made it through the entire song in less than ten min-utes. Antoine immediately began the mix down, adjusting the midtones and other audio levels. Junior sat in a nearby chair, nervously bouncing his leg. Fifteen minutes later, Antoine played the completed song for us. Given my own background in music production, I was impressed by the engineer's proficiency—his skills were obvious. I was less impressed with Junior's performance. To my ears, his vocals sounded off-time and off-key. I cringed more than a couple of times. I assumed that Junior shared my reaction.

I was wrong.

"Right there," I said in Junior's direction at one point in the song. "You're a little off-time right there." I offered my critique as gently as I could.

"It's good enough," Junior replied indifferently. He pulled out his phone and started writing lyrics for the next song he intended to record.

"But you're gonna re-record that part, right?" I asked, a bit more forcefully.

"Naw. It's good," he replied, consumed by his search for lyrics.

I was surprised at Junior's response. The two of us had spent long after-noons talking about music. I always assumed that he enjoyed it when I introduced him to classic hip-hop tracks and broke down the fundamen-tals of music theory. I remember one listening session in my car, with Ju-nior nodding along in appreciation as I explained how lyrical cadence worked in tandem with beats. Today, he simply brushed off my advice.

Ego slightly bruised, I pressed on. "Dude, you sure you don't want to—"

"Bro." Junior cut me off with a hard stare. "Stop tweakin'. It's *good enough*." His voice was louder now.

"But you want it to sound *really* good, don't you?" I asked.

Junior was growing more agitated. "You don't even know, bro. It's *supposed* to sound like that."

"It's supposed to sound *off*?" I asked.

"Forrest," he said, using my name to signal his seriousness. "It's *supposed* to sound like that. Like some real street shit." I could tell he was angry now, because he began criticizing my own musical tastes. "You be listenin' to that bubblegum rap," he said, making fun of my fondness for more mainstream hip-hop songs. At the time, the multi-platinum rapper and vocalist Drake had recently released an ear-catching song called "Back to Back." It was all over the radio, and on steady repeat in my car. "This ain't that," Junior said, referring to the Drake song. "This is hood shit. This is what *real* street nigga music sound like. You ain't know about this."

The two of us went back and forth a few more times before AJ loudly intervened. "Ay Forrest," he called out. "Back up, bro. Leave it alone." I bristled a bit at his orders. He turned to Junior to lend support. "Go 'head, boy. Do your thing. He ain't know what we doin'." Our argument was now threatening to cut into AJ's precious recording time. Even if Junior had taken my advice to jump back in the booth to re-record his vocals, it's unlikely that AJ would have allowed him to follow through with it.

I've thought a lot about this interaction over the past few years. On the one hand, I can't help but feel a little embarrassed about arguing with Junior. On the other hand, our dispute provided rare insights into the aesthetics of the drill world. I later realized that I *had* misunderstood what they were doing in that recording session. I had assumed that they were following older, more traditional conventions, when artists treated the musical process as a grinding quest for sonic perfection. Throughout the early 2000s, before the massive proliferation of streaming content platforms, up-and-coming rappers devoted incredible patience to lyric writing and recording sessions. The sociologist and hip-hop scholar Jooyoung Lee describes how rappers disciplined themselves to "think in rhyme" through strict repetition and practice. It allowed them to make word associations quickly and on demand. Their dedication included spending long nights reviewing and memorizing pages from dictionaries.[25] Conducting interviews in the early 2000s, the sociologist Geoff Harkness quotes the words of an up-and-coming Chicago rapper who described a monastic approach to the recording studio. "There's take after take," the young man told Harkness, "and you have to constantly be in there 'til you get it right. . . . You have to really work at it. It's time and commitment and dedication."[26] The drive to "get it right" was often so intense that it cost aspiring rappers friends, girlfriends, and other joys of life. Lee relays the story of an aspiring rapper who angered his girlfriend because he continued to rhyme words at the most inappropriate times, including moments of intimacy.[27]

Fast forward to just a decade later, to our current social media age. Rather than use his hour-long session to craft a single song as flawlessly as possible, Junior used his time to make *two* songs that were merely "good enough." On first blush, it might seem as though today's production process is simply about quantity over quality. But this view is too simplistic. Drillers still aspire to create high-quality products. It's just that "quality" means something different in the drill world. As both AJ and Junior were quick to instruct me during our disagreement, drill lyrics and vocals are *supposed* to sound off-time and off-key. They're *supposed* to sound raw, unrehearsed, and homemade. Time and time again, drillers presented the do-it-yourself quality of their songs as a conscious aesthetic choice, intended to convey that these products were made by a "real street nigga," as Junior put it. Rather than treat their amateurism as a liability, these young men exploited it as a vital asset in the attention economy. Outmatched by mainstream, radio-friendly rappers in financial capital, industry connections, and marketing capacities, drillers effectively rewrite the rules of the game. They make it more about street authenticity than sleek and seamless production. Through the low-fi quality of their songs, they convey the sense that they are "street niggas" first, musicians second.[28]

For some drillers, the production process stops here, with a completed song. They can now upload the MP3 file directly to streaming audio platforms like SoundCloud, Spinrilla, or DatPiff. But if a driller truly wants to attract a fan base and build micro-celebrity, he needs to record a music video to accompany the song. Music videos allow drillers to enter the heavily trafficked world of YouTube and increase their reach. Take the example of one of AJ's most popular songs. It amassed an impressive hundred thousand plays on SoundCloud. On YouTube, however, the video drew almost four times that number in views. Perhaps even more important than the additional exposure, music videos provide drillers with one of the most powerful means for verifying the authenticity claimed in their lyrics.

Music Videos: A Glimpse Inside the Ghetto

If drillers intend their beats and songs to conjure what the street *sounds* like, music videos are designed to capture what the street *looks* like. But unlike the amateurish feel of lyrics and vocals, drillers go to great lengths to make their videos look as professional and polished as possible. This is because music videos provide drillers with the first opportunity to provide *visual* evidence for the deeds and lifestyles they proclaim in their songs.[29] As the hip-hop scholar Tricia Rose reminds us, validating authenticity, or "keeping it real," is always a two-step process. "Rappers," she writes, "not only have to tell compelling stories about being in the [street] life but also have to convince listeners that they know that life personally and intimately."[30] The history of rap music is full of artists who have lost credibility (and their careers) not because they lacked talent, but because they couldn't adequately authenticate their claims of criminality, gang affiliation, and ghetto biography. Thanks to the democratization of cultural production, however, drillers possess new resources for satisfying audiences' continual expectations of autobiographical proof. With the assistance of skilled support personnel, these young men don't just take viewers into the exotic no-go zones that dominate nightly news and urban legends; they do so in ways that convey their own deep familiarity, ease, and stature within these social worlds. According to the Corner Boys, the best music videos don't just allow audiences to *see* their social world; they let audiences *experience* it in a visceral way.

Once, while sitting in a Burger King drive-through line, killing time watching YouTube, I asked Junior his thoughts about what makes an ideal video. In his words, the best videos are those that "take you there." To demonstrate this point, Junior grabbed my phone and cued up one of his favorites. It's a music video called "Shit Real," made by two South Side drillers known as "Fredo Santana" and "Rondo Numba Nine." The video, which has gained more than two million views since its upload, brings viewers into what appears to be Fredo and Rondo's evening routine. It opens with the two young men walking through one of the many corner liquor stores that dot the South Side landscape. The footage cuts to the interior of a small, dark apartment. Here, the young men appear to be cutting and sorting various drugs for distribution. The camera repeatedly pans across a small mound of marijuana buds sitting on a kitchen table. These striking scenes are recorded using slick camerawork and editing. The camera pulls in and out of focus. The song's gunshot sound effects are exaggerated by rapid jump cuts that give the entire video a chaotic and dizzying feel. Footage of the drug stash is distorted via disorienting red, blue, and green halos around all the images, simulating increasing intoxication.

"I love this," Junior said through a big grin as the video ended. "He showin' what the hood like. What it's really like. The fans always want that. They wanna see how we livin'." Noticing my interest in his comments, Junior cued the song up from the beginning. "Watch it again, bro. Imma show you. The rappin' and the video be workin' together." At first, I didn't quite understand. But as the video progressed, I caught Junior's meaning. Every few seconds, Junior paused the video to point out key features. He drew my attention to how each scene presented specific visual evidence for Fredo's claims. For example, early in the song, Fredo brags about the inventory of guns he keeps in his drug house. As Fredo delivers these lines, the video reveals a black 9mm pistol resting next to his pile of drugs. Then, he describes himself driving into rival gang territory and shooting his enemies:

> Nines, AKs in my trap, boy this shit real.
> Pull up on your block, boy this shit real.
> Hop out with them 30s and just lettin' out shells.
> Pouring up a pint of lean, boy this shit real.

As Fredo speaks, the video shows him exiting a car and hurrying across a street as though sneaking up on one of his intended targets. Keeping with the running pattern of tell-and-show, when Fredo raps about preparing doses of promethazine and codeine, the camera pans to a baby bottle and a tall Styrofoam cup, the two items most closely associated with its sale and consumption.

"It's like he say," Junior instructed as the video finished, "it's all real. He really in the field [violently street hustling]. All that shit's real." I suddenly understood the meaning of the song's title, as well as the repetitive phrase that punctuates nearly every one of Fredo's lines—"Shit's real." Somehow, I hadn't put it together until that moment. For any viewers that have missed Fredo's displays, the driller has taken additional steps to convey authenticity. As a longtime consumer of this content, Junior was more than convinced.

"See," he exclaimed, "that's why I *love* Fredo. He a *real* savage [violent criminal]. It's like you right there with him—slidin' on [shooting at] the opps and mixin' up that lean. That's how I want my videos to be like!"

Junior's gleeful commentary helps to explain why drillers covet well-produced music videos. This content holds the power to convince audiences that the young men on the screen aren't *talking* about street life; they're *living* it. To borrow a term from film and theater scholarship, these are videos that perpetually sustain the "fourth wall"—the invisible, imagined barrier that separates a performer from the audience.[31] When the fourth wall is "broken," so to speak, the audience is reminded that the performance is fictional. Viewers are reminded that they're watching actors, on a set, reciting a script. The longer the fourth wall remains intact, however, the more completely the audience will suspend disbelief. As anyone who has ever suffered through a poorly acted, low-budget movie knows, maintaining the fourth wall is no easy task. It takes a significant amount of preparation, staging, editing, ingenuity, and practice. The same is true of drill music videos. Drillers enlist a number of techniques to turn their music videos into short, seemingly transparent documentaries about their daily lives.

One of the best strategies is to hire one of the drill world's established videographers. In addition to their well-trafficked YouTube pages and impressive viewer statistics, these young men possess the equipment, skills, and experience necessary for authenticating drillers' claims. Over the course of my time with the Corner Boys, Chicago's videographers were engaged in an arms race to acquire state-of-the-art cameras, image stabilizers, color-correction software, effects plug-ins, and related recording supplies. I recall one summer when word spread throughout Taylor Park that a well-known videographer had acquired a flying drone, which allowed him to use dramatic aerial shots in his music videos. The Corner Boys spent the following weeks desperately trying to scrape up enough money to afford the videographer's newly elevated fee, which they reported to be between six hundred and one thousand dollars per video. AJ already had one particular scene mapped out in his head. It would open his music video and set the tone. The drone shot would begin at a high elevation, showing the Chicago skyline in the distance. Then, the drone would move downward, revealing a broad shot of the entire South Side before eventually descending down into the courtyard in front of AJ's apartment. There, it would zoom in on AJ and the other Corner Boys waiting for their rivals to show up.

"They gon' see we *stay* on the block," AJ said proudly as he sketched his vision for the group of us standing in the location he hoped to film. "Fuck these haters. We out here." AJ was referring to a constant criticism facing mainstream hip-hop artists who, despite their claims of street authenticity, actually come from middle-class backgrounds. Through his proposed scene, AJ hoped to preempt such attacks. By documenting the city, the South Side, Taylor Park, and the Corner Boys in one continuous shot, he could provide strong evidence of his steadfast presence in the neighborhood. It's a scene that would be difficult, if not impossible, for a nonresident to pull off.

Not long after AJ shared his vision, the Corner Boys hatched a different plan to capitalize on one of their favorite videographer's high-tech camera stabilizers.[32] In the span of just thirty minutes standing in the parking lot, the group pieced together a detailed storyboard of a lengthy scene. Shot from a dramatic ground-level perspective, the camera would smoothly follow the group of men as they walked through the surrounding neighborhood, interacting with various residents. It would include shots of the Corner Boys affectionately greeting a large contingent of young men standing guard on a corner, calmly selling drugs to passersby, generously doling out rent money to needy mothers, and shooting hoops with wide-eyed schoolchildren. The Corner Boys anticipated that this collection of images would portray them seamlessly transitioning between the various activities they describe in their song lyrics.

The videographers I met were upfront about their intentions to deliver these overdramatized representations. In fact, most wore it as a badge of pride. It helped them attract clients who were constantly searching for the video man who could make them appear the most "savage." During video shoots, the most experienced videographers spend considerable time directing the action, blocking out scenes, and barking instructions. During one session, a videographer encouraged Xavier to gather as many guns and fellow gang members as possible. Once the recording began, he instructed Xavier to peer down the street and act as if his enemies were nearby. On other occasions, I've watched videographers convince drillers to simulate shoot-outs, robberies, and prostitution rings.

Videographers refine these portrayals in the editing process. Terrance, the videographer from earlier in this chapter, explained several powerful techniques one afternoon as we sat at a café down the street from the University of Chicago. He explained that early in the editing process, he looks through the footage to flag any scenes that might make his client appear awkward or fearful.

"The camera shows *everything*," he told me. "When that camera is on, it's gonna catch a moment where you look goofy. Where you look vulnerable. Smiling where it doesn't call for it. It could be the way you stand. It could be like the way your posture is at that particular moment that may look a little feminine or a little suspect."

Using my tablet, Terrance pulled up an example from his own YouTube page. He clicked on a music video featuring two of Chicago's most notorious drillers. It was one of his most popular videos to date, with more than four million views at the time. The video shows the two men and their friends flashing gang signs along one of the sidewalks of their neighborhood. The lyrics, camera angles, and general mood of the video give the impression that the gang defends its territory to the death. As Terrance noted, however, the coherence and strength of this message doesn't happen naturally, or without his help.

"It's just fake," Terrance said abruptly. "They're actors." He explained that when he began to edit the footage, he discovered that a lot of it was unusable. Terrance noticed that one of the drillers seemed overly fearful as he stood on the sidewalk, where he was vulnerable to a potential drive-by attack. "He just had a look in his eyes," Terrance described. It was a look that directly contradicted the video's underlying claims. To camouflage the young man's apparent insecurities, Terrance slowed the footage to half speed—a common editing technique in drill rap music videos. When done correctly, the slow-motion effect creates a cinematic and striking quality that makes drillers look more confident and intimidating.[33]

In addition to amplifying drillers' violent dispositions and familiarity with street life, videographers also work to exaggerate the danger, poverty, and desperation of drillers' neighborhoods. This is best accomplished through the strategic inclusion of "B-roll." In contrast to "performance scenes," which show the driller rapping his lyrics in front of the camera, B-roll captures the general setting and context. I first learned about B-roll from a middle-rung videographer named Javelle, known in the drill world as "Big Bang Films." Although he had grown up in a neighborhood a few miles north of Taylor Park, he shared several family ties with the Corner Boys, which helped facilitate a collaboration. It was just after 11 PM when Javelle arrived in Taylor Park to record their newest music video. I stood with Junior and a couple of others in an alleyway, waiting for everyone to arrive. I noticed Javelle quietly step away from the bunch and walk to the far end of the alley. He turned on his camera and began recording short, three- to five-second shots of different items that caught his eye—a discarded mattress, an empty plastic drug baggie, and a burned-out streetlight.

"Getting some more shots?" I asked quietly as I approached.

"B-roll," he answered, scrutinizing the viewfinder on his camera. Knowing that I was interested in the nuts and bolts of video production, Javelle expanded. "That's really the secret to making a good video. It's all about B-roll. That's how you set the mood. If I could, I would make a video that was *all* B-roll. No rappers, just stuff like this." He pointed his camera toward the opening of the alleyway, where the busted streetlight created an ominous darkness. Javelle continued recording B-roll as we walked back toward the group. He showed me his favorite technique of adjusting the camera's f-stop settings, which has an effect of blurring the background and bringing the subject into razor-sharp focus. This allows him to direct the viewer's attention to the most eye-catching images.

Throughout my time with CBE, I witnessed Javelle, Terrance, and other videographers go to great lengths to collect B-roll footage that would bring these South Side neighborhoods even more in line with the popular imagination. The running list of items included: the brick façades of local housing projects; abandoned, boarded-up, and half-demolished houses; cramped and food-stained kitchens; dark passages found under railroad viaducts; addicts staggering down the sidewalk; muscular pit bulls straining against thick chains; flashing police lights; and crime scenes cordoned off by bright yellow tape. I also discovered that videographers routinely gather B-roll footage on their own time, storing hours of stock B-roll on their computer hard drives for use in future music videos. This means that a fair share of the scenes purporting to depict Taylor Park aren't actually recorded in the neighborhood. This irony is nowhere more pronounced than when videographers film entire music videos in their own middle-class neighborhoods.

I experienced this odd simulation of ghetto streets when Junior coordinated a music video shoot with one of the most respected videographers in the drill world—a man named Chucky. The twenty-seven-year-old operated a popular YouTube channel out of his two-bedroom apartment in a quiet suburb north of Chicago. About a year into my relationship with Junior, once the young man had uploaded a half dozen music videos, he began soliciting Chicago's elite videographers. He typed up a stock message and sent it to them all via Facebook Messenger and Twitter direct message. In his pitch, Junior asked them to record, edit, and upload his music video free of charge. In return, Junior promised to deliver future collaborations with the entire roster of Corner Boys, whose popularity was at an all-time high.[34] I was surprised when Junior reported the news that Chucky had agreed to his terms, though I soon learned why. Apparently, Chucky had hit a low point. His car was in the shop, which made it virtually impossible to commute into the city to record music videos. His videography services made up a large part of his income, so Junior's guarantee of future work with the Corner Boys appealed to him. There was a catch, however. Junior would have to find a ride to Chucky's home, located about an hour from Taylor Park.

Lacking other options, Junior called me. Two days later, we drove to meet Chucky at his apartment. Junior's eyes grew wide as he took in the lush greenery and spacious homes that lined the peaceful streets of Chucky's suburb. He vowed that he would move to a city like this when he "made it" as a famous musician. When we met Chucky, Junior made his excitement clear. He had never worked with someone of this stature, so he told Chucky he would gladly defer to any and all of the videographer's creative decisions.

"Imma do whatever you say," Junior insisted. "You just tell me what to do, bro."

Chucky seemed to expect as much, and began brainstorming ideas for the music video. There was a problem, however. In their earlier exchanges over Facebook Messenger, the two had decided to record a music video for one of Junior's most hardcore songs to date—one where he boasts about his love of killing rivals. But this kind of imagery would be hard to create on Chucky's quiet suburban street.

"That's a straight drill song," Chucky said as they brainstormed, "so we need some straight gutter scenes. But we don't got nothin' out here like that. All we got is nice parks and shit. We can't shoot a video like that out here."

"What about like some abandoned buildings or something?" Junior asked.

Chucky laughed a little at this. "Out here, bro? Naw. Ain't none of that shit. But maybe we can find some alleys. Like behind a store. We can make it look real."

We spent the next hour cruising up and down the commercial streets of Chucky's neighborhood. When Chucky spotted locations that could pass for an impoverished neighborhood, he and Junior unpacked his gear and quickly recorded a scene before attracting too much attention from pedestrians and passing motorists. We ended our trip back at Chucky's apartment, where the two decided on a final scene—a dark basement where a prosperous drug dealer might be expected to keep his supply, count his profits, and store his guns. To pull it off, Chucky removed all the furniture from one of his bedrooms and positioned Junior in the corner. To make the footage look even more realistic, Chucky handed Junior a few canisters of weed from his own recreational stash. With a thick, freshly rolled blunt hanging from his lips, Junior performed the role of successful drug dealer, sorting his stash in his simulated trap house.

■ ■ ■

Three weeks after our trip to the suburbs, Junior and I watched the completed music video. Judging from the young man's reaction, Chucky had done his job perfectly. The video provided visual proof for Junior's talk of violent street hustling. Ironically, videos like these are successful precisely because they *mis*characterize the conditions of Taylor Park. If they were accurate representations of daily community life, they would capture a far broader range of experiences and events. Much to the disappointment of voyeuristic consumers, they'd paint a far more ordinary and mundane picture. They'd portray young people getting up in the morning and heading off to school and sports practice. They'd show mothers, teachers, and coaches working to improve their neighborhoods. They'd highlight the joys of family reunions, graduations, and birthdays. And they'd juxtapose drillers' toughness with their vulnerability, creativity, and friendships.[35] Like their gangsta rap forebearers, drillers aren't "just representing" their communities; they're accentuating the most distressing aspects for the sake of shock value.[36] But as sensationalized as these songs and music videos may be, they're only the first step in drillers' larger quest to build online infamy. To win in the attention economy, they need to enlist additional social media platforms, where they provide even more evidence of their authenticity.

3

. . .

Keepin' It Real

I knew a lot about the Corner Boys before I ever met them in person. Or, at least I thought I did. For nearly two years, I had spent my afternoons watching teens in South Side community centers devour CBE's Instagram photos, Twitter uploads, and Facebook profiles. Titillated by the Corner Boys' music videos on YouTube, these young consumers had flocked to these additional platforms in search of even more tales of shoot-outs and robberies. Like most online audiences, these teens imagined that these platforms provided unadulterated windows into the Corner Boys' routine behaviors and true identities. Seeing how consistently drillers upload their shocking displays, it's easy to walk away assuming they might actually be the heartless victimizers and money-hungry hustlers they claim to be.

I'm embarrassed to admit how heavily these images weighed on my own mind when I first met AJ, Xavier, and the others. On more than one occasion, I worried that their generous text messages inviting me to the neighborhood were ploys to hustle or even rob me. Needless to say, my fears never materialized. Instead, the more time I spent with them, beyond the view of cell phone cameras, the more I learned just how inaccurate audience impressions can be. In fact, I discovered that a good majority of drillers' online displays of violent criminality are gross exaggerations and, at times, complete fabrications.

This realization came during my first several months with CBE. During that time, I developed an unexpectedly close friendship with AJ—a young man whose intimidating online profile had become a regular topic of conversation among youngsters in my after-school program. From our first meeting, AJ and I routinely spent entire days together. We played dice, listened to music, and generally passed time in the parking lot of his apartment building. I peppered AJ with questions about all kinds of topics, typing out his answers on my cell phone while he spoke. He was surprisingly forthcoming. AJ shared long, emotional stories about growing up in Taylor Park, his deep depression following the murder of his childhood best friend, and his efforts to improve his relationship with Charmain, his girlfriend and soon-to-be mother of his child. Despite his typical openness, however, AJ always grew quiet when I asked him about his involvement in local gang violence.

"I ain't really gon' talk on that," AJ said one time, after I asked him about several shoot-outs he discussed in his music videos. He quickly changed the subject. As if to distract me, he pulled out his phone, showing me YouTube videos and online gossip that discussed his involvement in local violence. Each time AJ sidestepped my questions in this way, I felt as though I was falling short as a researcher, as though the young man didn't trust me enough to share such sensitive information. I continually reminded AJ that I would keep any incriminating information strictly confidential. It didn't work.

Over time, I learned the real reason AJ had been dodging my requests. It had nothing to do with a lack of trust. The truth was that AJ wasn't actually involved in the violence he claimed. Contrary to his boisterous tales in songs, music videos, and across social media, the young man was not "droppin' opps" or "totin' the pole." In fact, as his fellow Corner Boys would later divulge in frustration and annoyance, the young man had likely never fired a single bullet at a rival.

I recall one notable afternoon, when I accompanied several Corner Boys on a road trip to Cincinnati. An up-and-coming driller had invited AJ and Xavier to make cameo appearances in his new music video. One of their closest friends, a twenty-year-old named Johnny, accompanied them as a kind of bodyguard and assistant. When we arrived at the video shoot, the Cincinnati driller distributed about a half dozen replica pistols to give the music video a more menacing and authentic appearance. He invited AJ and Xavier to brandish the fake firearms throughout their respective scenes. The two were giddy with excitement. They immediately pulled away from the group and took turns uploading Instagram pictures of one another posing with the replicas and firing off blank charges. AJ barked instructions to Xavier as he filmed the simulated gunplay with his phone. At one point, he ordered Xavier to avoid including the videographer, the video camera, or any other signs that this was a manufactured scene. AJ planned to give the impression that these photos and videos were providing an intimate and faithful glimpse into his daily life.

For Johnny—one of the CBE members with arguably the most experience with guns—AJ's performance fell short. Standing at my side, the young man let out a disappointed sigh.

"Man," Johnny complained under his breath. "Look at this goofy right here."

I was surprised to hear him refer to AJ in this way. This term, *goofy*, is a serious insult in the drill world. It refers to someone who claims to be more violent and gang-involved than they actually are.

"What do you mean?" I asked, hoping he'd elaborate.

"Just look at this nigga. This nigga don't even know how to hold a fuckin' gun, bro!" Johnny was worried that online audiences might recognize it too. "The fans gon' get down on us if he puts this up [on social media]." Johnny knew that once audiences began poking holes in AJ's violent persona, they might start questioning the authenticity of CBE as a whole. In the hope of preventing ridicule, Johnny walked over to AJ and instructed him on how to hold, load, and fire the gun with more expertise. Satisfied with AJ's progress, he returned to my side. "Now this nigga actually look like what he doin'."

Johnny's intervention worked. Despite the glaring inconsistency between AJ's offline behavior and his online performance, his Instagram photos attracted hundreds of "likes." He received praise from his followers who bought his displays at face value. They added their own comments to the images:

real shooter

dey in da field

droppin stains

In their efforts to validate their authenticity as violent criminals—as people who "really do what they rap about"—drillers like AJ use social media platforms to corroborate their song lyrics and music videos. Instagram, Facebook, and Twitter allow them to provide essential proof that their music videos aren't merely artistic expression, but rather transparent, documentary accounts of their daily behaviors, neighborhood conditions, and social relationships. By exploiting the unique affordances provided by digital social media, drillers have seized on a historically new tool for overcoming an age-old dilemma facing urban artists, particularly aspiring rappers. On these platforms, drillers can more forcefully convince audiences that they aren't just *from* the streets but also *in* the streets at this very moment.[1]

SOCIAL MEDIA AND THE PURSUIT
OF MICRO-CELEBRITY

According to new media scholars, electronic communication technologies create new forms of self-presentation and interaction. During "nonmediated," face-to-face interactions, we tend to have a relatively large and stable amount of control over the kinds of information that others can learn (and *cannot* learn) about us. In the words of Erving Goffman, the preeminent theorist of social interaction, we live our lives as a series of theatrical "dramas," performing different roles, on different stages, for different audiences, all over the course of a single day.[2] When I enter my university classroom, for example, I take on the role of authoritative professor. After work, I behave as a dedicated husband and father. On holidays, I become a dutiful son and sibling. Each of those roles demands distinct linguistic styles, dress, and other outward behaviors that might be inappropriate if I performed them on a different social stage. Luckily, there are relatively consistent boundaries segregating these different audiences and their particular expectations. There's also separation between what Goffman calls "frontstage" regions, where we actively perform our ideal social selves, and "backstage" regions, where we rehearse and relax.

In his pathbreaking work *No Sense of Place*, the media theorist Joshua Meyrowitz argued that electronic media disrupt this conventional arrangement by "collapsing" seemingly disconnected stages, roles, and audiences while making backstage regions more visible and accessible to the public. In the 1980s, Meyrowitz studied how politicians, celebrities, and other high-profile people were pressed to negotiate such "context collapse" caused by the advent of broadcast television. Mass media forced those in the limelight to restructure their actions, speech, and expressions so as not to alienate or anger the multiple audiences who were now simultaneously "eavesdropping" on their lives. As it became harder to hide backstage behaviors from the public, high-profile people lost not only aspects of their privacy but also their ability to play certain frontstage roles altogether.

Yet, this increase in visibility carried some powerful benefits. As Meyrowitz noted, electronic media created a "middle region," or "sidestage," where audiences simultaneously witnessed staged performance *and* seemingly natural, behind-the-scenes behavior. As audiences learn what their favorite celebrities eat for dinner, who they're dating, and where they travel on vacation, they develop an unprecedented level of intimacy and fandom. Viewers suddenly feel as though they are witnessing a genuine slice of celebrities' lives. "Although the relationship is mediated," Meyrowitz wrote, "it psychologically resembles face-to-face interaction. Viewers come to feel they 'know' the people they 'meet' on television in the same way that they know their friends and associates."[3] This helps to explain why the deaths of our "media friends" like John F. Kennedy, Michael Jackson, or Heath Ledger can cause people to experience feelings of loss that are as deep as (and sometimes even deeper than) what they might feel following the death of a close friend or relative.[4]

In today's digital age, the dynamics Meyrowitz described are no longer limited to politicians and public figures. Virtually anyone who maintains a social media profile can exploit context collapse to stimulate their own popularity and fandom. Digital platforms allow ordinary people to create a public persona, produce content, and build popularity among online followers and fans.[5] Aspiring micro-celebrities must constantly provide evidence that they embody the particular skills, knowledge, and competencies—the cultural capital—that their relevant communities and audiences value most highly.[6] Audiences tend to gravitate toward micro-celebrities precisely because they seem more authentic than traditional celebrities, whose images have been manufactured by marketing executives, agents, and industry tastemakers. As the new media scholar danah boyd reminds us, displays of sincerity and intimacy are cumulative, becoming more convincing and corroborated with each successive upload.[7] Audiences frequently evaluate a micro-celebrity's "realness" by comparing past and present uploads for consistency.[8]

In many respects, drillers operate much like other micro-celebrities. By this I mean that they similarly manipulate the heightened visibility of middle and backstage regions. They too offer (what appears to be) an unadulterated view into their inner lives and private social roles. But though these efforts share a common *form*, drillers differ dramatically from other micro-celebrities in terms of *substance*.[9] By definition, drillers saturate social media with extreme displays of violent criminality. By flooding social media with this kind of content, drillers create the impression that they maintain their unflappable toughness, hustler mentality, and homicidal dispositions at all times, even behind closed doors.

GUNS, DRUGS, AND DEAD HOMIES

The most common technique drillers use to authenticate their violent personas is to upload images of themselves brandishing guns, drugs, cash, and other items related to street hustling. Whenever the Corner Boys got their hands on any these items, they snapped dozens of photos, sometimes wearing a variety of outfits and set against different backgrounds. By accumulating collections of titillating photos on their phones, they can strategically post them whenever their violent reputations need a boost. This particular form of embellishment—often referred to as "flexing"—is convincing enough that I initially took it at face value. I routinely assumed that the pictures the Corner Boys were posting to their social media accounts were accurate reflections of what they were doing at that very moment.

Apart from AJ, Junior "flexed" more than any other young man I met. He spent most of our relationship homeless and broke, even after he had accumulated local fame as a driller. I did what I could to help. I often packed extra food to make sure he got at least one meal a day. Among other things, I helped him to get a new state ID card and to re-enroll in school. So, when I checked his Facebook profile late one evening and saw a string of photos of him holding a large stack of cash, a dozen bags of marijuana, and a shiny pistol, I assumed that his economic situation had improved. Though I worried about his apparent return to crime, it looked as though he'd at least be able to afford a proper meal. He could even start renting a room, or at least a spot on a neighbor's couch, until his mother took him back. He wouldn't be forced to sleep in apartment stairwells anymore. I was eager to see him the next morning to ask about his sudden change in fortune. But when he climbed into my passenger seat, he relayed a very different story.

"It looks like things are getting better," I said, referring to the Facebook photos.

"Hell naw, big bro," he replied. "I'm still fucked up [broke] as hell."

"But I saw your pictures last night," I continued. "You got some money and bought another pack."

He laughed a little. "You talkin' 'bout them pictures on Facebook?"

"Yeah."

"You believed that shit?" he asked me with an amused smile.

"Yeah!"

"I ain't even gonna lie," he confessed. "I be flexin', man. All those pictures is old, from back when times was better. You didn't see how short my hair was? That was from like two or three months ago!" He told me that the cash, drugs, and gun weren't even his. "Tell you the truth, one of the big homies had the roll [of cash] and I was like, 'Hey big homie, let me see the roll,' and then I had him take the pictures. All that flexin' shit is for the fans. If I don't flex, then they gonna know I'm out here broke. They'll stop fucking with me. I'm steady rappin' 'bout trappin' [dealing drugs] and stackin' paper [making money], so the fans wanna see that shit. They wanna see how I'm livin'. I gotta put that shit up so bitches and motherfuckers think I got it like that."

Junior's admission captures the pressure drillers feel to continually corroborate the bold claims they make in their songs. In an interesting twist, the identity drillers strive to perform on social media is one that is increasingly difficult to maintain in their offline lives, given the changing conditions of urban poor communities. Take guns, for example. At least in their teenage years, drillers have far less access to firearms than their YouTube videos, Facebook posts, and Instagram photos would have us believe. During my years in Taylor Park, the Corner Boys had only a small handful of guns at any given time—typically between one and five. They purchased these communal firearms, or "block guns," with collective funds, and used them in a kind of time-share agreement. Although one or two young men became the main custodians of a particular gun, it was almost always kept in a concealed location within the reach of others, whether under a stoop or in a nearby lot.

Unlike in the past, the neighborhood's older gang members are often unwilling to help the younger generation acquire weapons. Most of Taylor Park's big homies not only refuse to loan their individually owned firearms, or "personal guns," but also have stopped selling or brokering firearms to local youth. I witnessed the big homie's reticence firsthand, after members of the nearby Pharaohs gang drove through Taylor Park and fired several opportunistic shots at a half dozen Corner Boys who had been gathered at a dice game. Although no one was hit, the Corner Boys spent the rest of the afternoon panicked by their inability to fight back. They had been caught without any block guns on hand. Over the next two days, I watched one of the youngest members of CBE, sixteen-year-old Demonte, canvass the neighborhood, asking the big homies for their help in acquiring a high-powered pistol. The Corner Boys had been able to pool $160 in cash, which Demonte showed to the older men to prove his seriousness. Although the big homies didn't deny him outright, they all conveniently found ways to postpone the transaction to a later date. Two of them said that they had a gun they would consider selling, but that Demonte would need to come back in a few hours. When he did, they were nowhere to be found. Another man instructed Demonte to check back later in the week, after he had contacted his "gun hookup." Over the ensuing week, Demonte continued pestering the men, who continued to postpone the sale. Two weeks later, and still without a new gun, Demonte gave up. Even if one of the big homies had been willing to finally make the sale, the transaction would have been impossible. After only a couple of days, the Corner Boys started tapping into their communal gun fund, which was now down to just seventy dollars.

The big homies' refusal to provide firearms mirrors their unwillingness to integrate the younger generation into their drug enterprises. Most are too worried about prosecution. As Lewis, one of the neighborhood's former Black Counts, continually reminded me, the City of Chicago's recent prioritization of gun seizures has created a situation where prosecutors are willing to cut deals for arrestees to trace firearms back to suppliers and straw purchasers. Facing an increasingly unpredictable set of neighborhood youth, the big homies aren't willing to take the risk.

As Lewis explained, "You give him some work and a gun to protect himself, and he goes off and kills a little kid on accident. They get him up in the station like, 'We'll just charge you with discharging a firearm if you tell us who gave you the gun.' Then they come to my house trying to get *me* on first-degree murder. I'm not about to go to the pen for his dumb ass."

The generational split is only compounded by the big homies' disapproval of what they see as the younger cohort's obsessive, unhealthy relationship with social media.[10] Lewis and his friends are quick to snicker at the Corner Boys when they see them gathered together, staring at their phones rather than speaking to one another. It's no wonder that Lewis's generation trivializes the feuds that routinely erupt on social media between rival neighborhoods and peer groups.

Big Mo, a big homie in his early forties, was one such critic. Big Mo had been one of the few older Black Counts willing to loan his personal gun to the Corner Boys after the shooting death of one of their core members. Only a year later, Big Mo had decided that CBE was becoming embroiled in frivolous gang wars best left, as he put it, "on the social networks." Big Mo liked to complain about the "thin skins" of today's social-media-obsessed youth. "Nowadays," he griped, "it's all about 'You made a rap about me, and now I'm gonna shoot you. You put a ugly picture of me on the social networks and now I'm gonna shoot you.'"

This all limits the Corner Boys' access to guns, at least until they reach their twenties and can establish gun supply networks on their own. Up until that point, their block guns are often older, less powerful, and, in some cases, hardly operable. Only three of CBE's block guns lasted throughout the entire duration of my time with them. The Corner Boys found each highly disappointing. Two of them were .22 caliber revolvers—a black "snubnose" with old, fraying athletic tape on the grip, and a longer-barreled, vintage pistol that looked straight out of an old western movie.

For the uninitiated, .22 caliber bullets are among the smallest (and least lethal) ammunition sizes available on the consumer market. Revolvers carry six bullets, or "rounds," in a circular, revolving magazine. These guns take a longer time to fire multiple consecutive rounds, requiring a two-stage process of pulling back the hammer, which "revolves" a new round into place, and then pulling the trigger. CBE's third gun—a newer 9mm semiautomatic pistol—had an extended magazine that held sixteen relatively larger rounds, but was known to jam after several shots. The rumor was that one of the Corner Boys had left the gun in an abandoned lot, where it filled with mud during an overnight thunderstorm. Throughout my time with CBE, they acquired a series of other firearms from friends and family—including a .40 caliber semiautomatic pistol with a fifty-round magazine and even an AR-15 assault rifle—but they sold them for extra cash, lost track of them, or lost them during police stops within a matter of weeks.

Again, this relative shortage of weaponry means that drillers spend far less time in possession of firearms than appears online. In fact, some of the *only* times these young men handle the block guns is when they pose for photos and videos. As I witnessed during the video shoot in Cincinnati, the result is a serious ineptitude with firearms. As someone who grew up owning and handling guns from an early age, I soon saw that this inexperience wasn't limited to AJ. On separate instances, I watched Xavier, Dominik, and Junior all try to load pistols with the wrong bullets. They didn't realize their mistakes until the magazines jammed, causing rounds to spill all over the floor. In a different, and far more frightening show of inexperience, AJ almost shot me. I had accompanied him one late evening to a raucous gathering at Dominik's cousin's apartment. The air was thick with weed smoke, and a few of the Corner Boys started snapping photos of themselves for social media. A couple of minutes later, someone retrieved two of the block guns from a nearby hiding place. For the next few minutes, the Corner Boys took turns flaunting them for the camera. At one point, AJ pointed one of the pistols at my face. I cursed at him as I stepped out of the line of fire.

AJ laughed. "Relax, bro. It ain't loaded."

"How do *you* know?" I asked.

"Because I took the clip out." He held the full magazine in his other hand. "See," he continued in a mocking tone. "It ain't loaded, so quit actin' like such a little bitch." As he spoke, he pointed the gun at my face again, as if giving me a chance to redeem my honor. Panicked, I batted his arm down and grabbed the gun from his hand. Between curses, I pulled back the slide to make sure that the gun was unloaded. My jaw dropped as a single bullet flew out of the chamber.

AJ was as shocked as I was. He apologized profusely. "Bro! I am *so* sorry. I had no idea there was still a bullet in there. I didn't know I had to check that. My bad, bro. My bad."

Looking back on it now, it was the most contrition I had ever seen out of him. If I wasn't sure about AJ's inexperience before, this near disaster confirmed it. Contrary to his online persona, this was not the behavior of someone who engaged in regular shoot-outs with his enemies.

Much to the relief of us all, there are ways of flexing that don't rely on deadly weapons. Another prevalent technique is to *re*-present otherwise mundane, day-to-day activities as directly related to street hustling and gang violence. As much as drillers want their audiences to believe that they are "on the block" or "sliding on the opps" every moment of every day, they aren't. As Goffman's theater metaphor reminds us, these young men spend the majority of their waking hours performing a range of nonviolent social roles as fathers, sons, lovers, and friends. AJ is a prime example. The young man spends a considerable portion of his day in a domestic capacity, helping Charmain take care of two toddlers from her previous relationship. With all the care of an adoring father, AJ helps dress, feed, and entertain them while Charmain is at work, napping, or cooking. This role as caring partner and parent, often carried out with tender words of encouragement, never shows up online. In fact, as far as social media audiences are concerned, that role doesn't exist for him. He works hard to maintain this impression. I remember one frigid and snowy winter afternoon, when AJ and I sat in his dark apartment looking after the toddlers. We lounged on the couch, scrolling through our social media feeds. As he fetched the kids orange juice and crackers from the kitchen counter, I noticed that AJ had posted a series of photos to Instagram just a couple of seconds earlier. They depicted him outside on the corner, with a half dozen fellow Corner Boys, taunting one of their nearby rivals to attempt a drive-by. I immediately recognized the photos from previous weeks. Yet, by uploading these particular images at this particular moment, AJ created the impression that not even Chicago's punishing winters could stop him from standing on guard, protecting the Corner Boys' turf.

Once I started documenting this form of flexing, I realized that I had become unwittingly implicated. Virtually any time that I gave one of the Corner Boys a ride—whether to court, probation appointments, or their grandmothers' homes—they immediately started snapping pictures and videos of the street scenes we passed. Regardless of the actual purpose of our car rides (which were *never* for the sake of perpetrating gang violence), they used social media to insinuate that they were traveling through enemy territory for the express purpose of committing a drive-by or otherwise causing trouble. Once, as I drove Junior to borrow some cash from his aunt, he took a blurry photo as we sped past an intersection located on the edge of rival Murderville territory. He immediately posted the image on his Facebook page. The caption simply read:

OPP huntin

With this concise statement, Junior overtly (and untruthfully) claimed that he infiltrated enemy turf for the purpose of attacking his enemies. Although we were clear of Murderville turf within a matter of seconds, Junior received applause from his followers for the next week. And although the date and timestamp on the post was clearly visible, the fact that the image was a permanent fixture on his Facebook page gave the added impression that his incursion was routine, daily behavior.

In addition to recasting their mundane activities in a more violent light, drillers use social media to exaggerate and publicize their social ties with others who are engaged in newsworthy violence. There is perhaps no better association they can make than with drillers slain in gang violence. When Marvin "Capo" Carr, a twenty-two-year-old driller and close associate of Chief Keef, was killed by rivals, news of his death circulated throughout the country's most mainstream news outlets, including *Rolling Stone*, *People* magazine, and major cable news programs.[11] Carr's death—captured on bystanders' cell phone cameras—was a constant topic of conversation throughout Taylor Park. Among CBE's drillers, a common response was disappointment and regret. Mostly because of the loss of human life, but also due to the fact that none of the Corner Boys had the foresight to establish a visible online relationship with Carr before his death.

AJ was the most disappointed that he hadn't been able to take advantage of the incident. Several days after Carr's murder, the two of us sat in my car discussing the details.

"Have you seen the numbers Capo's videos is pullin' right now?" AJ asked. "His shit is straight *bustin'* since he got killed. His videos are smacking like three thousand views *every single day!*"

AJ was right. If anything, he had underestimated Carr's posthumous boost in popularity. Consider one of Carr's last music videos, called "Forced to Shooting." Prior to his death, the YouTube video tallied only about 250 total views per day. The day after Carr's murder, views soared to almost five thousand per day.

Seeing this spike in attention, AJ explained how a slain driller's attention (and views) spills over to his online friends and associates. "Right now," he began, "everybody that fucked [was associated] with Capo is blowin' up! All their videos is doin' big numbers and their followers is bustin'! See, when someone like Capo get shot, and they in the news, everybody goes and searches for their name. They go on his IG [Instagram], they watch his videos, they look at his Twitter. If he got pictures or songs with you, then they're gonna see you. Then they're gonna search *your* name and see who *you* is. . . . They're all lookin' for niggas that's in the field like Capo was."

AJ speaks from experience. In fact, the Corner Boys owe much of their own rising popularity to the widely publicized murder of their close friend and collaborator, a teen known in the drill world as "Young Merk." When Xavier was just beginning to make music videos, Young Merk agreed to feature Xavier in one of his music videos. It was a favor—Young Merk knew it would give Xavier's fledgling career a much-needed boost. The video was relatively successful, garnering around five hundred views per day. But when Young Merk was gunned down as part of a local gang feud, the video attracted a tidal wave of viewers, soon pulling in more than seven thousand views per day.

Recognizing this process, the Corner Boys strategically befriended and collaborated with drillers in other neighborhoods that were embroiled in particularly heated gang wars. They knew that if one of these young men was arrested, shot, or murdered, their own popularity would benefit. Sadly, I didn't have to wait long to witness this process in action, when one of AJ's newfound acquaintances was murdered. During a trip with AJ to record a feature in Missouri, we met one of St. Louis's more popular drillers, a tall twenty-seven-year-old known as "Killa Castro." AJ immediately asked Castro and his crew to take a few pictures with him. On the drive back to Chicago, AJ uploaded the pictures to all of his social media profiles. He made sure to "tag" Castro and mention his name in the photo captions.

I woke the next morning to an urgent phone call from AJ.

"Did you hear, bro?" he asked as soon as I answered the phone. "Castro is fuckin' dead! Somebody shot him."

"What happened?" I asked.

"I dunno," he replied. "But it was last night, right after we was with him. Damn, man. We was just with this nigga, and now he dead. Just like that." I could hear the pain in AJ's voice. The murder hit close to home.

Castro was one of AJ's heroes; he had been hoping to emulate Castro's success, especially as Castro was on the verge of signing a lucrative record deal. I could hear AJ struggling to process Castro's death. At one point in our conversation, AJ searched for a silver lining. "The only good thing," he began, "is that those pictures with me is the last ones before he got killed. I mean, I ain't wishin' the man dead or nothin', but my mix tape is droppin' soon. His fans is already on my page, listening to my music! They seen those pictures on IG and they're steady rockin' with me. His fans is my fans now."

In the following months, I watched AJ post and repost his photos with Castro. He memorialized him with heartfelt words. He also reminded online audiences of their friendship, which continued paying dividends even after Castro's tragic death. Given the grassroots, do-it-yourself nature of the drill scene, young men like AJ stay on the lookout for new ways to push past the noise of the internet and draw in new viewers. In their efforts to attract lucrative record deals and kick-start upward mobility, drillers capitalize on the old cable news adage that "if it bleeds, it leads." Sometimes, the Corner Boys brainstormed ideas for starting false internet rumors that one of them had abducted and murdered a high-profile Chicago-based celebrity. The running list of potential "victims" included multi-platinum recording artist Kanye West, television mogul Oprah Winfrey, and then-president Barack Obama. The Corner Boys reasoned that even if their hoaxes were disproven, they would still be able to "bait" curious audiences into clicking on their social media profiles and watching their music videos.

THE NEW REPUTATIONAL ENTREPRENEURS

By democratizing the process of reputation management, digital social media afford drillers unprecedented control over their public personas. Platforms like Twitter and Instagram free these young men to create and maintain robust self-brands without relying on the agents, managers, and other gatekeepers that once dominated the creative industries. With the push of a button, from the safety of their bedrooms, drillers flood social media platforms with promotional material that is both timely and specific. Within minutes of an ally's death or a friend's arrest, they link themselves to the ordeal, boosting their own street cred. It would be a mistake, however, to assume that the massive democratization of these tools has given drillers complete autonomy or freedom over their personal branding. Instead, these digital aspirants have become beholden to a new and different set of reputational entrepreneurs, without whom it would be virtually impossible to build a consistent and visible online brand.

Dateline: Chiraq

One of the most pressing issues drillers face is dissemination. Sure, a single driller can upload hundreds of shocking, gun-filled images to social media platforms in a matter of minutes. But if only a few people ever see those photos, it won't do much to authenticate his violent persona and boost his following. To make their content more visible to a wider audience, drillers enlist the help of additional support personnel. In fact, there are now so many young men hoping to dominate the attention economy that a new industry has emerged to capitalize on their dreams. A growing list of bloggers and citizen journalists offer to deliver drillers' content to vast new audiences. Given the resources required to provide wide exposure, these individuals turn out to be quite distinct from their clients. Demographically, they tend to look a lot like those assisting drillers in making music videos—they're older, more middle class, and often college educated. Despite their social, economic, and sometimes racial differences, these people are increasingly responsible for curating images not only of their individual clients but of urban poverty more broadly. In fact, much of what the public knows about the city's urban poor communities is based on the work of bloggers who intentionally inflate and profit from negative stereotypes.

The internet is full of websites, blogs, and YouTube channels, with names like "Chiraq News" and "Chiraq Central," providing up-to-the-minute gossip about drillers' rivalries, court proceedings, and deaths. One of the most popular YouTube channels, called "The War in Chiraq," gained more than a quarter million subscribers and tallied more than ninety-four million views in just two years of existence. It's worth noting that even though The War in Chiraq proudly claims to provide "only content about the ongoing war in Chiraq," it is actually run out of New Jersey, by a twenty-four-year-old former Rutgers University radio DJ, Livingston Allen, also known as "DJ Akademiks." In order to maintain a constant flow of scintillating content, Allen closely monitors the Facebook, Twitter, and Instagram accounts of Chicago drillers and presents this information in the form of short video news reports. One of the site's most popular videos, which garnered more than two million views in just two years, is titled "Chiraq Savages Record Themselves Going to Pay the OPPS a Visit via a Drive By!"[12] In the video, Allen has taken a grainy cell phone video depicting a drive-by shooting, and has interspersed it with drill music videos. He narrates the drive-by for the viewer. At one point, Allen exclaims, "These niggas love doing drive-bys! . . . In Chiraq, this is normal!" With commentary like this, Allen draws viewers' attention to what he suggests is a tight congruence between young Chicagoans' shocking online content and routine offline behavior.

To better document drillers' daily scandals and edge out the competition, some of these bloggers have taken to the streets, venturing into notable neighborhoods and housing projects to record exclusive interviews, "day-in-the-life" documentaries, and "hood tours" with drillers and their gangs. Two particular YouTube channels—called "ZackTV" and "VladTV"—are among the best known for this kind of content. They offer up-close footage of drillers taunting their enemies and brandishing their latest firepower. Of the 1,700 videos on ZackTV's channel, one of the most popular is titled "Live from JoJo World." The hour-long, three-part series follows members of the late Joseph Coleman's Brick Squad gang faction around their neighborhood, which they renamed "JoJo World" in honor of their slain friend.[13] Throughout the video, the channel's host—a dreadlocked thirty-something named Zack Stoner—introduces the audience to several members of the gang. This includes one young man who proudly brandishes a pistol equipped with an extended magazine. Throughout the video series, Stoner provides a platform for Brick Squad to challenge their enemies. At several points, they openly dare their rivals to "slide" into their territory.

Providing forums for inflammatory content, YouTube channels like ZackTV have become one of drillers' most coveted resources for amplifying their brand. In turn, they've become highly profitable businesses. Like the young men they chronicle, the operators of these sites have learned that the more violence and criminality they portray, the more internet traffic they can entice to their sites. In today's digital economy, this translates directly into dollars, as YouTube channel owners monetize their sites through the Google AdSense program. Once channel owners enroll in Google's program, AdSense automatically reviews the site's content (e.g., video titles and descriptions) and determines which companies will be most interested in embedding advertisements on the page. For drill-related channels, these typically include shoe companies, adult education programs, alcohol brands, and products related to digital music production. AdSense then auctions off advertising space to the highest bidder and embeds their ads in the videos and site banners. At the end of each month, Google cuts a check to channel owners based on the number of clicks, views, and "impressions" they've generated for advertisers.

For the owners of the most popular channels, the monetization process can provide a steady stream of income. In his recent reporting, the Associated Press's Michael Tarm writes that the Google AdSense program provides some owners of drill-related channels with as much as fifteen thousand dollars per month in income.[14] Take Derrick, a twenty-eight-year-old black man I met through the Corner Boys. He operates his drill-centered YouTube channel out of his two-bedroom townhome in a middle-class neighborhood near Hyde Park. The channel has amassed more than one hundred thousand subscribers and more than fifty million views in just five years of operation. He relayed that one of his site's most profitable videos has cashed in nearly five thousand dollars over the course of just two years. When we met up for our first interview, Derrick had just lost his job and was relying heavily on the advertising revenue to pay his bills. His success at generating provocative content has become the difference between paying his rent and risking eviction. His livelihood literally depends on his ability to overdramatize drillers' violent personas.

Channel owners like Derrick draw additional income by charging up-and-coming drillers a fee—sometimes as much as one thousand dollars—to feature those drillers' content. As with music producers and videographers, these bloggers cut deals with those who are newsworthy enough to draw extra traffic. If a driller is particularly "on," someone like Derrick will offer his promotional services free of charge. I watched this process firsthand alongside the Corner Boys. In my first few months with the group, they solicited the owner of the YouTube channel "Chiraq Savages" to record an interview and hood tour in Taylor Park. The channel owner offered to conduct the interview for a fee of three hundred dollars—a serious discount, given his usual rate. Nevertheless, the price tag upset the Corner Boys. Some were willing to pay the fee, and pressed to begin compiling the necessary cash. Others, including Xavier and Dominik, took offense at the notion that they should pay anything. Their popularity was on the rise, after all. Rather than save up the cash, the two young men suggested that they "treat" the owner of Chiraq Savages for his disrespect. They would pretend to agree to his price, invite him to the neighborhood, and then rob him. Over the next week, as the Corner Boys gathered along stoops and sidewalks, they bickered about the plan. Without anything approaching a consensus, the issue eventually went unresolved as the Corner Boys turned their attention to other affairs.

The matter worked itself out a few months later. In the midst of a highly publicized Twitter feud with another hybrid gang faction / drill music group, several YouTube channels—including Chiraq Savages—contacted CBE requesting exclusive interviews. This time, Chiraq Savages offered the service for free. The Corner Boys made the most of their now-public feud. During the interview, they proudly brandished block guns, insulted their rivals, and boasted about how many opps [rivals] they had killed. As soon as Chiraq Savages posted the video on YouTube, the Corner Boys saw an immediate boost to their individual and collective view counts.

It Takes a Gang

Throughout these pages, I've highlighted the gross disjuncture that exists between drillers' online performances and their offline behaviors and identities. Despite what AJ claims on his Facebook page, he doesn't personally commit drive-by shootings. Junior doesn't control Taylor Park's drug economy. Dominik will likely never meet Kanye West, much less kidnap him. Most of drillers' displays are artifice—over-the-top performances designed to validate authenticity and promote their digital brands. This isn't to say, however, that drillers' lurid social media uploads are completely independent of their offline lives. As it turns out, drillers' efforts to authenticate their violent personas require them to continually satisfy a number of offline obligations. In fact, validating authenticity is virtually impossible without continual support from drillers' closest friends and fellow gang members.

As Erving Goffman pointed out more than a half century ago, virtually every social performance—whether face-to-face or online—is possible only with the help of "teammates."[15] These are the consorts and confederates who assist with the various tasks of impression management. Sticking with the theater metaphor a bit longer, someone has to work the door, someone has to draw the curtains, someone has to furnish the props. Although one member of a team is usually designated as the star, lead, or center of attention, it's a collaboration, nonetheless. So much so that the task of ensuring a convincing performance frequently becomes an organizing principle for group cohesion and culture. At every moment, each member has to fulfill his designated role. When necessary, teammates discipline one another with informal sanctions and rewards.

The importance of teammates for drillers' online posturing is perhaps nowhere more apparent than in the support they receive from "shooters." These are the young men who make good on the violence that drillers are so fond of flaunting on social media.[16] As the most frequent custodians of block guns, shooters are the most likely to carry out drive-bys, engage in robberies, and brandish weaponry for video and photo shoots. This arrangement confirms the sociologist Randall Collins's sobering reminder that even in the most violent social contexts, "only a small number of persons perform virtually *all* of the violence; this is a practical reality, known to those who are in violent situations."[17] It's important to note that even a cursory look at official crime statistics shows that even the most prolific shooters engage in far less violence than the daily scores of antagonistic songs and videos indicate. If this weren't the case, Chicago would have exponentially more bloodshed than it already does. This reality is almost completely hidden from (or perhaps conveniently ignored by) the vast majority of audiences.

Typically, one or two shooters will attach themselves to a driller, serving as his de facto bodyguard, assistant, and enforcer.[18] I easily discerned most of these pairings before I ever set foot in Taylor Park. One of the most revered practices is for a driller to praise, or "shout out," his closest shooters in music videos. In one of his songs, AJ pays respect to his shooters, rapping:

> FaceTime Zebo, he my shooter and he don't quit,
> Come to yo' block, wet your team with his extendo clip.
> You goofies fakin'. Naw, you ain't gettin' guap,
> Poo got that tool, catch a fool lackin' on his block.

As the song indicates, AJ's shooters included his longtime friend Zebo, along with Poo, a short-tempered nineteen-year-old with scratchy face tattoos. Xavier was typically backed up by Johnny, or by his twenty-two-year-old cousin, Slim. When Dominik showed up, either Demonte or Stevie wasn't far behind.

Listing driller-shooter pairings like this, it might seem as though Taylor Park is full of young men actively committing violence. In reality, it was rare for more than a couple of these young men to be in the neighborhood at the same time, or for a prolonged stretch. Some of this has to do with the general residential instability affecting urban poor residents.[19] Due to evictions, unemployment, shifting romantic relationships, and changes to household composition, shooters repeatedly moved in and out of Taylor Park. By the time I finished my time with the Corner Boys, more

than half of the shooters were living in other neighborhoods, only returning to Taylor Park when they had reliable transportation. Given their near
monopoly over a gang's means of violence, shooters also spend more time
in court, in jail, or on house arrest. The recurring lack of shooters was a
major source of anxiety among the Corner Boys, especially during conflicts with rivals. Drillers typically considered taking matters into their own
hands, carrying out violence themselves, only when they were completely
unable to muster their triggermen.

The bonds between drillers and shooters typically developed early in
childhood, at local playgrounds, basketball courts, and lunchrooms. Like
virtually all of the Corner Boys, shooters like Johnny and Stevie tried their
hand at rapping in their early teenage years. With Meezy's help, I dug up
grainy videos of them, freestyle rapping alongside those who would go
on to be the public face of CBE. The difference in musical talent is immediately obvious. The young shooters eventually recognized this fact and
eventually gave up on their rap dreams. As CBE transitioned into a recognized gang, and as external conflicts with nearby factions escalated,
these young men found new ways to contribute. They tethered themselves
to their most talented friends, bound by loyalty and the promise that when
the driller finally made it big, he'd bring his shooters with him.

This symbiotic relationship was on full display whenever I drove the
Corner Boys' shooters to their court appearances and probation appointments. Drillers' showed their appreciation for shooters' sacrifices by waking up early to join us on these half-day excursions to Cook County's
various criminal court buildings. When I began driving Johnny to pretrial
hearings for a gun charge, Xavier always accompanied us.

On one of these occasions, when Xavier and I ran outside to feed my
long-expired parking meter, the young man described some of the details
of their informal arrangement.

"Fuck, bro," Xavier said in a worried tone as we descended the grey
stone steps in front of the courthouse. In just a few minutes, the judge
would decide whether to send Johnny to prison. The thought of saying
goodbye to his best friend was clearly weighing on Xavier. "I don't want
them to lock my brother up." His words were heavy with guilt.

Xavier held himself responsible. A year or so earlier, he and Johnny had
been walking through Taylor Park to a friend's house party. Xavier had
brought one of the block guns in case they ran into trouble. As usual,
Johnny refused to let Xavier carry the pistol, in case they were stopped
by the police. It proved to be a prescient move when a police SUV slammed
to a halt in front of Johnny. He took off running, turned the corner,

and threw the gun. The officers gave chase. Still high from smoking PCP earlier, Johnny stumbled and the officers tackled him, cuffed him, and recovered the gun. They charged him with unlawful use of a weapon (UUW) and battery of a peace officer.

"He always be doing that kind of shit for me," Xavier explained. "He says it's for my own good." It had been like this for the past three years, since Johnny dropped out of high school. "He always sayin' that I got the best chance of anybody to make it up outta here. I'm the one doin' the most rappin'. I got the most followers [on Instagram]. I finished school, too. He ain't finished school. He say I can't afford to do years [prison time], but he could. Ain't no niggas rappin' from jail, bro. When he get out, though, he can just come to wherever I'm at. LA, New York, whatever. If I eat, then my boy gonna eat, too. I *gotta* be here [at court]."

The two were ecstatic when the judge reduced Johnny's charges. Instead of prison time, Johnny received a year of intensive probation, which mandated a 7 PM curfew and weekly drug tests.

Arrangements like the one between Xavier and Johnny illustrate how shooters take account of their own skills and biographies to come up with the best way to contribute to collective success. Shooters know that someone must illegally carry guns. Someone must pull the trigger. Someone will be arrested. Someone will serve time.

Of course, there are plenty of support roles that don't necessarily involve physical violence. On the periphery of the Corner Boys' informal organization is a larger group of young men referred to simply as "the guys." The guys represent a kind of residual category in the division of labor—they neither star in music videos nor commit violence at the level of the shooters. Typically, all that is required to be considered "one of the guys" is being physically "on the block" frequently enough to defend the neighborhood and the drillers from rival attacks. Among this group, closest to the drillers, is a small collection of young men who possess special skills, networks, or other resources that are valuable to the Corner Boys' collective pursuit of fame. As we saw in chapter 1, Gio sometimes serves as the Corner Boys' resident videographer. When CBE lacks better options, Gio records, edits, and uploads CBE's music videos to his own YouTube channel. Another young man, known in the neighborhood simply as "P-Money," occasionally uses his familial networks to buy handguns. DeRon, another one of the guys, has a friend on the West Side who gives the Corner Boys discounted prices on marijuana (provided that they buy in large enough bulk). Demarcus, one of Taylor Park's more tech-savvy teens, keeps the drillers supplied with the Wi-Fi passwords from the local school and

AT&T hotspots. Sometimes, he uses a police scanner application on his phone to keep tabs on pending police actions and neighbors' complaints to 911.[20]

By taking on such responsibilities, all of these young men communicate their investment in local drillers. This brings them immediate benefits. Like the shooters, the guys are entitled to a portion of drillers' earnings and perks.[21] In Xavier's words, these close collaborators "eat first"—a popular phrase that takes on both figurative and literal meanings on Chicago's streets. My occasional "food runs" during the daily dice games provided some of the best illustrations of this distribution system in action.

Once, after AJ received a fifty-dollar "gift" from one of his female fans, he went on a hot streak in a dice game, consistently hitting his points and winning the pot.[22] The rest of us complained as he scooped our bills off the sidewalk. Rather than entertain our demands to keep playing, he pocketed the cash. He also passed me five dollars. He hadn't eaten all day and asked if I would drive to McDonald's to pick him up some food. I agreed. He had been patiently tutoring me in dice for the past month, so I wanted to return the favor. Besides, I was hungry too. After losing most of their money to AJ, the rest of the young men kept their remaining cash in the game, hoping for a change of luck. Zebo's younger brother, Ryan, volunteered to ride with me.

When we returned to the dice game twenty minutes later, I passed AJ his regular order: McChicken sandwich, no mayo, add cheese, large fries, large Sprite. Everyone else at the dice game looked on with envy. Without another word, AJ began the redistribution ritual. He unwrapped the sandwich, split it down the middle, and handed half to one of his shooters, Zebo.

Zebo responded with a single word of thanks: "Gratitude."

Then, AJ reached into the bag and pulled out the fries. He nonchalantly handed the entire cardboard container to his other shooter, Poo.

"Thanks, bro," Poo responded. "Good lookin'."

AJ peered inside the grease-stained bag. A dozen or so fries sat at the bottom. He turned to Gio and Demarcus, who had helped him record, edit, and upload a new music video a few days earlier. He held out the bag. "That's for y'all."

Gio and Demarcus shoved the remaining fries into their mouths. "Gratitude," they said, almost in unison, half-eaten potato still stuck to their teeth.

At this point two fringe members of CBE, named Marco and YoYo, began to protest. "Come on, AJ," Marco pleaded. "Let me hold some of them fries. Let me get just a couple of them fries."

"Naw Marco," AJ said loudly, moving to Poo's side. He bit down on a handful of fries in a clear display of refusal. "Get your own damn fries."

"Aw come on, bro," Marco whined. "You know I'm fucked up [broke] right now."

AJ held firm, providing a lecture rather than food. "That's on you, Marco. Put in some work, then, bro. You seen these niggas. They out there *workin'*. Real niggas eat first, but y'all ain't on shit." Marco and YoYo grumbled to themselves but didn't argue any further.

Though brief, AJ's reprimand is unambiguous in this context. Marco, YoYo, and the rest of the Corner Boys will only be rewarded once they begin contributing at the level of someone like Poo or, at minimum, Gio and Demarcus. Until then, they'll be locked out. Whether it's cash provided by fans, freshly rolled marijuana blunts, sodas laced with lean, or silkscreened "#CBE" shirts, dispensation unfolds outward from the drillers—shooters first, then the guys, and then everyone else, if there's anything left.

In addition to eating first, supporters benefit from elevated status in social spaces beyond the immediate neighborhood. On their high school campuses, shooters gain notable respect from classmates. Shooters' prominent place in lyrics, videos, and other online content allows them to ride the wave of drillers' popularity. Even after Poo dropped out of high school in his junior year, he continued traveling to campus to escort AJ home. Poo relished his role as bodyguard—he received far more attention standing next to AJ than he did on his own. Mirroring the redistribution of other spoils, drillers routinely facilitate sexual liaisons for their most dedicated supporters. When drillers rendezvous with young women admirers, they almost always request that she bring along a friend to occupy his shooter.

Flexing Too Hard?

Once I realized how easily drillers exaggerate on social media, and after witnessing the influence their micro-celebrity gives them over their peers, I found myself asking a different question: Why don't drillers engage in even *more* online embellishment? Why not take their social uploads to even *further* extremes? Why not saturate Twitter and Instagram with even *more* insults, firearms, and bravado? The answer, it turns out, is written into the symbiotic relationship between drillers and their teammates. Through an informal system of sanctions, the shooters and the guys routinely place limits on drillers' online hyperbole. It's a response to a practical dilemma. Although sensational content yields collective payoffs, the blowback from careless and excessive uploads is seldom distributed equally. When drillers' online boasts intensify conflicts with rivals, the young men physically "on the block" can find themselves embroiled in conflicts they didn't start. It's only a matter of time before they direct their anger toward the drillers who put them there.

I watched this process unfold several times during my time with the Corner Boys. It shouldn't be much of a surprise by now that most of their frustrations were directed at AJ. Months after I began my relationship with the Corner Boys, several of them realized that AJ was nowhere to be found whenever rivals ventured into their territory looking to retaliate for AJ's online taunts. I first caught wind of their resentment after Murderville attempted a drive-by shooting. I arrived in Taylor Park a few minutes after the attack. After watching my approach from his apartment window, Xavier jogged to my car. He filled me in on the details as we sped away from the neighborhood. Following violent incidents, I made a routine of listing off the names of young men I knew, asking about their safety and whereabouts. When I mentioned AJ, Xavier clicked his tongue in disapproval.

"The truth is," he said with venom in his voice, "AJ don't really be on the block. He perpetrate like he be. He rappin' like he on the block, but he ain't out there like us." Although Xavier and the majority of the drillers leave most of the gang's offensive assaults to their designated shooters, they take pride in being outside and visible in the event that any rivals came looking for trouble. It was a responsibility that AJ had been shirking for some time.

"These niggas on the block got no respect for AJ," Xavier continued. "That's why niggas be talking to him the way they talking to him. He rappin' some shit that he don't do. And then he expect other motherfuckers—*us*—to take up for him just 'cause we his guys. That shit gon' hunt AJ down, bro."

Xavier's words proved prophetic, as the Corner Boys soon made AJ pay for his hollow self-promotion. I was able to piece the details together over the following week. Apparently, AJ and another Taylor Park resident, a muscular twenty-six-year-old known as Blue, got into a heated argument during one of the daily dice games. Fed up with AJ's arrogance, Blue grabbed him by the neck and slammed him into the ground. AJ laid dazed on the ground as his fellow Corner Boys and other neighbors stood laughing. Looming over AJ, Blue "ran his pockets," walking away with all of AJ's cash.

According to Tevon, another member of CBE who had witnessed the incident, Blue's attack was a direct response to AJ's out-of-control flexing, combined with his failure to help defend the Corner Boys' territory. "If you ain't on the block," Tevon explained, "then motherfuckers lose respect for you. Like, Blue didn't need AJ's money. But niggas know he rappin' 'bout some shit that he ain't really about. He tries to front on motherfuckers, but motherfuckers finna call him on it. Because they know who he *really* is!"

Xavier told me that he had arrived on the scene just as Blue was walking off with AJ's money. "AJ was like crying and shit," Xavier recalled in a disappointed tone. "I was like, 'Fight back, nigga. What's wrong with you!?'" But AJ never sought revenge, even when Xavier and several others pledged their support. Dominik even offered to find AJ a gun. But the young man ignored their suggestions to confront Blue and recover his money. "He's too scared to do *shit*," Xavier continued. "He's just a goofy. He ain't really on shit. I steady be telling this nigga that, too. If you gonna say that shit on IG, then you *at least* gotta be on the block when the opps come through blowin'."

The Corner Boys continued punishing AJ by subtly refusing to help him generate online content. I quietly looked on one afternoon as AJ tried recording a new music video in the crowded apartment building courtyard. As soon as the videographer pointed the camera toward the driller and hit record, most of the nearby Corner Boys either turned their backs, kept their heads down, or simply walked out of the frame. Blue had robbed him of his money, but now his friends were depriving him of something far more valuable: the props, teammates, and symbols every driller requires to validate his violent reputation and remain relevant in the attention economy. There was no gang amassed behind him. No shooters sang along with the lyrics. There were no guns. No money. No drugs. Without uttering a single word, they sent a clear message that AJ needs them as much as they need him. It didn't take long for the silent rebukes to accomplish their intended effect. Over the next few days, AJ scaled back his social media insults. Rather than challenge rivals and advertise his own toughness, AJ used Twitter and Instagram to repair his relationships. By retweeting links to Xavier and Dominik's videos, and by uploading old photos with his closest friends, he shared the spotlight that he had been monopolizing for himself. It only took a few days before things got back to normal. Water under the bridge. For now, at least.

■ ■ ■

On a cold February evening, twelve people, including myself, sat in a circle in the basement of a Taylor Park church. We were there for the neighborhood's monthly "beat meeting," which brings Chicago Police Department officers, aldermanic staff members, nonprofit leaders, and community residents together to discuss local problems and solutions. Like every other beat meeting, tonight's discussion was dominated by one agenda item over all others—gang violence. For twenty minutes, residents expressed their fears of local gangs and criticized the police department's inability (and perhaps unwillingness) to control local youth. As the room grew tenser, several residents, organizational leaders, and one of the police officers agreed that Chicago gang violence was now worse than ever before. Today's gangs are more ruthless, they lamented, taking turns providing testimony. Gangs own more guns and deal even more drugs, they complained. They defend their dope corners even more fiercely. They lure even more teens into their organizations with promises of big money and flashy cars. And they've grown so bold that they're flaunting their crimes on social media.

I've heard a version of this narrative in nearly every community meeting I've attended. And although I'd never marginalize residents' fears of victimization—South Side violence remains well beyond acceptable numbers—I find these depictions of local gangs, their organizational structures, and their relationship to violence puzzling. This is because homicide and violent crime rates have actually *decreased* to historic lows since their peak in the 1990s.[23] During my time alongside today's gang-associated youth, I saw a number of mechanisms driving this trend.[24] The dissolution of the crack economy helped tamp down the bloodshed. So too did the erosion of the corporate gangs that warred over that market. The current generation of South Side teens can no longer count on joining the local corporate gang and moving up the organizational ladder. The neighborhood's gang elders, it seems, want very little to do with them. This was nowhere more apparent than when the Corner Boys sought the big homies' help in acquiring more block guns. Compared to their predecessors in the 1990s, today's youth have far less of the motivation and means for engaging in full-scale gang warfare. Despite what HBO dramas and public imagination might suggest, our ideas about urban gangs are highly outdated. In places like Taylor Park, there are no sophisticated drug lords running multi-million-dollar distribution rings out of high-rise housing projects; they're not laundering money through local businesses; they're certainly not coercing fourteen-year-olds to join up as foot soldiers.

And yet, local residents, and even some of the city's foremost experts, hold tight to the notion that gangs and gang violence are worse than ever.[25] How is it that they continue making these claims, especially in the face of clear statistical evidence to the contrary? The answer, I've come to realize, is the Corner Boys. Or rather, the thousands of Chicago drillers, gangs, and peer groups like them who have learned to manipulate the context collapse inherent in social media. By providing the public what appears to be a transparent window into street life—often through the assistance of middle-class support personnel—drillers make themselves appear far more sadistic, organized, and dangerous than they truly are. It's all a part of their self-branding techniques, which they use to corroborate their musical claims of authenticity. In the process, they've convinced the public that they've taken over the drug and murder game from their uncles and older neighbors, and that gang warfare has reached unprecedented levels. Like most moral panics, this one has more to do with subjective impressions than objective reality. As the public frets, drillers amplify their over-the-top displays. The more violent we think they are, the more clicks and views they attract. And as these metrics of micro-celebrity increase, so do the rewards.

4

•••

Cashing In on Clout

Spirits were high as AJ, Zebo, and I sped down the expressway, headed to a Walmart supercenter. Against my useless pleas, they maxed out the volume on my car stereo, singing along to AJ's newest song. The modulated snare drums and hi-hats drifted out through the open sunroof. AJ beamed with excitement.

Today was payday.

When we arrived at our destination, AJ and Zebo jumped out of my car and rushed inside, straight to the MoneyGram counter. AJ was there to pick up a wire transfer from an aspiring driller from Atlanta, who had solicited him to make a guest appearance, or "feature," in a new song. At the MoneyGram counter, AJ and Zebo giggled in excitement. They nudged each other as the impatient employee counted out five hundred dollars in twenties. AJ picked up the stack and fanned his face with the bills.

"We just got paid, boy!"

AJ and Zebo practically skipped through the parking lot back to my car. Walking behind them, I couldn't help but chuckle a little. The two looked more like third graders at recess than the hardened street thugs they portray online. Back on the road, AJ started making plans for his newfound income.

It wasn't the first time that I had accompanied drillers to one of these money wire-transfer counters. It wouldn't be the last. Trips like these were routine whenever eager collaborators and adoring fans hoped to tap into drillers' popularity—what Chicago teens fittingly refer to as "clout." In these gleeful moments, I began to see why drillers are willing to go to such lengths to manufacture reputations as authentic gangbangers.

Every year, more "everyday people" are turning to the online attention economy in search of fame and fortune. Aspiring micro-celebrities—from Instagram fashionistas to Twitter muckrakers and YouTube karaoke singers—hope to become rich by monetizing their personal websites, attracting sponsorships from major brands, or landing full-time dream jobs in the cultural industries. There still isn't much systematic research on precise success rates, but most case studies agree: Even for those with large social media footprints, it's extremely unusual to receive meaningful financial rewards.[1] Despite the siren song of "getting paid to do what you love," only a sliver of fame-seekers ever come close to achieving such a lofty goal. In a study of social media influencers in the Silicon Valley tech scene, Alice Marwick reported that "notoriety did not translate into more money; there was no equivalence between micro-celebrity status and income."[2] In an aptly titled book, *(Not) Getting Paid to Do What You Love*, Brooke Erin Duffy similarly reports that even the most prominent fashion bloggers remain "un(der)-paid, remunerated with deferred promises of 'exposure' or 'visibility,' even when they work long hours to satisfy brands and convey authenticity to observant audiences."[3] Marwick, Duffy, and other new media scholars describe these digital aspirants as primarily engaged in "hope labor"—uncompensated work performed with the *hope* that it might pay off down the line.[4]

These sobering descriptions of micro-celebrity loom large throughout academic and public discourse. And yet, the more time I spent with the Corner Boys, the more I came to suspect that these accounts oversimplified matters. It's certainly true that drillers' online status-seeking fits much of the definition of hope labor. Indeed, most of their social media activities and online performances originated in the long-term (and admittedly long-shot) goal of stardom. But to assume that their digital cultural production practices are *merely* hope labor misses the more practical and, at times, profound benefits in drillers' daily lives. I personally watched as these young men leveraged their outlaw reputations to secure the financial, social, and emotional resources desperately needed for basic survival.

Why haven't existing accounts given more consideration to these kinds of mundane yet powerful rewards of micro-celebrity? At least some of the answer rests on the fact that digital production by urban poor residents has been largely overlooked by researchers. Instead, studies of micro-celebrity overwhelmingly focus on white, middle-class, and other privileged groups. These are people trying to break into the online attention economy from other employment sectors, or from relatively stable economic positions. The hopeful fashion bloggers in Duffy's research, for instance, already held jobs in finance, pharmaceutical sales, and marketing when they began their quest for online stardom.[5] It's no mystery why they were dissatisfied with the irregular and piecemeal earnings they received from their Instagram profiles and YouTube channels. When micro-celebrity failed to pan out for them, they were unlikely to skip a meal or bounce a rent check. And when their lofty dreams failed to materialize, they were free to simply give up their online pursuit, or to treat it like a hobby.

For those stuck at the bottom of the economic, social, and racial hierarchy, micro-celebrity looks and feels very different. The stakes are far more pressing. For drillers and their gangs, it's unlikely that this will ever be just a hobby. What more privileged micro-celebrities lament as under-compensated labor, drillers celebrate as one of the most practical, stable, and dignifying options available. In turn, the attention economy and the benefits it provides become increasingly difficult to leave behind. This contrast—between drillers and their more privileged counterparts—underscores one of the larger lessons running through these pages: If we want to understand how digital technologies produce and reproduce inequality, we have to examine their meanings, uses, and consequences in everyday lives. For drillers, these are lives that were structured by racial and class disadvantage long before Facebook or YouTube ever entered the equation.

WORKING FOR "FEATURES"

For the most part, drillers consider the cash they earn from features as their official source of income. They envision themselves much like mainstream recording artists, but on a much smaller scale. During my time with them, CBE's drillers scored features about once every month or so. As their individual and collective reputations grow, these opportunities come more often and bring larger returns. From the outside looking in, these might seem like infrequent and paltry payoffs. But drillers don't see it that way. For them, features represent some of the fastest and easiest money possible. For less than an hour of work, these young men can pocket more than their neighbors and peers make in an entire week working at their low-wage jobs or selling weed on the corner.

AJ's experience with the Atlanta driller is typical of the process. Along with the five hundred dollars, the aspiring collaborator sent AJ an email containing a digital audio file (an MP3) of the song—minus AJ's verse, of course. As typical, the Atlanta driller expected AJ to record his voice over the audio file and then email back the completed song. If Gio or one of the other tech-savvy Corner Boys happened to have access to a laptop and a microphone, AJ could record his verse in one of the makeshift studios they sometimes set up in their apartments. If need be, he could rent time at one of the city's warehouse studio spaces for about sixty dollars per hour. Even in this worst-case scenario, AJ still stood to net more than four hundred dollars.

Features bring immediate and substantial cash flow to young men who, like many in their community, wake up every morning unsure of how they will afford their next meal. AJ was flat broke when the Atlanta driller contacted him. He desperately needed the money, and soon. His cell phone had been disconnected, Charmain and the babies needed groceries, and AJ hadn't eaten much over the past couple of days. His breakfast that morning was a sodium-packed bag of Jay's brand potato chips. This all changed following our trip to MoneyGram. First, AJ treated Zebo to a McDonald's meal. Then, he settled his phone bill in full and reactivated his service. Next, he bought enough basic items to last his household for a week. Finally, he treated himself to a new outfit consisting of a bright blue Nike jumpsuit with matching shoes, which he planned to wear during his upcoming music video shoot.

It's hard to overstate the importance of such a large influx of cash in the lives of urban poor residents. In *Nickel and Dimed*, Barbara Ehrenreich famously revealed the range of additional, "special costs" paid by those living on the bottom rungs of the socioeconomic ladder. Many basic products and services are *more* expensive for those with infrequent and irregular paychecks. "If you can't put up the two months' rent you need to secure an apartment," Ehrenreich reminds us, "you end up paying through the nose for a room by the week. . . . If you have no money for health insurance . . . you go without routine care or prescription drugs and end up paying the price."[6]

The cash from features allows drillers to offset these additional costs. If AJ hadn't had the lump sum from his Atlanta feature, he wouldn't have been able to renew his expensive, premium phone plan, which provides him with unlimited minutes, text messaging, and data. Given his poor credit history, he would have been forced to purchase an inexpensive, base-level plan with strict limits on usage. In the end, the seemingly cheaper plan would have actually been *more* expensive because of the steep overage charges he'd owe for each minute or megabyte over the limit. His bill would have gone unpaid for an even longer period of time. In the meantime, AJ wouldn't be able to connect with fans and potential collaborators via social media. He'd lose key opportunities to land more features and grow his reputation. By spending a large, one-time sum to purchase a week's worth of sundries at a discount grocery store, AJ was able to buy more groceries at a cheaper per-unit price. Otherwise, he and Charmain would have been forced to buy their groceries on an as-needed, daily basis from the nearby gas station or bodega, often at double the price. Lastly, without the larger one-time sum necessary to purchase an entire outfit,

AJ would have had to wear older clothes in his upcoming music video, making it more difficult to convince audiences that he is as successful at street hustling as he claims.

At the same time, this sudden influx of cash can create new dilemmas for drillers. With bills and expenses put aside for so long, the money goes as fast as it arrives. As a result, drillers frequently fail to uphold their end of the transaction. By the time AJ finally turned his attention to recording his verse, the money was gone. He searched around for cheap options to record his voice over the audio file, but quickly struck out. None of the Corner Boys had easy access to a computer, microphone, or audio production software at the moment. With no remaining cash, booking a studio was out of the question. As days turned into weeks, AJ lost interest and redirected his attention to other matters. He never recorded the feature. When the Atlanta driller started pestering him for a refund, AJ simply deleted his messages and blocked him on all of his social media accounts.

I routinely watched AJ and other drillers accept money for features that they never completed. I couldn't help but wonder about the negative repercussions of their fraudulent business practices. Word spreads quickly on social media. Weren't they worried about losing the trust of potential collaborators? When I asked them about this, they brushed off their dishonesty as "just part of the game." If anything, they *celebrated* it. They reminded me that any online rumors of extortion actually *helped* to authenticate their criminal personas. Besides, they told me, most of these upstart drillers requesting features were, as Xavier liked to put it, "just fans." In drawing this sharp dichotomy between themselves and "fans," drillers appeal to the asymmetrical and potentially exploitative nature of micro-celebrity. As Marwick importantly notes, "micro-celebrity is a way of thinking about oneself as a celebrity, and treating others accordingly. . . . The people [micro-celebrities] interact with . . . are thought of as *fans*, rather than friends."[7] In the attention economy, where drillers' online connections greatly outnumber their offline connections, the dynamics of micro-celebrity lead them to rewrite a whole host of social interactions as fandom. So, although drillers are certainly dependent on the enduring love of their Facebook "friends" and Twitter "followers," they tend to view them instrumentally, approaching them as a readily exploitable resource.

This orientation was most visible when drillers engaged in more violent forms of extortion. I recall arriving in Taylor Park one afternoon just as Xavier and two other members of CBE put the finishing touches on a scam to rob one of their customer-collaborators. A relatively unknown driller from another South Side neighborhood had solicited Xavier to record a feature on a new song. Xavier insisted on face-to-face payment. He set up a meeting near his apartment, and then the two would head to a nearby studio together. According to the plan, once the man arrived with the cash, one of CBE's shooters would rob them at gunpoint. Xavier would play along, offering up a bit of his own cash to make the stick-up look more convincing.

When we spoke about the plan, Xavier justified the robbery by appealing to what he saw as an underlying disingenuousness on the part of fans and hopeful collaborators.

"He's just a *fan*," Xavier said. "He ain't shit to me but a stain. These fans don't *really* care about *us*. If I get locked up, you think one of these fans gon' bond me out? They gon' take care of my OG [mother] if I get killed? Hell naw, bro! They gon' find some other rapper to listen to."

Although many of the Corner Boys' interactions with their fans tended to be exciting and optimistic occasions, I noticed an intense cynicism lurking just under the surface. When Xavier dipped into his more depressive periods, he spoke resentfully about the need to continually perform for a fickle and insatiable audience. This was one of those times when Xavier's own feelings of powerlessness shone through his outward veneer of emotionless, coldhearted hustler. Although the Corner Boys didn't end up going through with the robbery, the plan was as much a catharsis as it was a moneymaking scheme.

"This lame-ass nigga," Xavier continued, referring to the man they were planning to rob, "you really think he give a shit about me? Hell naw! He's just on my dick 'cause I got that clout right now. He's wants some of *my* clout. He's tryna' use *me*! He just a clout head, bro. Fuck him!" The others nodded their heads in agreement.

During my time with CBE, I hardly went a day without hearing this term—*clout head*. It's a pejorative label referring to a subset of fans who latch onto popular drillers and their gangs for the sake of "clouting up," building their *own* micro-celebrity and online popularity in the process. Drillers consistently doubt the loyalty and sincerity of clout heads, whom they see as willing to do just about anything for a bit of the spotlight. This includes paying for features, providing intelligence about rivals, and giving discounts on drugs, guns, and phones. Although I never observed a so-called clout head inflict any serious harm on CBE, local lore was full of stories about clout heads gaining intimate access to popular drillers and their gangs, only to give up vital information to rivals and the police. These cautionary tales enable drillers to justify their treatment of fans. Once someone is labeled as a clout head, it's acceptable to exploit them. In fact, between their sporadic paydays for features, drillers rely on the manipulation of clout heads for making ends meet on a day-to-day basis.

FINESSING CLOUT HEADS

Drillers typically discover the everyday rewards of micro-celebrity well before they ever attract a lucrative feature. There is perhaps no more alluring benefit than the elevated attention they gain from young women in their schools and neighborhoods. As their popularity grew, the Corner Boys learned that they could leverage their status to persuade adoring classmates and neighbors to provide them with all kinds of things—from cell phones to clothing, sex, drugs, and cash. On the streets of Chicago, this scam has a name: *finessing*. Treating these women much like hopeful collaborators soliciting features, the Corner Boys justify romantic exploitation by reframing women as manipulative clout heads, only interested in drillers because of their elevated status and potential pathway to upward mobility.

It wasn't long after Junior began his drill career that he noticed his newfound power to finesse. In the course of just a few months, Junior had managed to produce three new music videos and even land an interview on a popular drill blog and YouTube channel. Young women in Taylor Park took notice of his growing stature. I watched as he invited a steady stream of young women to his mother's apartment. I sometimes sat on the couch with Junior, interviewing him and watching new music videos as his female companions cooked, cleaned, and did general housework. In private, I asked Junior about these budding relationships. Where had all this amorous attention come from? With a self-congratulatory laugh, he described what I was witnessing as an instrumental arrangement where both parties were trying to "get over" on one another.

"It's all about the clout," he began. By associating with an up-and-coming driller, he explained, these women were busy elevating their *own* social status and public recognition. "It's all about bragging rights. You know that I ain't got shit. You know I ain't got no money. But to other people? To other people, I'm *that* nigga. And every girl wanna be with *that* nigga. Bragging rights. So they can say, 'Yeah, that's *my* nigga. Yeah, I fucked him.' . . . They just want attention, bro. They just wanna be *that* girl."

"How do they do that?" I asked.

"Look at Gena's Facebook," he answered, pulling out his phone. Gena had been Junior's on-again-off-again girlfriend for the past two years. "That's all she do. All she do all day is talk about me on Facebook." He explained how, following the release of his recent music videos, Gena had become increasingly intent on posting pictures to Facebook and Instagram of the two of them engaged in affectionate behaviors. He pulled up a few of these on his phone. "Look," he instructed. "She says shit like, 'I'm laying up with Junior, woo woo woo. Junior's mamma so funny, woo woo woo. Junior this, Junior that.'"

For me, Junior's explanation didn't quite add up. I had spent a decent amount of time with the two over the previous months. To me, Gena seemed genuinely in love with Junior. I had witnessed her generosity and self-sacrifice. She took care of Junior when others—including his Corner Boys "brothers"—had let him down. She supported him financially and emotionally before he had established his name as a legitimate driller. Junior saw it differently, however. He was convinced that even if Gena had real feelings for him, she was finessing him nonetheless. To me, it seemed like his own practices of misrepresentation—where he lied about his success as a violent hustler to gain attention—had colored his view of women.

"See," he complained, referring to one particular picture on Gena's Facebook page with more than forty "likes." "Now she's got *my* clout. The thing is, people recognize her on the street or at school or whatever from pictures that she takes with *me*. Then, those picture go all over social media and people see it, and then they recognize *her*. So it's like she gets to get famous off *me*! Because she's *with* me."

By viewing women as fame-seeking hangers-on, drillers give themselves license to go on the offensive, turning the tables in their favor. They dangle the prospect of a monogamous, long-term relationship with a future superstar to extract whatever cash or goods they might need in the moment. Drillers constantly "remind" women that they will be making it big soon, that they're "getting out of the 'hood," and that they're bringing their loyal girlfriends with them.

I witnessed Junior repeatedly unleash this strategy. Each time he needed quick money, he'd spend an hour or so firing off compliment-filled text messages to dozens of women, asking to "hold" some cash. I once watched as he wrangled hundreds of dollars in the span of a single afternoon. Junior had been so confident in his ability to extract money from the women in his life that he booked an afternoon recording session at a local music studio without knowing exactly where, or from whom, he would get the sixty-dollar hourly rental fee. We sat in my car, waiting for replies. Less than two hours before the scheduled start of his studio session, he received a response from a young woman named Shana, whom he had met and slept with the week before. She was currently at school. But, she told him, if he could meet her before her next class period, she would give him the cash he needed. We made our way to her location—an alternative high school on a quiet street near Chicago's Bronzeville neighborhood.

On the way, Junior bounced up and down in excitement. "Watch this finesse, bro," he bragged. "These girls, they want my clout. That's fine. I'm about to finesse her ass. Give a girl some dick and some clout, she be giving you money and all kinds of shit. Bet."

Shana bounded down the front steps of the school when she saw us pull up. The two teens embraced and Junior playfully kissed her neck and cheeks. I awkwardly busied myself a few steps away, replying to emails on my phone. Without any additional prompting, Shana handed Junior three rolled-up twenty-dollar bills. Junior slid the cash into his pocket and pulled in for another round of kissing. I noticed his eyes lock on a white iPhone sticking out of Shana's back pocket. He perked up at the sight of it. He was in a desperate search for a new phone after shattering half his screen a couple of days earlier. Without warning, Junior grabbed the phone out of Shana's pocket. He playfully dangled it just beyond her reach as she hopped up and down trying to grab it back.

"I need this phone, girl," he told her, asking if he could keep it. She didn't seem to be listening. Instead, she continued desperately reaching for the phone. "I'm gonna take it," he told her, "I need this phone, girl." She already had a phone, he insisted; why did she need a second one?

Despite his pleading, Shana was steadfast in her refusal. After a few minutes of his teasing, I made the decision to step in. The two were starting to cause a scene and a nearby security guard had taken notice. I was relieved (and a bit surprised) when Junior finally acquiesced and returned Shana's phone. I turned to head back to my car when two young men suddenly appeared at the top of the stairs. They called out in our direction, interrupting Junior and Shana's goodbye kiss.

"Hey," one of them yelled, "ain't you Junior?"

"Yeah," Junior answered in a defensive tone. He shot them a hardened look, sizing up if they were looking for a fight.

"Yo," the other one said. "I fuck with your music. You be goin' hard, shorty. I fuck with you." I watched Junior's shoulders relax. This would be a peaceful, even flattering, encounter.

Junior began smiling again as two young women also appeared at the top of the stairs. One of them recognized Junior and similarly complimented his music. "Shana," she called out, "is Junior your boyfriend?"

Rather than answer, Shana pulled in close to Junior and nuzzled her nose in his neck. As her four classmates looked on in envy, she pulled out her other phone, a black Samsung, and took several selfies with Junior. Then, she recorded a video of the two of them kissing. Shana was clearly relishing the attention Junior had brought her. The six teens stood chatting for another five minutes, mostly about Junior's newest music video and his rising stock in the drill world. Finally, the school bell chimed. As Junior and I walked back to my car, Shana sprinted up behind us. She grabbed Junior by the wrists, opened his arms, and pulled in close to his chest. With a flirtatious smile, she placed the white iPhone in his hand. Amid all the praise from her classmates, she had changed her mind.

"Here," she told him, "you can have it. You're gonna call me when you're done at the studio, right?"

"You know it," he answered, "especially now that you gave me this phone."

"Promise?" she asked.

"Promise," he assured, kissing her goodbye.

We returned to my car, where Junior broke into a fit of laughter. He gave me a playful shove. "Faneto!" he yelled—another word Chicago teens use to describe a successful con. "You see that?" he asked. "I told you! I be finessing these girls. I knew I had her when those niggas recognized me. Shana be lovin' that clout I give her. Watch. She gon' be livin' large in that school now that everybody think she with me." Within minutes, Junior had proof for his claims. Shana posted her kissing video on Facebook, along with the caption: "Me and my man." Junior clicked "like," adding his own public show of approval.

"Now I got her," he said. "I'm 'bout to finesse her ass out of all kinds of shit." And that he did. Junior kept his promise to call Shana after he finished at the studio. On the call, he asked her for more cash. Later that night, she obliged.

Junior isn't unique in this extractive practice. Time and again, I observed drillers enlist amorous young women to provide all sorts of vital lifelines. AJ, arguably the most accomplished "finesser" in the neighborhood, turned to his network of admirers when Charmain suspected he had been seeing another woman and kicked him out of her apartment. AJ needed a place to stay. Despite his looming homelessness, AJ quickly solved his predicament. For the next month and a half, he rotated among several women's homes across the city until Charmain took him back. During this period, I sat with AJ outside Charmain's apartment nearly every afternoon as he methodically worked his way through his contact list. At the top were women who had been communicating with him via Facebook or Instagram. He dialed them up, one by one, using the FaceTime application on his iPhone. In the sweetest tone possible, he ran through his routine script. He complimented their beauty. He gushed about his infatuation. He insinuated that he wanted to try a monogamous relationship.

"Hey girl," he began one of these calls. "I've been thinking about you a lot. I wanna see if we can really make this work. I really wanna see you tonight. You think I can come over?" It sometimes took a few of these calls, but AJ always found a woman who was both interested and available for the evening. As a testament to the effectiveness of this tactic, AJ never spent a single evening sleeping in stairwells or in the back of parked cars, which was routine for the other Corner Boys who lacked his level of clout. Instead, AJ converted his micro-celebrity into a home-cooked meal and a warm bed every single night.

REPUTATION, UNBOUND

In many respects, drillers' tactics of manipulation aren't so new. Even before the arrival of digital social media, the politics of teenage popularity could take on an instrumental quality. Young men and women have long used their elevated social statuses to gain favor with, and extract favors from, admiring schoolmates and peers. What *is* new, however, is the way that social media disrupts previous spatial dynamics and constraints. In the past, status hierarchies were overwhelmingly local, limited to a single neighborhood, school, or other physical area. In fact, this boundedness was one of the hallmark themes for urban research conducted throughout the twentieth century. Ethnographers, in particular, described hierarchies, roles, and statuses as expressly *local* phenomena. "The sense of personal identity," Elijah Anderson famously wrote in the late 1970s, "is not immediately transferable to just any street-corner. When group members travel to different areas of the city, they must negotiate a place anew."[8] As anyone who ever had to transfer between schools can attest, the acclaim and accolades gathered on one campus rarely follow to a new one. In the predigital era, teens were forced to start over, building their new reputations from scratch.

Things are different now. Today, the clout drillers develop online ac-companies them as they move beyond their local neighborhood. I was re-minded of the unbounded character of micro-celebrity whenever I ac-companied the Corner Boys on road trips to other cities. I marveled at how easily these young men leveraged their elevated social media status to not just survive, but thrive (for a few days, at least) in far-flung locales. When AJ, Xavier, Dominik, and I departed on one of our trips to Indiana to record a feature with an up-and-coming Indianapolis driller, the three men barely had twenty dollars between them. They had no food and no idea of where, exactly, they were going to sleep for the two nights they planned to be there.[9] If they were worried, they certainly didn't show it. They had done this plenty of times before. It was all part of the thrill. As soon as we got on the road, they alerted their tens of thousands of social media followers that they were headed to Indianapolis. Within minutes, they were FaceTiming young men and women whom they had never pre-viously met in person. By the end of our three-hour drive, they had lined up two groups of young women who promised them weed, liquor, and beds for the duration of their stay.

The unbounded character of drillers' micro-celebrity is amplified by another one of social media's unique affordances—namely, the permanent and searchable character of online content. Platforms like Instagram and Facebook provide a repository of all those images, posts, and other uploads that drillers use to validate their violent personas. So long as their smartphones are handy, drillers can remind others of who they "really are."

I watched this process unfold during one of the Corner Boys' trips to Atlanta, after two upstart drillers there solicited AJ, Xavier, and another CBE driller named Ricky to collaborate on a feature and perform together at a concert. A week before the trip, the Atlanta drillers had agreed to pay CBE a total of twelve hundred dollars. As promised, they sent a six-hundred-dollar deposit via Western Union to defray costs of the long road trip from Chicago. They pledged to pay the remaining six hundred dollars on arrival. But when the Corner Boys pulled into town after hours on the road, all they received were excuses and delays. After two days of waiting around in a cheap motel, they were finally fed up. Ricky, a twenty-one-year-old driller prone to emotional outbursts, called up their Atlanta hosts and ordered them to meet him at a nearby Waffle House. I tagged along. I could feel the tension in the air as I sat down at the next table over. I sat quietly, just within earshot. I kept my eyes forward as Ricky confronted the two men. He laid out the consequences if they continued delaying his payment. First, CBE wouldn't show up to the recording session or concert. The Atlanta drillers wouldn't just lose their deposit, they'd lose this chance to establish public ties with "real" Chicago drillers. Second, CBE would launch an online smear campaign to ruin the Atlanta drillers' reputations. Ricky insinuated that they might even resort to more violent forms of recourse.

To put teeth to his words, Ricky shared a series of the Corner Boys' social media posts. He slapped his phone down on the table, scrolling through his Instagram feed. In photo after photo, he drove home the message that the Corner Boys don't just make violent music; they *are* violent.

"See this?" he asked them. From my position I could see that it was an image of Benzie, a member of the Corner Boys who had been murdered years earlier. "This is the nigga Benzie right here. This nigga dead over this shit we're into. The opps came and took him from us. I don't like talking about that shit, but that's the way it is. We're really out here in these streets. We ain't just rappin' 'bout this shit." He scrolled to a different picture, this time of Zebo holding an assault rifle. "See this?" he asked again, more forcefully. "We really do this shit. We got the choppas [machine guns] on deck. That's why niggas up in Chicago know not to fuck with our money. We're straight Chiraq demons out here. You could go Google that shit yourself." Over the next few minutes, Ricky pulled up a half dozen more photos that depicted fellow CBE members with guns, drugs, and stacks of money. "We really live this life," he kept repeating.

I knew some of these photos to be exaggerations, manipulated to make CBE appear more ruthless and sadistic. Judging from the contrite expressions of the two men across from Ricky, however, his demonstration had its desired effect. They immediately apologized. They confessed that they were having trouble scraping up the rest of his payment. To restore the relationship and avoid retribution, they offered alternative methods of payment. The first was a shiny new pistol—a silver .45 caliber semiautomatic, worth about $250 on the street. They also agreed to hand over the profits from the concert's ten-dollar entry fee. The tension at the table eased as Ricky accepted the terms and confirmed the new deal with a handshake. His mood lifted even more once we returned to the motel. He spent the afternoon snapping selfies holding his new gun. In the end, Ricky's ability to validate his violent persona via his existing social media content ensured him the material compensation owed to him. It also delivered to him an additional prop for authenticating his violent persona well into the future, perhaps during out-of-town trips like this one.

MICRO-CELEBRITY AS A SOURCE OF
LOVE AND SUPPORT

Micro-celebrity also provides drillers with powerful emotional benefits. Like every young person, they yearn to feel appreciated, loved, and cared for. Unfortunately, urban poor neighborhoods like Taylor Park are often characterized by a hypermasculine street culture that frowns on outward displays of emotion. Amid the daily threat of violence, residents, particularly gang-associated youth, constantly assess which of their peers they can depend on to defend them. Who will hesitate when the shooting starts? Who will run in fear? Who will stand tall, fight, and potentially pull a trigger? This constant calculation inhibits young men from talking about their feelings or asking for help. It turns displays of insecurity and weakness into a liability.[10] Those deemed as too "in their feelings" face ridicule and ostracism. By deterring young men from seeking the emotional support they need, this street culture robs many of America's most traumatized youth of healthy avenues for working through grief and pain. It's here that micro-celebrity provides yet another reward. As drillers amass increasing levels of clout, they gain new opportunities to express emotions, ask for assistance, and deepen relationships, all without appearing weak. Ironically, the more toughness drillers flaunt online, the more emotional support they're able to obtain offline.

I learned more about the constraints on emotional expression as my relationship deepened with the Corner Boys. As I increasingly played the role of confidante and sounding board, I also saw how heavily the expectations of masculinity weighed on them. After swearing me to secrecy, they opened up about some of their deepest secrets and self-doubts. I was one of the first people that Stevie, AJ, and Junior told when they found out that their girlfriends were pregnant. They each confessed that they wished they could move out of Taylor Park, relinquish their gang ties, find good-paying jobs, and start providing for their growing families. After the shooting death of a close friend, Junior shared his recurring nightmares, in which he replayed the scene as his friend died in his arms. AJ talked about the sorrow he felt every time he walked past the corner where Benzie, his closest childhood friend, had been gunned down. During a particularly violent period in the neighborhood, Xavier shared his secret plan to simply pack his bags and leave in the middle of the night. He would turn his back on CBE for good.

"I'm sick of this shit," Xavier told me as we sat in front of his apartment. "I can't be doin' this no more. I can't even walk across the street without niggas tryna' get at me." Xavier went on to describe how his af-filiation with the Corner Boys made it dangerous to leave the neighbor-hood. He felt like a prisoner, constrained to the four-block area around his apartment. "I'm done, bro. I'm done with this gangbanging shit."

Xavier was midsentence when he spotted Johnny and Dominik on the other end of the courtyard, walking toward us. "You can't be telling that shit to nobody," he warned me. "I don't need niggas around here talkin' 'bout me, like I'm some kind of little bitch or something." No matter how overcome Xavier and the others were with these feelings, they knew they had to maintain an air of unflappable dependability.

Bidding for Emotional Support

By creating viral online content and amassing micro-celebrity, drillers open new, previously unavailable opportunities for soliciting help and commu-nicating their feelings, all while maintaining the coolness demanded by street masculinity. One of drillers' most common bids for emotional sup-port unfolds in a kind of informal ritual. After recording a new song or video, drillers gather their friends and fellow gang members to debut their newest creation. They amass along local stoops and sidewalks, playing their tunes on repeat for an hour or so. Holding his phone out for everyone to see, the driller provides constant commentary on the beats, lyrics, and visuals. One of the more memorable occasions unfolded early one morning as I drove Xavier to a court hearing for a trespassing charge he received while standing in front of his apartment without ID. We were joined by two other CBE drillers, named Adam and Ocho. The two had talked me into driving them to their various errands and appointments after Xavier's hearing. For Ocho, these errands were only a marginal concern. His goal was to get his friends to listen to his new song on my car stereo. He had recorded it a few days earlier and was eager to share. From his position in the back seat, he grabbed my auxiliary cord, plugged it into his iPhone, and cued up his song. He gave some introductory commentary.

"A'ight," he began. "Ya'll need to listen to this. Everything you need to know about my life right now is right here in this song." With that, he hit play. The beat was slower and more melodic than his usual high-energy, sinister sound. The first couple of verses covered a range of intimate top-ics. He rhymed about feeling abandoned by the world; that he was being lied to by those close to him. He rapped that he was struggling to take care of his family, that he had stopped attending school to try his hand at drug dealing. The song eventually transitioned away from his talk of struggle to boasts about killing rivals. Just as it began to change directions, however, Ocho pushed pause. He was clearly annoyed that Xavier and Adam hadn't been paying much attention to the lyrics.

"Naw, naw," Ocho complained as he poked his head into the passenger seat and nudged Xavier, who had been busy writing a text message. "I can tell y'all ain't really listening. Listen to what I'm saying in my music. This some real shit right here."

"A'ight bro," Adam said, apologetically. "Lemme hear it again."

Ocho started the song over. By the middle of the first verse, Adam was nodding his head, listening intently. "Hell yeah," he said at one point, before repeating one of the lines of the verse out loud. "That's some real shit."

Now that he had the full attention of his friends, Ocho paused the song once more. "I'm sayin'," he repeated. "Everything you need to know about my life is right here." With that, he played the song two more times, so that we could all listen carefully.

By the third round, Adam had memorized a couple of the lines. I watched through my rear-view mirror as the two young men danced up and down in the back seat, rapping along to the song. They leaned into one another. At first, they took turns nudging each other with their shoulders. But by midway through the song, Adam had thrown his arm around Ocho, who was practically sitting on his lap. The instant the song ended, they returned to their respective sides of the car. I had never seen the two behave so affectionately toward one another. For at least a few moments, Ocho's musical content served as a kind of emotional camouflage, allowing him to solicit and receive support without violating the norms of street masculinity. It provided them both with the cover they needed to express physical affection that would otherwise be seen as too effeminate. It's important to recognize that these opportunities aren't evenly distributed among the gang. They're open almost exclusively to drillers, increasing in frequency as a young man uploads more content and as his peers increasingly consume and interact with his online products.

Gaining Support through Loyal Deeds

In their bids for love and support, drillers have also learned to capitalize on the evolving structure of drill-oriented gangs. As we saw in chapter 3, during AJ's calculated redistribution of the McDonald's meal, the shift to the attention economy creates new bonds of obligation. As the gang's public face and meal ticket, drillers are uniquely positioned to demand outward displays of loyalty from their peers. Those who contribute to drillers' well-being and success earn a cut of the spoils. Drillers also glorify their backers in music videos and Instagram posts. They promise to bring these "real niggas" with them when they finally make it. Those who fail to demonstrate devotion, however, are locked out, at least until the next chance to step up and redeem themselves. Among the Corner Boys, this arrangement is perhaps most visible in the wake of traumatic events, which tend to leave these young men feeling powerless and vulnerable. In such moments, drillers are uniquely positioned to enlist their closest peers to help them cope and regain a sense of control. Given the hypermasculine norms of street culture, supporters convey their devotion not in words, but in decisive acts. The more daring and dangerous those acts, the more compassion they communicate. Sometimes, if the emotional turmoil is great enough, drillers may expect their friends to engage in what they view as the sincerest act of support: violent retaliation. Drillers call on their friends to "slide" for them, enlisting their help in drive-by shootings.

Junior leveraged his elevated status in precisely this way following the tragic murder of one of his best friends, a young woman named Destiny. Among the Corner Boys, Destiny's death hit Junior the hardest. In contrast to his antagonistic stance toward Gena, Shana, and other so-called clout heads, Junior treated Destiny with kindness and respect. Neighbors since childhood, the two had grown up side by side. They routinely walked to school together and spent afternoons on the local basketball courts. Over the years, their bond remained thoroughly platonic, unhampered by the drama of teenage romance. When Junior gained popularity in the drill world, Destiny was among his first and most ardent fans. She proudly shared his music videos on her Facebook wall. She posted on Instagram pictures of herself wearing silkscreened "#CBE" t-shirts and flashing their gang signs. Junior and Destiny's deep fictive kinship had blossomed well before his micro-celebrity, leaving Junior with little doubt about her underlying intentions. She wasn't in it simply for the clout.

Destiny's murder did more than rob Junior of one of his closest friends. It made him doubt his ability to protect his loved ones, and himself. His feelings of loss and guilt were exacerbated by the reactions of Destiny's family. Amid their own grief, they held Junior responsible for her death. They came to believe that Destiny's visible online ties to the young man had made her a target for CBE's rivals. At one point, they accused Junior of sacrificing Destiny for the sake of his own online stardom. In the weeks following her death, Junior and I routinely found ourselves sitting in my car, reading her family's hate-filled Facebook messages and wall posts. Junior rejected their accusations, but understood why they had come to this conclusion. Across social media, he watched his fellow Corner Boys embellish their friendships with Destiny. To him, these posts were purely instrumental. His peers were merely trying to claim proximity to a murder victim to boost their own street authenticity.

"You see all these niggas talkin' 'bout 'RIP the dead homie,'" Junior complained as we scrolled through a series of their tweets. "But they wasn't even fuckin' with her like that. She was *my* homie, not theirs. They wasn't cool with her like that. And now they're flexin' like 'I miss my girl, woo woo woo.' All for that clout. But they don't even miss her like I do, bro. I done lost a piece of me."

Junior felt the need to prove to Destiny's family, and to himself, that he was different—that he truly cared for the young woman. But he didn't quite know where to turn.

"Who have you talked to about all this stuff," I asked during one of our conversations.

"Nobody," he responded without hesitation. He filled me in on his current coping strategies. "To be honest, bro, I smoke and I drink. I don't be talking to nobody about this shit. I ain't gonna lie, bro, I was just tweaked."

"What about the guys," I probed, hoping to identify a couple of the Corner Boys who might serve as confidantes and talk him through his grief. Junior shot me a disapproving look. He shook his head, relaying a sense of abandonment. "If I feel like nobody else give a fuck, why would I explain myself, pouring my heart out to people? I just say fuck it, bro." He shoved a thumb to his chest. "I keep my shit inside. That's how I feel. Look at my face, bro. I ain't even shaved. I just been in the gutters. I'm in a very rough place in my life right now, bro. Real shit, bro. It don't feel too good."

Junior's emotional health (along with his personal hygiene) continued to deteriorate over the next couple of months. That is, until he came up with a new way to ease his pain. He decided it was time to avenge Destiny. He recounted the decision while the two of us sat in a downtown coffeeshop, miles from Taylor Park. The distance seemed to free him to speak more openly. He reminded me that a drive-by shooting wasn't something he could pull off on his own. He needed help, which would provide a chance to test his friends' dedication. Who was willing to slide for him?

"That's when yo' niggas' true colors come out," he instructed me. "Who gon' turn up with you? That's how you know who got yo' back. I ain't even gonna sugarcoat it, bro."

Junior explained that he made his appeals for help as reasonable as possible. He knew it was a lot to ask. He knew that some of his peers weren't willing to commit murder, no matter how deep their love for him. But there were other ways they could contribute to the deed and prove that they cared about him.

"I ain't sayin' you gotta be the one blowin' [shooting]," Junior reasoned, listing off the necessary roles in a drive-by shooting. "You could do other stuff. Somebody gotta drive. Somebody gotta get the pole [gun]. But you gotta do *somethin'*. Or else you ain't really my mans."

According to Junior, at least three others heeded his call. It was a lower turnout than he had hoped for, but it gave him definitive proof of his true friends. The first was Johnny, one of CBE's longtime shooters. Although the two had always been friendly, their bond tightened when Junior featured Johnny in his latest music video. It signaled Johnny's new role as Junior's unofficial bodyguard and enforcer. Gio also stepped up to lend support. As I would learn, he was intent on improving his status in the group. He hoped to become a shooter. He communicated this desire by carrying the block guns and accompanying Junior whenever he ventured beyond CBE territory. I was most surprised to hear that Xavier lent his support. Like most of the other drillers, Xavier rarely engaged in violence. But Junior had provided him the chance to contribute without pulling a trigger. Xavier was particularly useful because he was one of the only Corner Boys with a valid driver's license. Through his family members, he also had access to a dependable car with up-to-date registration documents. Between the four of them, Junior amassed what he needed to avenge Destiny, quiet his self-doubt, and confirm his friends' love.

Having watched Junior's evolving relationship with his fellow Corner Boys over the previous year, I could see that his recent ascent to micro-celebrity status helped his recruitment efforts. When I first met the young men of CBE, Junior occupied a rather peripheral role. It wasn't so long ago that some of his current supporters had stolen his drug stash and sabotaged his efforts to make ends meet. Now, amid his growing success in the drill world, they were risking their own lives to solidify their place at his side, and in his online content. The fact that they were willing to risk their lives for him was enough to make him feel valued and supported, regardless of their underlying reasons.

Popular Drillers, Worthy Sons

The intangible rewards of micro-celebrity extend beyond drillers' immediate peer groups and collaborators. By distinguishing themselves in the attention economy, these young men also unlock powerful resources for conveying their value and self-worth to their families. They can finally show that despite their failings in school, the job market, and the justice system, they are ambitious, hardworking young men. For some, the rise to micro-celebrity status offered one of the few times since childhood that their families had ever showered them with praise.

Recall that Junior's decision to become a driller stemmed in large part from his hope of earning the love of his mother, who had banished him from her home. Without any additional run-ins with the law, he successfully completed his probation. He excitedly shared the news with his mother as soon as he received word from the judge. She was still frustrated with him, but she extended an olive branch. She invited him to accompany her on an afternoon shopping trip to Walmart. She could use an extra pair of hands. Junior recounted the events of that afternoon to me. He described how he and his mother spent much of the time catching up, with Junior filling her in about his new songs and videos. As they stood in the checkout line, his mother received some unexpected proof of the new life Junior was trying to create for himself. Out of the blue, a wide-eyed teenage girl walked up to Junior and tapped him on the shoulder. The young woman had recognized him from his YouTube videos. She was a big fan, she told him. In fact, he was one of her favorite rappers. Junior's mother looked on with a smile as her son interacted with the star-struck teen. As they left the store, Junior noticed that his mother's demeanor toward him had completely changed. He beamed with pride as he recounted the details.

"I just seen the joy on her face," he recounted, "to feel like her son is *somebody*. Like, she feels like her son has an effect on other people, you feel me? That I make people wanna turn up."

When Junior and his mother returned home, she invited him to move back into her home. As Junior explained it, she saw his turn to music as a dramatic improvement over his previous trajectory as a stick-up artist.

"Did that help your relationship with your mom?" I asked him.

"Hell yeah," Junior responded immediately. "It changed for the better." He went on to describe how his mother even began seeing many of his "old" attitudes and behaviors in a different and positive light. Her reaction to guns is a case in point. Previously, she saw firearms as an essential component of his robberies. It angered her whenever one of the Corner Boys brought guns into her home. Now that her son had given up robbing for rapping, she saw these same items as necessary for her son's protection. Her son was gaining popularity. He was earning a small income. And he was finally contributing to the household financially. But he had also attracted competitors who would love to do him harm.[11]

"Now," Junior explained, "if I'm riding in the car with my mama, she'll ask me if I got my joint [gun]." He patted his waistband. "If I don't, she'll be like, 'Why? Why not?' She wants me to keep this bitch on me, 'cause she know. She know how motherfuckers be on my ass. She know motherfuckers will just shoot me 'cause I got that clout."

In addition to allowing Junior to bring weapons into her home, his mother occasionally loaned him the resources he needed to continue building his self-brand. In fact, she even offered up her living room for Junior's music video shoots. She kept to her room on the second floor while Junior and the rest of CBE piled onto her brown sectional couch, circulating thick blunts, blowing smoke toward the camera. After receiving a modest tax refund, Junior's mother even lent him a stack of twenties and tens to flash in Facebook photos. Only months earlier, she had hardly trusted him in her home. Now she was trusting him with her hard-earned cash.

"She done put up with all my bullshit," Junior confessed during one of our conversations about his rekindled relationship. "I been a real asshole. But with this rap shit, though, I can finally give her what *she* be needing. I'm tryna' put her in a mansion out in the suburbs or out in LA or something." If anything, this renewed motherly love encouraged Junior to pursue micro-celebrity with increased intensity—to "go harder," as he described it. "I gotta feed my family," he reminded me. "I gotta make my mama proud."

■ ■ ■

Among the material, social, and emotional rewards drillers derive from micro-celebrity, there is one benefit that can't be overemphasized. Online infamy not only allows these young men to be seen and heard; it also allows them to finally feel *special*. Whether it's an out-of-town driller hoping to enlist them for a feature, or a fan stopping them on the street for a selfie, these interactions are incredibly fulfilling. We have to remember that these young men have grown up in a world that has labeled them as worthless and lazy, as a menace to society. They've heard it at school, in court, and at church. But now, thanks to social media, they've unlocked the means to hear a very different message—one of respect and appreciation. Both online and off, they're being told that they're worthwhile. They're unique. Given the demeaning experiences in the low-wage service economy and the meager payoffs of the illegal drug economy, this reward is becoming more attractive than ever.

And yet, we shouldn't over-romanticize this payoff. If we zoom out a bit from Taylor Park, and consider *everyone* involved in the drill world, we encounter a range of other people reaping far larger rewards, squarely off the backs of drillers and their gangs. We start to notice the dubious and exploitative reward structure that undergirds this particular branch of the attention economy. In fact, compared to everyone else profiting from drill videos and associated content, drillers often stand to make the *least* money from their own digital products. Indeed, the drill world's support personnel—the videographers, music producers, and bloggers—are far better positioned to accumulate profit in the digital economy. On a good day, a driller might take home five hundred dollars for recording a feature. This might happen a couple of times per month at best. Meanwhile, support personnel like videographers charge dozens of clients these same sums for every video they record. They also receive recurring monthly checks once they monetize their YouTube channels via Google AdSense and other "per-click" advertising arrangements. The fact that drillers and their gangs seldom own their own YouTube channels means that they completely miss out on these kinds of opportunities. Because they don't operate their own channels, they *have* to rely on existing highly trafficked channels to host their content. When they invite videographers to record, edit, and upload their music videos, they effectively give away ownership of their musical products. It may bear their likeness, but as far as the digital economy goes, the videographer holds the copyright. Every penny made through advertising or licensing goes directly into his pockets. Whether it's at the hands of videographers, producers, engineers, or bloggers, drillers' vulnerability to exploitation isn't much better than it was in the traditional music industry. The arrival of social media has changed the parties doing the exploiting but, much to the chagrin of techno-optimists, it certainly hasn't eliminated it.

Zooming out even more, we see others who stand to benefit even more handsomely off drillers' efforts. I'm talking about social network platforms, their CEOs, and their shareholders. Advertisements—like the ones videographers attach to drill music videos via AdSense—make up 84 percent of the annual revenue of Google's parent company, Alphabet, totaling roughly thirty-two billion dollars in 2018.[12] Drill content, especially violent content, creates buzz. It attracts clicks, views, and dollars. In this way, drillers provide what the media theorist Tiziana Terranova calls "free labor."[13] By handing over their digital products, drillers offer their labor freely, willingly, even happily. And as in age-old forms of labor-capital relations, the surplus value squeezed from digital products virtually never finds its way back into the hands of its producers.

Drillers' digital disadvantage creates additional problems beyond labor exploitation. Young men like the Corner Boys bear virtually all of the most serious costs associated with their digital production practices. The more content they create and the more micro-celebrity they build, the more constantly they have to watch their backs. As these young men come to learn, online infamy brings increased attacks from competitors hoping to make a name for themselves by challenging, and sometimes even killing, the drill world's most recognized figures.

5

...

When Keepin' It Real Goes Wrong

The text message came in just as I was turning off my phone and climbing into bed.

"They killed Javon."

My heart sank. Javon was Junior's best friend, inseparable since childhood. Whenever I spent time with Junior, Javon was never very far away.

I scrambled to get ahold of Junior, sending messages to everyone I knew in Taylor Park. It was early morning before I finally got him on the phone. I grabbed my keys, hopped in my car, and drove to his mother's home. I arrived to find him propped up in his twin-sized bed, staring blankly at the wall.

Through tears, Junior told me what happened.

Barely twelve hours earlier, he and Javon had been walking down a quiet South Side street. The two were on their way to a friend's house. They were several miles from Taylor Park, so they didn't expect to run into any trouble. They were also beyond rival territory. Or so they thought. Just as they reached their friend's block, a car full of unfamiliar teens pulled up to the curb in front of them. The young man in the passenger seat called out to Junior by name. Seeing Junior's response, he lifted a pistol from his lap and aimed it at him. Junior turned to run as the bullets whizzed past him. The shooter turned his gun on Javon, who stood frozen in shock. Junior hid in an alley until the shooting stopped and the car sped off. He raced back to Javon, who lay lifeless on the sidewalk. Junior fell to his knees, and cradled his best friend in his arms as he breathed his last breath.

"Javon's dead because of *me*," Junior said, wiping his eyes. "They were after *me*. They recognized *me*. And now *he's* dead." Junior's remorse only deepened as police detectives began showing up at his door at all hours of the day and night. He could clear his conscience, they apparently told his mother, if he would identify the shooters and testify in court. In this difficult time, Junior's closest friends started pulling away from him, worried that he might "turn snitch."[1]

Amid all the vital benefits the Corner Boys and other drillers derive from their public visibility, Javon's death and Junior's lasting trauma are chilling illustrations of the drill world's darker side. The sudden tragedy highlights the dangers that drillers encounter in their efforts to compete in the attention economy.

I'm certainly not the first to point to negative consequences of micro-celebrity. Over the past decade, new media scholars have documented some of the less-than-glamorous aspects of digital self-branding, particularly the difficulties associated with maintaining an "always on" persona. Ironically, the same technological affordances that make digital social media so effective at conveying authenticity are also what render it so perilous. The dynamics of context collapse—which digital aspirants use to convey a singular, coherent identity across multiple social contexts—make it increasingly difficult to fully separate their online, branded self from their offline lives.

As I've previously pointed out, virtually everything we know about micro-celebrity's consequences comes from just a handful of studies, all of which were conducted alongside rather privileged populations. This research focuses mostly on the "psychic damage" these digital hopefuls encounter when their online performances start contaminating their offline social roles and relationships. In the most frequently cited study, danah boyd profiles several teens who face intense scrutiny and derision from schoolmates as a result of their growing social media popularity.[2] These young people grow anxious and depressed as they find themselves on constant guard, questioning the true motives of new acquaintances. By definition, Alice Marwick reminds us, a micro-celebrity "lacks the protections available to an actress or model. She does not have a bodyguard, a press agent, or a stylist."[3] Other research illustrates the difficulties micro-celebrity causes for intimate relationships. Brooke Erin Duffy, for instance, relays that up-and-coming fashion bloggers feel torn between their need to continuously upload content and their daily obligations as wives and mothers. Vacations, honeymoons, and other intimate moments get contaminated by the constant pressure to upload new photos and blog posts.[4] These micro-celebrities start weighing major life decisions—things as serious as filing for divorce—against the potential damage it might do to their online brand.[5]

Fortunately, such hazards aren't completely unavoidable or life-altering for most of these people. When the burdens of being always on grow too onerous, they can reduce or, in some cases, completely withdraw from the social media spotlight. Marwick details how one aspiring tech-scene micro-celebrity escaped the psychic damage of public scrutiny by physically relocating himself to rural New Hampshire. He now spends his free time tending livestock, brewing beer, and gardening.[6] In the end, even those who don't renounce their micro-celebrity seldom, if ever, face the possibility of violent death as the result of it.

As the assault on Junior shows, however, drillers sometimes pay a lethal price for success in the attention economy. Unlike middle- and upper-class micro-celebrities, these young men enter the attention economy from the very bottom of the social, economic, and racial hierarchy, which greatly exacerbates the negative consequences of context collapse.[7] Drillers build their online brands in neighborhoods where reputations for violence have long been coveted prizes. They portray themselves as willful offenders in communities that are already under intense surveillance and criminalization. By the time drillers realize the dangers of the social media spotlight, it's often far too late. Even if they wanted to, they lack the resources to shed their over-the-top reputations, which follow them into new spaces and interactions. With its capacity to pull these young men deeper into street violence, gang life, and criminal justice entanglements, online production intersects with long-standing inequalities to produce a distinctly digital form of disadvantage.

CODE OF THE DIGITAL STREET

Reputations have always been valued resources in urban poor communities. Facing inadequate police protection and blocked economic opportunities, residents have been forced to find alternative ways to resolve disputes, stay safe, and attain dignity and honor. One method is to adhere to what Elijah Anderson famously called the "code of the street." "The code," Anderson wrote two decades ago, "revolves around the presentation of self. Its basic requirement is the display of a certain predisposition to violence. A person's public bearing must send the unmistakable . . . message that one is capable of violence, and possible mayhem, when the situation requires it."[8] Resembling a zero-sum game, successfully building a "name" requires challenging others and discrediting their reputation. As the criminologists Bruce Jacobs and Richard Wright confirm, "bringing someone down . . . raises your personal market worth in the eyes of your peers."[9]

Before the arrival of digital social media, reputational struggles conformed to particular spatial and temporal rules. First and foremost, they almost always unfolded in face-to-face interactions. This required both parties to be in the same place at the same time—usually busy public settings, or "staging areas."[10] If combatants hoped to impress onlookers and build names for themselves, retaliation had to be swift and visible. As Jacobs and Wright note, "waiting before striking back against an aggressor can . . . make you look afraid. . . . Intolerance earns respect and makes you look strong."[11] Throughout the twentieth century, these dynamics were responsible for much of the bloodshed that gripped urban America. At the same time, however, they also provided key opportunities for de-escalation and desistance. Combatants could bring an immediate and potentially lasting end to a conflict by simply moving out of the local neighborhood, eliminating the possibility of a public run-in.[12] In a different neighborhood, they could forge a new public identity, freed of obligations to engage in violence. If moving wasn't feasible, one or both parties could simply "lay low," retreating into private and otherwise neutral spaces where public challenges were less likely to erupt. There, they could relax their outward displays of toughness while performing their other social roles—as fathers, sons, or lovers, for example.[13] Public hostilities dissipated while young men enjoyed moments of vulnerability and "softness" beyond the gaze of challengers and judgmental onlookers.[14]

Stealing Clout

As the assault on Junior tragically illustrates, times are changing. Digital social media disrupt the spatial and temporal dynamics that once governed reputational struggles. In a perverse twist, drillers have become victims of their own success. Their underlying goal, after all, is to build durable reputations as violent street hustlers that stretch well beyond the boundaries of their local neighborhoods. But as they do, they become more recognizable and vulnerable to anyone, including complete strangers, hoping to build their own reputation. Former safe havens and private spheres—places like work, home, and neutral territory—become sites for opportunistic ambushes as challengers strive to invalidate their rivals' authenticity and claim it for themselves. As young Chicagoans refer to it, challengers hope to "steal" their clout.

These dynamics were on full display following the attack on Junior. Mere hours after the shooting, three different young men, affiliated with three different South Side gangs, used Twitter and Instagram to claim responsibility for the attack. They also dared Junior to retaliate and avenge Javon's death—to prove that he was as "savage" and intolerant of disrespect as he proclaims on social media. Such challenges have become even more pressing in the social media age, now that they are permanently archived and searchable. Public affronts, along with their targets' responses, live on indefinitely. If someone like Junior fails to refute challengers' claims and reaffirm his authenticity, he'll be forced to live with this stain on his reputation. He'll lose fans and followers. His YouTube views will plummet. He'll be outed as a fraud—as a "computer gangster."

This newer, digitally mediated brand of reputational struggle has become so prevalent that it now has its own vocabulary. Junior and Javon were merely the latest victims to be "caught lacking"—that is, confronted in non-gang-related situations, engaged in non-gang-related behaviors and roles. It's a well-known truth that even those with the fiercest reputations for violence can't live up to these personas during every minute of every day. They have to let their guard down at *some* point—perhaps riding the bus home from school or running weekend errands with family. It's in these moments that drillers, their shooters, and their closest supporters are most vulnerable—when they're missing the protection of their gangs and guns. Challengers use these opportunities to capture vulnerabilities on their camera phones and upload them to social media platforms for the rest of world to witness and ridicule. In the most egregious cases, they capitalize on these moments to assault, injure, or kill their targets.

Even a cursory Google search for the term *catch opps lacking* returns thousands of videos depicting young men caught off guard in a variety of mundane settings—at the mall, at Memorial Day picnics, and along residential streets.[15] They show challengers chasing their victims, beating them up, forcing them to their knees, making them beg for mercy, and compelling them to say disparaging words about their own gang, neighborhood, and recently slain friends. Across social media and throughout their songs and music videos, drillers underscore their toughness by claiming that they have never been caught lacking. They boast that they are "never lacking," are members of "no lack gang," or are part of "team no lack."

Of course, a young man's ability to continue making such claims hinges on his success in avoiding being filmed in such compromising situations. As Junior's experience confirms, this becomes increasingly harder as his popularity and brand recognition grows. Aside from the attack on Junior and Javon, the Corner Boys have been generally successful at avoiding being caught lacking. During my time in the neighborhood, they were documented in this manner only one other time. Given the details of that incident, however, they typically brush it off as insignificant. This response has a lot to do with the identity of the victim—a Taylor Park resident in his early thirties, known throughout the neighborhood as Crazy Nicky.

Chiraq Savage Catches a Opp Lacking on the
Wrong Block and Chase Him Down the Block.

The War In Chiraq

▶ Subscribe 331,147

672,807 views

➕ Add to   ➤ Share   ••• More   👍 5,246   👎 227

A screenshot of a "caught lacking" video, recorded on a challenger's camera
phone and uploaded by a third-party YouTube channel. (https://www.youtube
.com/watch?v=8Z__poSsUs0, accessed January 14, 2017, later "removed for
violating YouTube's Terms of Service")

Up until the afternoon in question, Nicky had played a peripheral role in
CBE. He was an occasional participant in their music videos, where he
was fond of standing in the back of the scene, flashing CBE's gang signs.
He wasn't involved in much more than that, so long as the rest of the Corner Boys got their way. As his nickname suggests, Nicky was known
throughout the area for his severe mental health and substance abuse issues. According to multiple residents, he was prone to interjecting into
conversations and dice games with slurred non sequiturs that annoyed
everyone present. The first time I met Nicky, he greeted me by showing
off a handful of bright pink Ecstasy pills. After jokingly offering me one,
he threw four into his mouth, chewed, and swallowed them down. Whenever Xavier and Dominik fell into their periods of deep depression, they
usually spent a lot more time with Nicky, self-medicating with PCP-laced
blunts. Nicky also cycled through the criminal justice system more fre-

quently than most other neighborhood residents, and was well known by local patrol officers. Whenever Nicky showed up, unwanted drama was never too far behind.

Despite Nicky's tenuous affiliation with CBE, his various social media profiles greatly exaggerated his role in the Corner Boys. His username across Facebook, Twitter, and Instagram was "CBE Nicky." On social media, the man appeared as central to the Corner Boys as people like Stevie, Gio, or Demarcus. It's perhaps no surprise that Nicky eventually drew special attention from CBE's rivals who were looking to steal their clout.

The incident occurred one late afternoon when Nicky visited a Family Dollar store located in a nearby area controlled by the Murderville gang faction. As Nicky left the store, four young men associated with Murderville cornered him, flashed a gun, and started recording the interaction. His attackers went through the now-familiar steps. First, they verified his identity, making him confirm that he was in fact CBE Nicky. Next, under threat of death, they forced him to "diss" the Corner Boys, coercing him into shouting "Fuck CBE." With sufficient cowardice now on record, they let Nicky go. He ran all the way back to CBE territory, where the video was already circulating on Facebook. Seeing Nicky's failure to "take a jump"—stand up for himself and defend their reputation—the Corner Boys immediately disowned him. They demanded that he remove any mention of his affiliation from his social media profiles. From that moment on, they maintained even more physical and social distance from him, running him off from social gatherings and music video shoots.

Having addressed the incident at home, the Corner Boys turned to social media, where they wrote posts denying that Nicky was ever a "real" member of CBE. They also belittled Murderville's attempts to catch them lacking.

"We let those foo niggas know that they're a bunch of lames," Junior said as he, Stevie, and I sat discussing the video. "This nigga Nicky ain't right. He's *retarded*. You've seen his ass. Murderville *know* he ain't right." Junior pointed at himself and Stevie. "They know that if they tried that on one of *us*, we woulda smoked their asses. Real niggas ain't goin' out like that."

Using the comments section on the video, Junior and other Corner Boys relied on this logic to insist that Murderville hadn't *actually* caught them lacking. They had merely assaulted a mentally handicapped neighbor, who was only loosely affiliated with the group. Therefore, CBE had no reason to feel humiliated. If anything, they had reason to laugh. This was simply more evidence that Murderville was full of cowards, unwilling to challenge one of the actual members of CBE. Murderville contested the Corner Boys' reframing, but ultimately lost the online war of words. The video, along with its potential to diminish the Corner Boys' reputation, eventually faded from public debate. There are now only a few traces of it online.

Nicky's ordeal provides additional insights about efforts to document prominent drillers and their gangs in compromising situations. First, these incidents don't automatically spark violent retribution. This is especially true if drillers and their close supporters can easily rebuff these attacks via online methods. But just because they don't lead to bloodshed doesn't mean that they have no lasting effects. Like Nicky, young men who have been caught lacking face repercussions, including ostracism by their friends and neighbors. Fearing this, drillers and their peers avoid leaving the neighborhood without their shooters, a few of the guys, or a block gun, if it's available. This, in turn, has created a new urban reality where social-media-oriented gangs like CBE are confronting each other in new and additional public spaces, backed by additional combatants and firepower. The Corner Boys reported that shoot-outs now erupt in locations where they had expected to escape from gang violence—places like Chicago's downtown Loop, along lakefront beaches, and at the Six Flags Great America and Wisconsin water parks, where these youth once found temporary respite from the drama of inter-neighborhood beefs.

Second, Nicky's ordeal reveals the dilemma facing those who instigate these challenges. Often, would-be challengers have to rely on serendipity, crossing their fingers for chance run-ins with the young men whose clout they hope to steal. This is what happened during the attack on Junior and Javon. Junior's assailants happened to recognize him as they drove down the street. In the attack on Nicky, I suspect that if Murderville had had their way, they would have caught AJ, Xavier, or another prominent member of the Corner Boys lacking. But none of these young men were at the Family Dollar that day. It was only Nicky—a peripheral member, whose documented assault ended up doing very little to increase Murderville's clout. In this case, Murderville suffered from a difficulty long identified by criminologists and other violence scholars: Contrary to public belief, would-be assailants must overcome mundane, yet powerful logistical obstacles if they want to assault a specific person.[16] A drive-by shooting, for example, requires not only access to an operable firearm, a car, a driver, and someone to pull the trigger but also accurate knowledge of the exact whereabouts of the intended target.[17]

Social media allow challengers to overcome this last obstacle. Today, thanks to the always-on quality of micro-celebrity, challengers no longer have to rely as much on chance. By closely monitoring drillers' social media uploads and activities, aggressors can gather actionable intelligence to make their assaults more immediate, precise, and deadly. Stevie, one of the Corner Boys' primary shooters, has made a daily routine of secretly monitoring the social media activities of his rivals—a form of lateral surveillance that teens refer to as "lurking."[18] His goal is to piece together his potential targets' habits, whereabouts, associations, and vulnerabilities in real time. This increases his likelihood of locating, confronting, and harming them when he desires. I once asked Stevie to explain how shooters use social media to locate their targets.

"Right now," he began, "somebody is out there lurking on somebody, getting ready to put a bullet in 'em. And shit, social networks make it even easier! People know what you doing, what you eating, that you out in front of yo' house. It's mad easy. Everybody is doing their homework. People takin' pictures in front of their house not even realizing that their opps is steady waiting and looking at their Instagram."

Anticipating my next question, Stevie offered a hypothetical scenario to demonstrate how social media provides an additional level of granularity. "It's like this," he continued in a slower, more instructive cadence. "The opp used to know which *block* you live on, but he didn't know which *house*. He didn't know what yo' *house* looked like. But now he *know*. Now he know *exactly* what yo' crib [house] look like. And now he up on you. Now he gaming you and you don't even know he out there with that kind of information. It's all about information!"

On other occasions, these young men stressed the importance of committing their rivals' social media content to memory. They made it a point to memorize the features of their target's home, the color and make of his car, his favorite outfits, and the faces of his closest friends and family. The savviest shooters also pay close attention to the timestamps and locations of their enemy's social media updates. By doing so, they can begin predicting when and where he will be alone, unarmed, and unprepared for an ambush.

Given my close relationship with the Corner Boys, I wasn't in a position to ever observe their rivals gather intelligence on them. However, the Corner Boys told me how they used seemingly innocuous social media content to coordinate an attack on an up-and-coming driller known in the drill world as "Smoky-P." After the attack, several of the Corner Boys relayed that they had been monitoring the man's Facebook, Instagram, and Twitter profiles. They said they had assembled a rough picture of Smoky-P's daily routine. Because of Smoky-P's habit of posting selfies, the Corner Boys were able to discern that he routinely walked alone to a nearby liquor store in the afternoons, multiple times per week. They stated that they then began driving past the location on those particular days and times. Their lurking apparently proved effective when they spotted Smoky-P exiting the store by himself. As the Corner Boys tell it, one of them snuck up and shot Smoky-P multiple times. Smoky-P survived the attack, but only after being hospitalized in critical condition. To this day, the Corner Boys refuse to tell me who, exactly, pulled the trigger. Nevertheless, they openly celebrate one key detail—that they shot Smoky-P while he was absentmindedly staring at his phone, preparing to take yet another selfie.

A second common technique for challenging others' authenticity entails what the Corner Boys sometimes referred to as "calling bluffs." We've seen repeatedly how drillers exaggerate their violent personas and deeds on social media. Alongside their friends and fellow gang members, they upload sinister statements and photos depicting themselves protecting their turf, or "on the block," flashing guns and gang signs, daring rivals to "slide" into their neighborhood for a shoot-out. In response, challengers try to expose these displays as artifice, daring them to act on their claims. This often entails traveling to a driller's supposed location and documenting that he is absent, less supported, or less armed than he purports. Using their camera phones, challengers take care to record street signs and relevant landmarks to verify their counterevidence.

In my first month in Taylor Park, one of the Corner Boys' nearby rivals, a gang faction known as Crown Town, repeatedly tried to call CBE's bluff. In one of the first instances I ever witnessed, one of the Crown Town members posted a short, grainy video to his Facebook page that showed him and several friends driving completely unmolested past one of the corners where CBE routinely films music videos. Drawing an explicit contrast to the images the Corner Boys upload to social media, the Crown Town video captures several hundred yards of empty sidewalks, accompanied by the following caption:

y CBE block dry asl lol

In this concise comment, Crown Town calls attention to the dishonesty of the Corner Boys' reputational claims. The caption rhetorically asks why ("y"), despite the Corner Boys' recurring claims of guardianship over their turf ("block"), the area is completely empty of gang members ("dry asl [as hell]"). This evidence of CBE's inauthenticity has apparently caused Crown Town to laugh out loud ("lol").

Like all targets of this technique, the Corner Boys faced a tough choice: Either remain quiet and hope the online challenge goes unnoticed, or create and upload their own evidence to refute the exposé. On this occasion, they chose the latter. I followed behind the Corner Boys as they gathered more than a dozen members and walked to the same corner where Crown Town had recorded the earlier video. There, they recorded their own video, which they uploaded to social media. It depicted the group standing boldly on the sidewalk, flashing CBE's hand signs, looking into the camera, daring the Crown Town to attempt their incursion again. In doing so, the Corner Boys effectively reversed the challenge, calling Crown Town's bluff. After two hours passed and no Crown Town members had returned, the Corner Boys returned to social media to criticize the inaction of their rivals. For the next few weeks, the Corner Boys reposted screenshots and photos to remind online audiences of Crown Town's cowardice.

At the time, I was concerned about getting caught in any ensuing crossfire, should Crown Town accept the Corner Boys' challenge. I pulled AJ aside for a private conversation, taking him up on an initial promise he made to let me know when the neighborhood was "too hot" for me to be there. To my surprise, AJ brushed off my concerns. He was confident that Crown Town wouldn't return.

"They ain't gon' do shit," he reassured me. "They just talkin'. To tell you the truth, they don't want no smoke [violence]."

Over the following weeks, I spoke with other Corner Boys about the incident. They confirmed AJ's statement. According to Demitri, one of the young men who used his camera phone that afternoon, everyone knew that there was only a very slim chance that Crown Town would return.

"We *knew* they wasn't about to slide right then," Demitri explained. "You got damn near twenty of us on front street. Even *they* ain't stupid enough to try sum'. We woulda let off shots before they even turned the corner. They know that. I don't care what nobody say, ain't nobody who *likes* gettin' shot at. Hell naw! They gon' wait 'til we clear out. Just like I ain't about to slide on *them* when *they* all outside. We gon' wait 'til maybe one or two out there, but not their whole crew! That's suicide."

As Demitri remarked, the very structure of the video—portraying a large mass of potentially armed men—was itself a deterrent. Demitri's assessment was bolstered by his knowledge that at least two of Crown Town's shooters were indisposed at the time. As he remarked, "I seen [on their social media profiles] that their main shooter was OT [out of town]. The other one locked up. The rest don't want no smoke. They only come through recording when they know we ain't out there, but they ain't really tryna' blow."

It's important to remember that these calculations are completely hidden from online audiences. In the absence of such ground-level information, the Corner Boys appear *even more* violent than they actually are. They seem wholly unafraid of death, despite the fact that they strategically worked to reduce the possibility of a shoot-out.

As I would learn during my time with the Corner Boys, the vast majority of efforts to steal clout unfold just like this—*without any bloodshed*. This is because drillers and their gangs often take conscious steps to ensure that challenges *don't* spill into the streets. In fact, the most common form of stealing clout stays entirely confined to online space. There, challengers leverage the affordances of social media to publicly contradict, compromise, or otherwise cast doubt on the personas drillers and their gangs meticulously curate. Acting like fact-checkers, challengers scour their target's social media profiles, continually comparing current claims of violent criminality against past content. It usually isn't too hard to find compromising material. As the media theorist Bernard Harcourt reminds us, every social media upload, photo, or self-admission—no matter how seemingly innocuous—always emits little puzzle pieces, allowing others to assemble and expose inconsistencies in online performances.[19] Among the Corner Boys, several young men play the role of social media watchdog. It's a delicate task. There's a strong norm against following rivals on Instagram or "friending" them on Facebook. These things don't just add to rivals' popularity metrics, they're read as a sign of envy and insecurity. It's not uncommon for gang-associated youth to snap screenshots when their rivals send them friend requests, using these opportunities to humiliate their enemies on a public stage. To avoid embarrassment, young men typically create fake accounts, or borrow the accounts of young women friends and family members, to covertly lurk on their rivals. When they encounter particularly damning information, they spring into action, disseminating it as widely as possible.

As arguably the most tech-savvy member of CBE, Gio routinely engaged in this practice. Hardly a week went by without him greeting his friends with the latest gossip about which Chicago driller has been arrested, shot, or insulted. One of Gio's favorite hobbies was creating and spreading crude online "memes"—small pictures with comical captions and statements—that poke fun at rivals' physical appearances or the circumstances surrounding their deaths. Social media platforms are full of these attacks. For instance, although it's been several years since the death of Joseph "Lil JoJo" Coleman, his rivals continue to circulate memes disrespecting him and undercutting his gang's claims of toughness and supremacy. Several of the most popular memes mock the fact that Coleman was gunned down while riding what is rumored to have been a child's bicycle.

A homemade meme mocking the death of Joseph "Lil JoJo" Coleman. The acronyms in the last line stand for "Shaking my damn head" and "Laughing my ass off." (https://wallpapersafari.com/w/AwOLfk, accessed November 8, 2016)

One of Gio's most popular memes took direct aim at a rival driller known as "Boss Roc." At the time, Boss Roc was one of the best-known members of a gang faction located about a mile from Taylor Park. None of the Corner Boys had ever met Boss Roc, but their dislike (and jealousy) seemed to grow by the day. His popularity had skyrocketed over the previous two years, and now surpassed that of the Corner Boys. Boss Roc was receiving attention from international music blogs and hip-hop magazines on the heels of a series of inflammatory diss tracks and music videos that insulted several mainstream rappers based in Los Angeles and New York. The Corner Boys complained that Boss Roc's sonic assaults, as well as his drug kingpin persona, were highly disingenuous. It was easy to pick fights with out-of-town rappers, they criticized, because Roc would never be forced to back up his words.

Amid the Corner Boys' disgust, Gio devised a plan to put Roc's inauthenticity "on blast." Gio spent an afternoon searching through Boss Roc's various social media profiles, looking for evidence that might prove CBE's contentions. He soon found what he was looking for. It appeared that Boss Roc had grown careless as he uploaded Instagram and Facebook photos that depicted him hugging women, flashing gang signs, and generally posing for the camera. Gio noticed that many of these, which had been taken over the course of multiple weeks, showed Boss Roc wearing what looked to be the same pair of boxer shorts. Gio used his phone to take screenshots of a half dozen of these photos. He quickly cropped, resized, and assembled them in a collage using a photo editing application on his phone. He uploaded the finished product to Facebook with the following caption:

Dis fu Nigga got one pair of boxers How he a drug lord 😊

Gio's message is straightforward: If we were to only listen to Boss Roc's songs, watch his music videos, and look at his social media uploads, we might imagine that he is swimming in profits from robberies and drug sales. Yet, at least according to Gio's meme, it appears that Boss Roc can only afford a single pair of boxers. If this is true, then Boss Roc's claims of a lucrative criminal career are fabrications. Boss Roc, it would seem, is a fraud. Gio knew that Boss Roc was likely wearing a single pair of boxers, day in and day out, precisely because Gio and the rest of the Corner Boys do exactly the same thing. Throughout my time with the Corner Boys, most members of CBE owned only three or four outfits. Despite how they may appear on social media, these well-worn "fits" were often stained and threadbare. When it was time to perform for the camera, they'd slip on their prized sweatshirts, luxury brand jeans, and glittering pieces of costume jewelry. When those weren't available, they'd simply go shirtless. There's a popular saying on the streets of urban America: Real recognize real. These new, digitally mediated challenges suggest that the inverse is also true: Unreal recognize unreal.

Gio's meme went viral over the following twenty-four hours. First it spread among the Corner Boys, and to other young people in Taylor Park. Then it circulated to other Chicago neighborhoods, eventually stretching to users across the United States. All the while, the various social media audiences piled on, questioning Boss Roc's hygiene along with his online persona. I watched to see how he would respond. I was somewhat surprised to see how easily he shrugged off the meme, reframing it as insignificant. He even reposted the meme on his own page, along with a few strategic captions. First, Boss Roc took the opportunity to remind online audiences that boxers come in packs with multiple pairs. He claimed, contrary to Gio's meme, that he was actually wearing a brand-new pair of boxers in every photo—proof that he had plenty of cash on hand. Boss Roc then went one step further, turning the tables on the Corner Boys. If anything, he remarked, their attempt to soil his name had actually served to *increase* his popularity. When the meme went viral, it piqued public curiosity and drove traffic to his social media content. He experienced a surge in new followers, and his YouTube videos received a wave of new views. He went so far as to thank the anonymous creator of the meme for inadvertently helping him to build even more clout. This irritated Gio, but he wasn't upset for long. He was soon back to work, making fresh new memes about Boss Roc and other drillers he disliked.

Sticky Reputations

Javon's murder had a profound effect on Junior and his family. As Junior wrestled with the trauma of losing his best friend, Junior's mother, Tasha, made plans to move her four children as far away from Taylor Park as possible. Unlike some of the Corner Boys' parents, Tasha was highly active on social media. On Twitter, she saw the continual threats on Junior's life. She read the Facebook posts by rivals boasting about finding her address and killing her family. She had grown weary of the detectives knocking on her door, pressing Junior to identify the shooters. She knew the price he'd pay for cooperating with the police.

So, three months after Javon's death, Tasha packed up her entire home in a U-Haul truck and headed to Chicago's North Side. Her niece agreed to let the five of them crash at her apartment, some ten miles away from Taylor Park. Tasha was beyond relieved; her children would finally be out of harm's way. Junior shared the sentiment. On the eve of their move, the two of us sat in my car, reminiscing about Javon. Junior openly admitted his desire to give up on his drill music dreams.

"I got shot at over this drill shit," he said at one point. "And I *still* don't got a record deal!" Although Junior had received a wave of feature requests from other aspiring drillers in the months after the shooting, he questioned whether they were worth losing his best friend over. For Junior, Javon's death was an "awakening moment"—the sociologist Nikki Jones's term for the "brief episodes of reflection triggered by external events that encourage a person to think, even in the most fleeting ways, about changing the direction of their lives."[20] "This drill shit ain't workin' for me no more," Junior continued. "I'm done. Music. Gangbanging. All of it. Even the guys. I'm out this bitch. Imma just finish school and get the hell out of Chicago."

I found myself as optimistic as Junior and Tasha. This move would finally let Junior put some distance between himself and Taylor Park, the Corner Boys, and their long list of South Side rivals. He could finally start fresh in a new neighborhood and a new school.

We were all mistaken.

Junior received a lesson in the stickiness of online reputations the moment he climbed out of the U-Haul in front of his new home. According to Junior, a group of young men approached him from a nearby stoop. Although he didn't recognize them, one of them addressed him by name. As the stranger spoke, he formed an "A" and a "K" with his fingers, signaling affiliation in the Almighty Knights—the "parent" gang of Murderville, one of the Corner Boys' fiercest rivals. Apparently, a small Almighty Knights faction controlled Junior's new neighborhood.

Junior and Tasha panicked, quickly unloading the rest of their belongings before any more Almighty Knights arrived. Once inside, Junior reformulated his plans. For now, school would have to wait. Without the protection provided by his fellow Corner Boys, this new neighborhood was even *more* dangerous for him than Taylor Park. Deciding that he needed a gun to protect himself, Junior called up one of the other Corner Boys, who made the trek north to deliver a pistol. Junior carried the gun in his waistband whenever he ventured outside. He told me that he had to "up" it on the Almighty Knights two times in his first couple of weeks.

If the attempt on Junior's life captured how micro-celebrity pulls young men into new, unexpected, and sometimes deadly conflicts, the Almighty Knights' thinly veiled threats outside Junior's new home shows how micro-celebrity creates new obstacles for drillers trying to leave digital production, gangs, and crime. For young men who came of age before the proliferation of digital social media, the spatially and temporally bounded character of the code of the street allowed for what criminologists commonly refer to as "ageing out." "Most antisocial children," the sociologist Walter Gove famously wrote more than three decades ago, "do not become antisocial adults."[21] As they enter adulthood, most young people pass through key "turning points"—such as moving to a new neighborhood, having children, getting married, securing a career, or pursuing higher education. New and stronger emotional attachments to family, work, and education disrupt previous patterns of offending and reduce the influence of the code of the street by increasing informal social control by adult social networks, and by replacing delinquent peers and identities with pro-social ones.[22] As Nikki Jones argues, these vital turning points are almost always preceded by awakening moments, like Junior's. Awakening moments act as a kind of pre–turning point. They prime young people for change, creating the emotional, social, and material conditions for turning points to take hold.[23]

Unfortunately, digital production and micro-celebrity short circuit this process. Sticky reputations sever the link between awakening moments and turning points. Social media platforms act as permanent archives of young men's violent deeds and appearances. As a result, even if drillers experience awakening moments—even if they decide to leave their former neighborhoods, return to school, start families, and enter formal employment—they have to deal with the fact that their previous online content lives on, sometimes indefinitely. Even when they shut down their social media profiles and withdraw from online activity, rivals and potential assailants may have already committed their likeness and identifying information to memory. In fact, it's during this hopeful period of ageing out that young men are *most* vulnerable. This is when they're most likely to be engaged in non-gang-associated activities and social roles, unarmed and without the protection of their gang. In the social media age, awakening moments can get a young man killed.

Among the Corner Boys, there is perhaps no better illustration of this dilemma than nineteen-year-old Stevie, one of CBE's most feared shooters. Stevie's online persona prevented him from transitioning into a more conventional, law-abiding trajectory. Stevie's change of heart occurred about a year into my time in Taylor Park. I noticed that he had begun spending less time hanging out in the neighborhood. When he did show up, he was even more reserved than usual. When the Corner Boys recorded new music videos, he tended to stand off to the side or outside of the frame altogether.

It wasn't until the two of us were alone in my car, on the way to his weekly meeting with his probation officer, that I confirmed my suspicions. About halfway into our drive, Stevie reached out with a slender finger and turned down the volume on my car stereo.

"I got something to tell you," he confessed. I could sense him relax. He took a deep breath. He let it out with a long exhale. "I got a baby on the way, bro. I'm about to be a dad."

"That's awesome" I replied, congratulating him.

We discussed the due date, his relationship with the baby's mother, and his thoughts about becoming a father. He was excited, he told me, but he was feeling overwhelmed with the sudden responsibility. "I can't be out on the block gangbangin' no more," he said with conviction. "I got a baby on the way. I gotta take care of my kid and his momma. I can't do that if I'm dead or locked up."

Stevie described his efforts to pull away from the Corner Boys. He had moved out of Taylor Park, and in with his grandmother. She lived on the Far South Side, closer to the mother of his child. After weeks of looking for employment, he had finally secured a graveyard shift at a frozen food warehouse about an hour outside of Chicago. The commute was horrible, he said, but the company ran two shuttles per day between the warehouse and the city. Without a high school diploma and a spotty work history, Stevie was grateful for the steady income. I was excited to hear him describe his plans to become, as he put it, "a family man." According to the research on desistance, Stevie was doing precisely what he needed to build a new life away from violence and crime. Following his awakening moment, he was separating himself from his delinquent peers. He had established a new, pro-social identity for himself. He was spending more time with family and at work. He was on the verge of a turning point.

Yet, thanks to Stevie's large social media presence, the road to redemption was far rockier than he imagined. He couldn't shed the online reputation that he had worked so hard to create. A couple of months into his new job, Stevie stood at the shuttle stop with his coworkers. The shuttle soon arrived, unloading tired employees from the previous shift. One of these men noticed Stevie. The stranger walked up to Stevie and confidently asked if he was "CBE Stevie." With Javon's death fresh in his mind, Stevie refused to answer. But his reaction was all that the stranger needed, smiling in satisfaction as he walked away.

The brief interaction left Stevie rattled, and for good reason. "I didn't know him," Stevie recalled. "But he knew *me*. Niggas know me from the [music] videos. They be steady studying that shit." Stevie sighed in frustration. "The way he looked at me, I could just tell he was one of the opps. Now he knew where I was working at. He knew I was at that *same* bus stop every day at the *same* time." Fearing an ambush after work, Stevie didn't board the shuttle that day, or any day afterward. Despite his efforts to break away from the Corner Boys, he was still an opportunistic and worthwhile target. "I ain't just gonna let the opps pull up on me while I'm getting off the shuttle," he vowed. "I ain't just gonna let them catch me lackin'." The low-pay job wasn't worth his life.

Fortunately, Stevie was able to land another job in a little less than a month. It was another manual labor position in a warehouse in the Chicago suburbs. But only a week into his new job, another stranger recognized him from the Corner Boys' social media content. Again, fearing an ambush, Stevie quit his new job. He wasn't going to take any chances.

A couple of weeks later, Stevie's inability to escape his online identity became even more apparent. A passing car opened fire on him during one of his visits to Taylor Park. In the aftermath, he called AJ, Xavier, and Junior to make a bold request. He was tired of looking over his shoulder, so he asked them each to re-record or delete their most recent music videos and online photos that portrayed him associating with the gang. I was with AJ when the call came in. He refused Stevie's requests without hesitation. He even called Stevie a "bitch" for being scared of an attack. Given the discussion so far, AJ's reaction makes sense. AJ needs Stevie, and Stevie's reputation as a fearless shooter, if he wants to maintain his own authenticity as a violent street hustler. Helping Stevie "make good" would deprive AJ of one of his most powerful resources for validating his authenticity.

AJ's refusal reveals an additional difficulty that drillers and their peers face when trying to shed their violent reputations. Much of the content bearing their likeness doesn't actually belong to them. Recall that, given their relative lack of resources, these young men rely on various third parties—videographers, bloggers, and YouTube channels—to upload, host, and disseminate their content. This makes it virtually impossible for them to erase the images of guns, drugs, and criminality circulating on the internet. These displays will remain online, at the content owner's discretion, as long as they continue drawing clicks, views, and dollars. It's yet one more way that non-gang-associated, "mainstream" individuals contribute to micro-celebrity's potentially lethal consequences.

Sometimes, the negative influence of these third parties is undeniable. An increasing number of blogs and YouTube channels are now dedicated to providing curious viewers with up-to-the-minute news about gang wars and "beefs" between rappers. Titillating details on the latest taunt or shooting generate clicks. Clicks generate revenue from advertisers. In order to keep profits flowing, bloggers closely monitor the social accounts of prominent drillers. When they notice a conflict brewing, they upload news about it to their websites and channels. The most common technique is to snap screenshots of heated social media exchanges between gangs, compile these images into short video sequences, overlay these videos with foreboding drill beats, and upload them to their YouTube channels. They title the videos "Twitter Beef" and list the names of individuals and their gang affiliations. As these conflicts escalate, channel owners post additional videos, adding the most recent tweets alongside reports about subsequent retaliation.

From the outside, it might seem as though these blogs and channels are merely documenting ongoing conflicts. But these third parties are actively sparking new antagonisms while fanning the flames of those already underway. In fact, thanks to one of these channels, the Corner Boys unexpectedly found themselves embroiled in a war with a gang called Young Thug Entertainment, or YTE for short. YTE controls a small territory located more than twenty blocks away from Taylor Park, known as "Dee-Town," in honor of one of YTE's slain members. Over the past five years, several of YTE's rappers have gained a national following, with multiple YouTube videos boasting well over two million views.

Although the war between CBE and YTE would escalate quickly, it had begun rather unintentionally, with a casual cell phone video. Like countless teens, the Corner Boys are fond of documenting themselves smoking weed. They stare at the camera, taking long drags from blunts, letting the thick tendrils of smoke leak from their mouths. On a lazy afternoon, Xavier and Ricky sat in a neighbor's apartment, uploading videos of themselves getting high. Between their high-pitched giggles, the camera catches Ricky making the offhanded comment that he is "smoking on Dee-pack." This phrase has deep significance among gang-associated youth in Chicago. According to every Chicago teen I've ever spoken with, it's arguably the most disrespectful insult someone can make. It means that they've sprinkled the ashes of the deceased (in this case, Dee) into a marijuana blunt (a "pack") and are smoking it, getting high on the thought of his death. The fallout from Xavier and Ricky's careless utterance came quickly. Within minutes, the video was circulating social media and reached YTE. Upset by the unprovoked affront, they responded by posting defamatory comments about Benzie, one of the Corner Boys' slain friends. Over the next few days, CBE and YTE hurled additional insults at each other via social media.

By the end of the week, multiple third-party blogs and YouTube channels had picked up the feud. This included Chiraq Savages, which uploaded its own videos chronicling the war of words. As I write this, one of these videos has already eclipsed two hundred thousand views. The feud escalated over the next month as fans and onlookers posted comments in support of their favorite "team." Throughout this period, each side dared the other to "slide" into their territory and deliver their insults in person. At one point, YTE called the Corner Boys' bluff and drove through Taylor Park trying to catch one of the Corner Boys lacking. Despite the fact that YTE's incursion was unsuccessful, the looming threat of attack raised the level of paranoia and anxiety in the neighborhood. At the height of the conflict, several Corner Boys expressed their frustration to Xavier and Ricky.

I stood with a half dozen of them one evening, listening to Dominik, AJ, and Demonte rip into the two. There was no need for this war with YTE, they lectured. Sure, CBE had gained some online attention, but now the entire neighborhood was embroiled in an unnecessary war. I was shocked to hear Ricky, one of the most stubborn of the group, apologize.

"Our bad," he told them contritely. "That shit got outta hand *real* quick."

Xavier was also apologetic, but argued that the conflict wouldn't have ever escalated to this point if the third-party blogs hadn't gotten involved. "How were we supposed to know that shit woulda' blown up like that? Niggas get high and say stupid shit all the time. We wasn't *really* tryna' diss on YTE. We just fuckin' around."

Dominik continued his scolding. "Y'all can't be puttin' us out there like that."

"True," Xavier conceded, "but it was fucking Chiraq Savages, bro. Once they got it, there was nothing we could do!"

"Yeah," Ricky chimed in. "Everybody was lookin' to see what we was gonna do. What would *you* do? These fools was dissin' Benzie, all on that 'Fuck Benzie' talk. We had to say *something*! We woulda looked foo [weak] as hell if we didn't."

By broadcasting their brazen displays to hundreds of thousands of on-lookers, third-party websites neutralize drillers' ability to de-escalate or otherwise settle online disputes before they spill into the streets. Thanks to blogs like Chiraq Savages, Xavier and Ricky's casual utterance was amplified and broadcasted on an even bigger and higher-stakes public stage. With the entire drill world looking on, Xavier and Ricky knew that backing down might harm the Corner Boys' individual and collective reputations. In the end, their efforts to maintain authenticity, combined with the interference by third-party blogs, put the entire neighborhood in danger. As the Corner Boys would soon learn, these reluctant efforts to preserve online personas can backfire in additional ways, especially when these online displays fall into the hands of the criminal justice system.

THE LEGAL COSTS OF MICRO-CELEBRITY

When it comes to drillers' online displays, it's hard to imagine a more unintended yet powerful audience than police, prosecutors, and judges. Since the declaration of the War on Crime in the mid-twentieth century, repeated and aggressive police contact has become a fact of everyday life for urban poor residents.[24] Since the 1990s, police departments across the United States have embraced patrol policies that instruct officers to stop and frisk pedestrians who appear suspicious. Black residents are twice as likely to be detained as whites.[25] By the end of the twentieth century, the number of Americans behind bars had increased five-fold since the 1970s, eclipsing two million behind bars, with another four million on probation or parole.[26] These staggering statistics are overwhelmingly borne by black residents, particularly young black men.[27] The mark of a criminal record brings a host of collateral consequences, including exclusion from public and government-assisted housing, barriers to employment, ineligibility for public benefits, voting restrictions, and deportation.[28]

The criminalization of urban poor communities, along with its multitude of detrimental effects, is exacerbated in today's digital age. Criminal justice actors have embraced social media to more aggressively investigate, indict, and convict youth designated as gang members.[29] In fact, by 2014, approximately 81 percent of law enforcement professionals reported using social media as a tool in investigations.[30] In the most common variant, officers manually search individual suspects' social media profiles for potential evidence that they have, or will likely, engage in violence. As one undercover narcotics officer confidently put it in 2016, "If someone were to tell me you get one tool to investigate crime right now . . . I'd pick Facebook every time. . . . In fact, over the past two years, I can't think of a case when I didn't use social media."[31] To improve the scope and speed of investigations, departments are also turning to machine-learning algorithms and contracting with technology vendors to scour social media for aggressive statements, images of guns, and other potentially violent content. Court personnel similarly rely on social media to secure indictments and convictions. In fact, nearly half of the evidence used in gang conspiracy cases is now drawn from social media.[32]

So although drillers and their gangs envision their music videos and other social media content building a pathway out of poverty, it's actually more likely to result in arrest and imprisonment. Unfortunately, most don't learn this lesson until far too late, until after they've already built durable online reputations. In fact, for much of my time with the Corner Boys, I seemed to be the *only* one who worried about the legal repercussions of their online behavior. In my earliest interviews with the Corner Boys, I asked each of them if they were concerned that the police might use their uploads against them. To a man, they waved off the possibility, claiming that the police were simply "too busy" to monitor their online activity in any meaningful way. At the time, they had little reason to believe otherwise. None of their posts had led to arrests or jail time. None had shown up in court. But this wouldn't last forever. As time went on, there were signs that they had attracted the attention of the Chicago Police Department. A few months into my relationship with the Corner Boys, officers detained Xavier and AJ while they walked down the street. During the stop, officers referred to them by their drill monikers, suggesting that local law enforcement had begun watching their music videos. Not long after that, a group of the Corner Boys' middle-school-aged neighbors relayed that detectives had stopped them on their way to school and pressed them for information about the time and location for CBE's next music video shoot.

And yet, the Corner Boys shrugged off these early warning signs. "That's the thing," AJ said with his typical cockiness. "They just tryna' catch us while we shootin' the videos. They know that's when we got the *guns*. That's all they really want. They don't care about us, bro. They just care about the *guns*." For AJ and the others, so long as they kept quiet about pending video shoots, and kept a sufficient lookout while recording their scenes, they had little to worry about. Given the potential rewards of their online activities, the Corner Boys pushed the possibility of criminalization from their minds. And besides, most of the drillers saw what they were doing as far less criminal than their past moneymaking pursuits, which included robbery and drug dealing.

As time wore on, however, the Corner Boys learned how easily online reputations and displays can follow them into the criminal justice system. Dominik was the first to experience the way micro-celebrity makes punishments more severe and less escapable. I traveled with him to his court hearings for a gun charge. Six months earlier, Dominik had been standing in front of his apartment building when officers detained and searched him. They found a pistol stashed a few feet away and arrested him. As in virtually all of the gun cases I observed, the judge sentenced Dominik to twelve months of intensive probation, which included a nightly 7 PM curfew and weekly drug tests. For the next few months, officers stopped by his home at random to ensure that he was inside, obeying curfew. Although he was thankful to avoid time behind bars, the probation conditions disrupted his ability to sustain his drill career. His criminal record boosted his authenticity and online following, but it simultaneously limited his ability to participate in any activity that kept him out past sunset, including out-of-town features, across-town recording sessions, or neighborhood video shoots.

Dominik's disappointment turned to depression when he was invited to perform his very first concert in a college town a few hours' drive from Chicago. It was one of the big breaks he had been waiting for. He was distraught when he broke the news to me. He cursed in frustration, brainstorming how he might be able to perform at the concert and race back home before his probation officer stopped by for an evening check-in. The more Dominik spoke, the more I worried that his plan might land him in prison. When I suggested that he call his attorney, he immediately dialed the number. Through the tinny speaker of Dominik's iPhone, his lawyer suggested that he write the judge a letter, asking for a temporary exception to the 7 PM curfew. If Dominik could prove that he was a legitimate musician, and that the concert was an important source of his regular income, the judge might waive the curfew for a few days. Dominik smiled hopefully as his lawyer explained the process.

But Dominik's frown returned only a few moments after he hung up the phone. The new plan had a serious flaw. To that point, the judge knew Dominik only by his real name. He was unaware of Dominik's violent online content and his drill music moniker, "Ruger," which was a tribute to his favorite brand of gun. If Dominik followed through on his attorney's plan, he would have to send the judge links to the concert flyer, maybe even some of his YouTube music videos. If he did that, the judge would get a very different picture of Dominik—an image of a young man obsessed with firearms, openly boasting of his purported gun crimes and unsolved murders. Dominik worried that the judge wouldn't just deny his request, but might even revoke his probation. In the end, Dominik decided not to ask the judge for leniency. He called the promoter and removed himself from the concert lineup. His online hyperbole had become a liability.

Dominik would come to appreciate the decision to withhold online content from the judge. Not long after, police and prosecutors began to use the Corner Boys' YouTube videos and social media posts more systematically in their investigations and prosecutions. When police officers drove past one of AJ's video shoots, they took the opportunity to search the driller and the four other Corner Boys who stood in the background of the scene. The officers found a pistol stashed near one of the young men, a peripheral CBE member named DeRon. They arrested DeRon on the spot. Over the next few months, I received updates from DeRon's friends and family. According to them, the officers found the YouTube video from that day and introduced it as evidence contradicting DeRon's claims that the gun wasn't his. Facing such incriminating evidence, DeRon decided not to fight the charge at trial, as he and his lawyer had originally planned. Instead, he took a plea deal that sent him to prison.

Of all the times that the Corner Boys' online content turned up in court, few were as frustrating as Junior's experiences. The year following Javon's death had been difficult for Junior. Little did he know that it would only get worse. Terrified to walk the neighborhood streets alone, Junior carried his pistol whenever he left his new apartment. Given the frequency of stop-and-frisks on Chicago streets, it wasn't long before officers detained and searched Junior. They immediately found the weapon. Like Dominik, Junior received intensive probation. It was yet another awakening moment. Determined to fulfill the mandates of his probation and stay out of prison, Junior steered clear of Taylor Park and the Corner Boys. He also recommitted himself to his pregnant girlfriend, re-enrolled in school, and even landed an entry-level job at a nearby fast-food restaurant. Much to Junior's frustration, the conditions of his probation—which required a three-hour round trip to meet with his probation officer and submit to mandatory drug tests—made it difficult to fulfill his school, work, and family obligations. Even so, Junior persisted. He successfully upheld his commitments.

Months later, I drove Junior to court. He was nervous but optimistic. Given his good behavior, he anticipated that the judge might terminate his probation early, or at least ease the terms of supervision. After all, he had completely avoided re-arrest, passed every drug test, and even carried a letter of support from his English teacher, who applauded his dedication to school. However, even despite evidence of self-transformation, Junior's probation officer recommended *against* reducing Junior's punishment. The reason: a series of recent Facebook uploads that showed Junior exchanging aggressive, profanity-laden insults with several rivals. The probation officer had been covertly monitoring his online activity. In his eyes, Junior's recent content provided the clearest evidence of Junior's immoral character and ongoing criminality. It trumped all other evidence of Junior's clean record, including his sterling school record, new job, and support letter.

Junior kept quiet throughout the proceedings, hiding his rage until we returned to my car. He knew that anything he said would be taken as yet another strike against his character. He released it all when we finally got on the road. He cursed his probation officer for completely misunderstanding his social media activity. According to Junior, the admittedly aggressive statements were actually part of his attempt to *avoid* future violence—to ward off opportunistic and potentially lethal attacks that would jeopardize his efforts to "get right."

"What he [the probation officer] want me to do?" Junior asked, rhetorically. "I ain't about to do somethin' to [physically attack] these clowns. I'm tryna' get right. But I can't let these niggas talk shit without sayin' none. If I do that, I'm dead. I can't stay in my mama's house forever. I gotta go to work. I gotta go to school. If these niggas see me on the bus, and they think I'm sweet [weak], they definitely gon' get down [attack]. But if they think I'm still poled up [armed], then they ain't gon' do shit!"

In the following months, Junior had difficulty balancing the terms of probation with his other obligations. He figured, why bother? His probation officer and the judge felt they already knew who he was. He had done everything they had asked of him. It didn't make much difference. It wasn't long before he stopped showing up to school and eventually gave up on his job.

■■■

Young men like Junior work hard to build online reputations as hardened urban predators. But once they've built them, it's hard to predict exactly how others will respond. On one side, they face competitors and rivals who doubt and challenge their authenticity, trying to catch popular drillers in vulnerable situations. On the other side, they face a virtual army of law enforcement professionals who take these same social media performances at face value. Instead of poking holes in drillers' online personas, these audiences treat them as straightforward representations of their moral character, pulling them deeper into criminal justice entanglements.

In the latter case, the online performances of young black men are *too* convincing. *Too* authentic. According to a recent study, 75 percent of law enforcement professionals report that they are "self-taught" in the use of social media for criminal investigations.[33] Like Junior's probation officer, they act according to their subjective and, at least in this case, inaccurate interpretations of social media content. As research on policing and punishment has long shown, law enforcement personnel typically lack the cultural competencies and knowledge required to understand the cultural practices of urban youth, whether online or off.[34] Instead, they fall back on popular stereotypes of young black men as coldhearted perpetrators.

One of the most egregious examples of this process occurred recently in New York, where a teenager named Jelani Henry was falsely arrested and incarcerated for nineteen months in Riker's Island (including nine months in solitary confinement) based largely on his social media activity. This included "liking" gang-related posts on Facebook.[35] In major U.S. cities, including Chicago and New York, police departments increasingly assign residents to gang and criminal databases based (sometimes exclusively) on social media activity.[36] Database inclusion carries disproportionate harm for black residents, in particular, who are seven times more likely to be wrongfully convicted than whites.[37] In addition to leading to gross violations of constitutional rights, database inclusion can exacerbate unemployment, deportation, and loss of housing.

In the end, it hardly matters that someone like Stevie has severed ties with his former gang networks, or that Junior has devoted himself to work, school, and family. For anyone scrolling through YouTube or Instagram—today or four years from now—these young men are likely to appear just as gang-involved and murderous as they did as teens. This is only amplified by the third-party blogs and YouTube channels dedicated to chronicling and profiting from Chicago violence. It's critical to note that young people hailing from more privileged backgrounds don't suffer from such indurate online identities. Over the course of high school, college, formal employment, and various adult hobbies, their achievements and successes will eventually crowd out most inappropriate content from their early years on social media. Embarrassing uploads will be relegated to the bottom of a Google search. Young people growing up in places like Taylor Park have no such luxury. Given their disadvantaged starting position, they're unlikely to create a digital footprint big enough to stamp out the sensational content they produced as teens. Their online pasts will haunt them well into the future.

This underscores one of the most harmful dimensions of digital disadvantage. Long-standing inequalities and moral hierarchies *between* social media users shape how their online content is evaluated and acted on by outside audiences. Police, prosecutors, and the general public hardly bat an eye when middle-class white users post photos with firearms and other dangerous weapons. I encountered just such images in 2018, as I finished writing this book. In May of that year, Kaitlin Bennett, a graduating senior at Kent State University, uploaded a series of photos to Twitter that showed her strolling comfortably through campus with an AR-10 strapped to her back.[38] The images show Bennett posing in a short white dress, her curly blonde hair flowing over the stock of the large assault rifle. She holds a graduation cap, where she's written a warning and challenge to anyone who disapproves: "COME AND TAKE IT." Unsurprisingly, Bennett hasn't faced any criminal justice consequences. If anything, she's benefited, becoming the newest darling of Second Amendment activism and American libertarianism. She's even spun her online notoriety into a correspondent position with the far-right news website InfoWars. Meanwhile, young black men face arrest, prosecution, and entry into gang databases for merely appearing in photos alongside guns, regardless of whether those guns are unloaded, inoperable, or fake. Bennett is free to threaten police and other state authorities without fear of consequences. Yet, when someone like Junior uses forceful language toward rivals, even if it's part of an attempt to avoid physical violence, it can cost him his freedom.

Despite the potential peril, more and more urban youth are joining the online attention economy every year. Their actions are a testament to their dreams of upward mobility, their rejection of other options available to them, and the attractiveness of micro-celebrity. Their pursuit of online infamy becomes even more seductive during their occasional interactions with privileged and powerful admirers, who provide grand glimpses of the world beyond urban poverty. These moments leave youngsters feeling as though mainstream success is within their reach—so long as they can stay out of jail and enemy crosshairs for just a little while longer.

6

• • •

Digital Slumming

Junior and I sat in a dark plane on the tarmac at Los Angeles International Airport, headed back to Chicago. Junior slept soundly in the seat next to me, his head resting on the flimsy plastic tray table. From top to bottom, he wore an expensive new outfit: red LA Dodgers cap, goosedown jacket, True Religion jeans, and matching suede Timberland boots. A conspicuous bulge on Junior's hip held $2,100 in crisp hundred-dollar bills. These items were all gifts he had received from one of his biggest fans—a wealthy, white, twenty-five-year-old man named Chad Campbell. A week earlier, Chad had flown Junior to his home in Beverly Hills. He wanted to meet one of his favorite drillers, learn more about Chicago gang wars, and, if everything went well, study how to become a popular driller himself. As I learned during our trip, Chad had become *obsessed* with the Chicago drill world and its over-the-top displays of street hustling. For the past couple of years, he had spent multiple hours per day watching YouTube drill music videos, dissecting blog posts, and swiping through Instagram.

Chad isn't alone in his fandom from afar. During my time with the Corner Boys, I met four different young men who had each traveled to California at the request of a wealthy fan. In fact, one of drillers most impressive accomplishments is that they've harnessed the attention and affection of audiences located well outside of their own Chicago neighborhoods. As the YouTube analytics for one of the Corner Boys' most popular videos reveal, only 14 percent of the roughly two million views came from within Illinois.[1] Although the state commands the largest share of views, the remaining 86 percent of viewers are located in other U.S. states and international countries. New York accounts for 9 percent of views. Almost 8 percent come from California. Canada and the United Kingdom account for 7 percent and 3 percent, respectively.

As Chad's fandom suggests, some of the most devoted out-of-town consumers live in places that look and feel nothing like Taylor Park. And yet, these are often the primary viewers that drillers hope to impress when they upload their menacing images and videos. It begs the question: Why, despite such physical and social distance, do these consumers gravitate so intensely to drillers' violent, gang-related content?[2]

Answering this question requires investigating the functions that drillers and their content play in consumers' everyday lives. It means asking what drill "does" for someone like Chad.[3] As I watched consumption unfold in places like Beverly Hills, I came to understand that drill provides privileged consumers with transgressive, intimate, yet safe opportunities to interact with the ghetto and its stereotypical residents. As drillers satisfy consumers' voyeuristic desires, they also supply people like Chad with the chance to build new identities and feel desired themselves.[4]

This mode of cultural appropriation isn't completely new. As one of the most segregated cities in America, Chicago has long been the epicenter for a practice known as "slumming." More privileged residents have continually penetrated these spaces in search of authentic urban experiences, sexual encounters, and other thrills. Beginning in the early twentieth century, black-owned clubs on the South Side sold well-to-do white patrons on romantic fantasies and stereotypical images of black poverty. According to historian Chad Heap, the Plantation Café and other aptly named cabarets curated "jazzed-up versions of the jocular mammies, shiftless urban dandies, and alluring jezebels" for slummers' delight.[5] The tradition continued throughout the late twentieth century, as jazz clubs commodified racially charged, stock images of poor blacks—as hypersexed, soulful, and naturally rhythmic—for white revelers hoping to "let loose" on their excursions to the South Side.[6] In fact, club owners, managers, and promoters intentionally hired entertainers who were skilled at acting out racialized stereotypes.

The democratization of the means of cultural production has ushered in a new era of slumming. Thanks to social media, the relationship between ghetto residents and slummers has become more direct. Through sites like YouTube, Instagram, and Facebook, those wishing to commodify their individual and collective stigma no longer need managers, music venues, record companies, and other intermediaries to connect them with people hoping to take a walk on the wild side. Likewise, with just a few keystrokes, today's slummers can access a virtually endless stream of such homegrown representations without spending a penny or leaving their couches. And when they desire more? As with other forms of internet-driven commerce, consumers can have their favorite commodity—in this case, drillers—delivered right to their doorstep, receiving unique and customizable experiences in the comfort and safety of their own home.

Alongside Taylor Park residents, I documented three related, yet distinct forms of this new brand of social-media-driven slumming. The first involves youth from more well-to-do communities hoping to stand out and overcome mediocrity by aligning themselves with stereotypical urban predators. The second involves an emerging variant of sex tourism, where affluent women enlist drillers for exotic sexual experiences. In the third variant, middle-class blacks recruit drillers as props in their performances of respectability, morality, and piety. It's important to point out that although these cross-racial and cross-class exchanges can be instrumental in character, they're not necessarily malicious. In fact, most of the interactions I witnessed were shot through with a benevolent tone. These consumers often positioned themselves as generous patrons whose money, affection, and influence were intended to support drillers' burgeoning artistic careers. Beneficence aside, this consumption carries important sociological ramifications. As the Corner Boys' experiences reveal, these relationships reify social difference, legitimize stigma, and undermine the long-theorized benefits of cross-cultural exchange.

DRILLERS AS GHETTO AMBASSADORS

Officially, Chad had invited Junior to LA to record a feature on a new drill song. As the trip unfolded, however, it was clear that this collaboration was about far more than music. In fact, Junior returned to Chicago a week later without recording a single verse or video scene. Chad reaped real benefits, nonetheless. He used Junior's time in Beverly Hills to help him cement his new identity as an authentic driller, both online and off. Leading up to the trip, I was concerned that my presence might make Chad uncomfortable. My worries proved unfounded. In Chad's eyes, the fact that I, a university professor, was writing a book about Junior only increased the young man's value and provided him with even more legitimacy. My presence led Chad to express even more excitement about his decision to fly Junior to his home.

From the first moment Chad introduced himself, his fascination with Chicago gang culture was evident. He was clad in a meticulously planned, monochrome outfit that looked eerily similar to the kind worn by CBE in some of their videos: a bright white pair of Nike high-tops, a plain white t-shirt, a pair of white True Religion jeans that sagged low around his hips, exposing half a foot of his plaid cotton boxer shorts. He capped off his color coordination with an accessory that I doubted I would ever see in any of CBE's content—a white Pomeranian named Harley, which he carried under his arm throughout our visit. Though Chad affected Chicago slang when he spoke to me and Junior, he continually spoke to Harley in swooning, high-pitched baby talk.

When he greeted us, Chad immediately pulled Junior into a lengthy, multistage handshake that bent their index fingers into various shapes and motions. I wasn't familiar with this particular variation, but Junior filled me in just moments later, when Chad excused himself to take a phone call.

"Did you see that?" Junior asked in a forceful whisper, similarly bewildered. "He just shook up with the Ks. That's the Almighty Knights handshake! Where the fuck did he learn that shit? Is he a Knight or something?"

Junior was paranoid. And for good reason. The Corner Boys were at war with several Almighty Knights factions. Back in Chicago, "shaking up" with a rival's handshake is an intentional sign of disrespect, and perhaps even an invitation to fight. But this wasn't Chicago, and Chad was clearly oblivious to the deep significance of what he likely assumed to be an innocuous greeting. It was the first in a stream of gang-related behavior, language, and aesthetics that he had plucked from drill music videos and adopted as his own. Here, in Beverly Hills, Chad seemed incapable of understanding their true meaning in the lives of Junior, the Corner Boys, and other Chicago youth.

As I watched Chad's excited appropriation of Chicago drill culture, I was reminded of the writings of the black feminist scholar bell hooks. In a provocative essay titled "Eating the Other," hooks argues that in our contemporary age, affluent white youth and other privileged groups have come to feel a kind of postmodern malaise, marked by unexceptional lives and unremarkable identities.[7] Within our commodity culture, however, close contact with "others"—particularly poor blacks—provides "a new delight, more intense, more satisfying than normal ways of doing things."[8] Race and class become a "spice," as hooks calls it, a "seasoning that can liven up the dull dish that is mainstream white culture."[9] The cultures and bodies of marginalized populations have become "alternative playgrounds," consumed as resources for pleasure, self-fulfillment, and even transformation. As Chad helps to illustrate, at least some of drill's most privileged consumers are drawn to it because it helps them overcome the ennui created by the safety and comfort of their daily lives.

Within minutes of our arrival, Chad began complaining about how uninteresting his life in Beverly Hills was.

"It's really different from Chicago, huh?" Chad asked, hoping to grab Junior's attention as he sat in the passenger seat of Chad's car, face pressed against the window, taking in the grandeur of iconic Rodeo Drive.

"Hell yeah!" Junior replied, captivated by the luxury cars parked in front of the Maserati dealership.

"Yeah," Chad said in a sour tone. "It's cool at first, bro. But it gets mad old after a while. Trust me. I've lived here my whole life. It's actually *really boring*. Not like what you got back in Chicago, though! It seems like the block is always bustin'!" Chad had slipped back into Chicago slang. "Always some shit going on. Fi-fis [parties] and shit. Slidin' on the opps. I want to come kick it with you in *Chiraq*!" Junior didn't answer. He kept his gaze out his window. I sat in the back seat, typing into my notetaking app, capturing as many of Chad's words as I could. From my position behind Junior, I noticed him roll his eyes at Chad's comment. I knew that he would gladly trade places with Chad—a sentiment he repeated to me throughout the trip.

Through his appropriation of gang culture, Chad had found a way to begin filling his life with the excitement, danger, and unpredictability that he ascribed to gangland Chicago. When we arrived back at his townhouse later that afternoon, he suddenly grew flustered, barking anxious orders at us as we got out of his car.

"Quick," he commanded, "get inside. Bitches be snitchin' out here!" He looked toward Junior, affecting more Chicago slang. "If they see you, they'll think I'm runnin' a trap house. They'll call twelve [the police]." Amid Chad's urgency, I took a look around. The surrounding streets were virtually empty, except for an elderly woman chatting on the phone in front of a Spanish-style mansion, and a lone Latino man loading a lawn mower into the back of a small pickup truck. Neither seemed to notice as Chad herded us inside.

Once in his living room, we sat down on large leather couches, nestled under framed modern artwork. "First things first," Chad said as he opened a blue canister of medical marijuana. He added a few pinches to a bong, and passed it to Junior. After five minutes of boasting about the quality of the weed, Chad got up and moved to a nearby window. He pulled back the curtain and peered out to the street. He suddenly jumped backward, frustrated with what he saw. "Ah fuck," he said quietly. "That's the opps [rivals]." Concerned, I rushed to his side. I took his lead and covertly peered around the window shade. I wasn't sure what to expect. Back in Taylor Park, alarms over the presence of opps are no joking matter. Upon hearing the word, everyone in the vicinity launches into action. Some take cover behind cars and buildings. Others move to retrieve a gun, if available. But this wasn't Taylor Park. The only person on the sidewalk was a slim brunette who looked to be in her early forties. She wore black yoga pants and a purple Lycra workout top. She pushed an infant in an expensive stroller. "That's the opps," Chad repeated to clarify. "She's gonna smell my weed and tell my dad again." He slid the window closed with an angry thud, hoping to keep the smoke from leaking out to the sidewalk. "Fuckin' opps."

Throughout the trip, Chad stretched this term, *opps*, to apply to virtually anyone who upset him. The loose-lipped neighbor? Opps. The driver in the BMW who beat him to a parking spot? Opps. The restaurant manager who refused to believe that Harley was *really* a service dog? Opps. It's critical to remember that for young men like Junior, having well-established opps is both a blessing and a curse. On the one hand, engaging in public rivalries is a necessary requirement for establishing authenticity as a violent gang member. On the other hand, these same rivalries make daily life perilous. The looming threat of running into an opp turns every bus ride to school and every trip to the grocery store into a potentially fatal outing. Seeing this dynamic on social media, Chad yearned to experience the social status and nervous rush he imagined came with having opps. So he simply made up his own, injecting otherwise harmless antagonisms with an emotional charge.

Junior and Chad spent the next two hours in his living room, passing blunts between them, watching YouTube videos, and discussing which Chicago drillers were the "hottest." Chad filled us in on his plans for building a drill career and "clouting up." He had an ingenious plan, he told us. First, he'd record a song with one of the Corner Boys. Then, a song with a different gang. Then a different gang. And so on, borrowing all these gangs' clout while tapping into their dedicated fan bases. He bragged that he was the first person to think of this strategy. However, this was just more evidence that Chad didn't fully understand the dynamics of reputation seeking and rivalries the way Chicago youth do. It wasn't that people like Junior hadn't thought of this tactic. Rather, such wide-ranging collaboration is incredibly unwise in a social world where befriending others and collaborating with them automatically thrust drillers into new rivalries. In Chicago, Chad's plan would open him up to new and unexpected attacks.

Oblivious to this fact, Chad rattled off a list of Chicago drillers he planned to solicit next for features. Already smitten with Junior, he invited him to join him in these future music videos. As he rounded out his list, he mentioned the name of a driller associated with the Almighty Knights.

"Bro," Junior interrupted, speaking slowly to emphasize his words. "That's. My. Opps."

Chad didn't understand. "But he's not *my* opps," he countered, defensively. "*I've* got no beef with him."

"Bro," Junior repeated in a stern tone, before taking a quick drag from the blunt. "He's *gonna* be your opps if you do a song with me. Now you *do* got beef with him." The two went back and forth for a minute or so, with Junior trying to explain the dynamics of gang rivalries in Chicago. He was growing visibly frustrated. Despite his multiple attempts, he couldn't get Chad to understand. He eventually gave up. "Never mind," he finally said. "You're tweakin'. You're too high, bro."

Junior was right. Chad was really stoned. But the source of their misunderstanding wasn't chemical; it was cultural. Participation in drill carries drastically different meanings and consequences for these two young men. When Junior and other Chicago youth upload drill videos, flash gang signs on social media platforms, and outwardly associate with well-known shooters, they face retaliatory gang violence, criminal justice entanglements, and mistreatment at the hands of teachers, security guards, and other adults. For Chad, in contrast, the aesthetic and material realms remain neatly separated. He can enact these same styles without fear of repercussion. In the words of the sociologist Mary Pattillo, Chad is living in a "ghetto trance." He and other privileged consumers can "practice their ghetto styles, recount authentic urban ghetto tales, and display their ghetto outfits," with the confidence that "no one will mistake them for real gangstas and turn their play into perilous reality."[10]

Chad's ghetto trance was even more evident once he finally understood Junior's point. After a few minutes passed in smoke-filled silence, Chad suddenly sat up from his plush leather recliner. "Wait," he exclaimed, hit by a sudden realization. "I get it. I get it. You're saying that if we do this song together, then the AKs will be my opps."

"Yeah," Junior replied, annoyed but satisfied.

I was surprised to watch Chad grow excited by the news. "Oh shit. I got opps now?" Junior nodded in agreement and took another drag from the blunt. "I got opps," Chad repeated with even more excitement. He stood up and jogged down the hallway to his bedroom, where he traded his t-shirt for a bulletproof vest. "Type 2–class body armor," he told us as he strolled back into the living room, "like what the cops wear." He also carried a large serrated military knife. "See, Junior," he said, holding it in front of him, "I always got something on me. I got you. You ain't got to worry about shit while you're with me." Chad seemed intent on letting his social media followers know whose "team" he had joined. He spent the next few minutes posing for selfies, arm around Junior, brandishing the blade. It struck me as a bizarre juxtaposition with the collection of Faulkner, Hemingway, and Twain novels on the bookshelves behind them.

Hoping to make sense of this scene, I reached out to several colleagues, asking if they had encountered or read about anything similar. Their responses suggested that although Chad's behavior may be surprising, it wasn't isolated. One of them pointed me to a series of *Los Angeles Times* stories about a wealthy white teen who had similarly grown obsessed with gang life, though with deadly results. In 2018, Cameron Terrell, a senior at affluent Palos Verdes High School, was charged with murder and two counts of attempted murder in connection with a gang shooting in South LA.[11] According to prosecutors, the shooting was part of Terrell's "LA gang binge," in which he joined the Rollin' 90s Neighborhood Crips gang, located some twenty miles north of Palos Verdes Estates. Terrell first developed ties with the gang faction in 2016, letting them borrow his luxury car and wear his clothes. As he grew closer with them, he adopted the nickname "Milk," tattooed a "W" on his chest to represent the gang, and appeared in the background of one of their YouTube music videos wearing a baby blue bandanna and flashing gang signs.[12] In 2017, he allegedly drove two fellow Crips in his father's black Mercedes SUV into rival territory, where they shot at three people, killing one. Prosecutors argued that the shooting was part of Terrell's efforts to gain status within the gang.

Although news reports contain significant details about Terrell's efforts to fit in, and the shooting that ultimately resulted, they don't say much about the teen's underlying motivations. Why would someone like him want to enmesh himself so deeply in gang life? My time in Beverly Hills provided potential answers. There, I saw how privileged consumers like Chad and Cameron Terrell enlist authentic gang members to help remake their own identities, in this case, from urbane upper-crusters to urban outlaws. As hooks reminds us, the process of "eating the Other" isn't merely about physical contact and possession. Privileged consumers routinely implicate the Other in a process of self-transformation; they desire to be changed in some way by the encounter, leveraging "otherness" for the sake of transforming their identity. "They call on the Other," hooks writes, "to be both witness and participant in this transformation."[13]

"Nobody gets me," Chad complained on one of our hour-long trips to pick up Kelly—his petite, platinum blond girlfriend—from her job at a day spa in the valley. "My dad, my friends, even Kelly. They don't understand this rap life I'm living. They're all stuck in that corporate lifestyle. But that shit's for suckers. I don't want that. I'm more about the streets and hustling. I can't be sitting in some office all day. They want me to do the school thing, but that ain't for me."

I learned a lot about Chad's biography during these drives. I could understand the concerns of his loved ones. After struggling through high school, Chad had dropped out of college on two separate occasions. With the financial safety net provided by his father, however, he put school on hold and went into business with his best friend, Cliff, selling discount Chinese-made iPhone covers on Instagram. Now, more than a year into the profitless venture, his father was on the verge of cutting him off. He mentioned that Cliff had taken away his company credit card. Kelly also seemed to be pulling away. The two argued nonstop throughout Junior's visit. The two of us got used to sitting quietly in the back seat of Chad's car, pretending to sleep or check Facebook while the couple exchanged verbal blows.

With his family and friends at their wit's end, Chad appeared to be using Junior's visit to convince them that his new career path wasn't the result of failure, laziness, or drug addiction, as they assumed, but rather a deliberate and defensible choice. This mission was nowhere more apparent than in his constant sparring with Kelly as we inched through LA traffic. When Kelly jabbed, criticizing his lack of motivation, Chad countered by pointing (sometimes literally) to Junior as proof of how successful drillers behave. Take their fights about his daily marijuana use, for example. It was a major source of contention. Kelly was annoyed that Chad and Junior spent their days together in a haze of weed and Xanax.

I recall one afternoon when we picked Kelly up from work. She immediately noticed that Chad was high. She laid into him, questioning his work ethic.

"This is what rappers do," he responded. "We smoke while we're writing. That's how we get into the flow. So we can write our lyrics." He motioned to Junior for confirmation, receiving a single syllable response. "You just don't understand," he said, turning back to his girlfriend. "I'm not just sitting around doing nothing. This is *work*! Junior and his guys always smoke. It helps their creativity. And look, now they're some of the most famous rappers in all of Chicago. I'm trying to get where they're at. You just don't get it."

I watched Chad apply this logic to a range of Kelly's gripes. Alongside Junior, his late-night partying became an opportunity to network with agents, producers, and fellow artists. His expensive shopping sprees became necessary for establishing his "look." His over-the-top Instagram posts were necessary for expanding his fan base and solidifying his brand. What looked like irresponsible play was, at least according to Chad, a vital part of a driller's daily work. Junior served a similar legitimizing function when it came to Chad's friends and business partner. Junior's presence in Beverly Hills, particularly as Chad's houseguest, suggested a deeper level of collaboration between the two than was actually the case. As he shared the Corner Boys' Instagram posts and YouTube videos with friends, he reworked the details of their collaboration. He conveniently left out the fact that he was paying Junior thousands of dollars to hang out.

For the most part, Chad's strategy worked. Some of his friends congratulated him on his newfound success. Chad told me that Cliff had even unlocked the company bank account. They were all fascinated by Junior. Seeing this, Chad's talk of Junior and CBE grew more extravagant and caricatured as the trip wore on. He bragged that these violent, ruthless criminals held a deadly grip on Taylor Park's drug economy. Their social media posts provided him with all the necessary evidence.[14] As I watched Chad's show-and-tell, I couldn't help but think of the countless hours I sat with Junior, listening to him confess how his own boastful uploads created new dilemmas. He had been robbed, shot at, and generally mistreated because others saw his online photos and assumed that he was wealthier, more heavily armed, and more violent than he actually was.

Halfway through the trip, I asked Junior how he felt about Chad's misrepresentations. "I don't like it," Junior answered, "but it's gonna make him give me more money. It's working." Junior went on to remind me that this new "friendship" was purely instrumental. Chad was just one more clout head. "I'm just playing my role," he reminded me. "That's it. Just playing my role."

It seemed that Chad wanted to meet an authentic gang member as badly as Junior wanted to give him one. For both young men, this meant essentializing Junior's identity. It meant pushing Junior's multidimensionality to the margins. This became fully apparent when I accidentally divulged compromising information about some of Junior's recent troubles. On one of our last days in LA, Chad, Junior, Kelly, and I sat in a trendy restaurant on Melrose Boulevard. Junior excused himself to buy a few last-minute items at the clothing store next door. In his absence, Chad marveled out loud about yet another of Junior's curious traits. Chad had noticed Junior's uncanny ability to fall asleep at a moment's notice, wherever he happened to be. Junior routinely dozed off in Chad's car, in restaurants, and even on the curb outside the medical marijuana clinic waiting for Chad to pick up the day's supply. Chad imagined that these sleeping habits were a necessary skill, cultivated in Chicago's infamous drug economy.

Without thinking, I offered an alternative and far less glamorous explanation. "It's sad, really," I began, momentarily forgetting the dynamics of the trip. "He's gotten good at sleeping in weird places because he's been homeless for so long. Stairwells and the back seats of cars aren't exactly the most comfortable places. So it's either that, or don't sleep at all."

Chad's expression changed from awe to disapproval. I immediately realized my mistake.

"Wait. He's *homeless*?" Chad asked, clearly displeased.

I silently cursed myself. I had just offered information that directly countered Chad's image of Junior. I backpedaled. "I mean, well, things are getting better for him." I took a big bite of my sandwich, hoping to stall.

Chad didn't let it go. "I thought he has lots of money. He has his own place, right?" Chad referred back to Junior's social media posts. "I see it in his pictures. He's out there trappin'. He's making big money."

I tried to keep my answers vague, hoping to end the conversation quickly. "You know," I said, "you'll have to ask him. The guys don't really like it when other people talk about them. It's kinda against their rules." Chad pressed me for more information, but I repeated that it was unwise for me to speak on behalf of Junior. Chad eventually relented, but I spent the rest of the day worried he might confront Junior, who would feel betrayed by my admission.

To my thankful surprise, Chad never brought it up with Junior. Looking back, Chad's silence makes sense. His newfound identity, street cred, and feelings of accomplishment all depended on Junior's authenticity. If Chad admitted that Junior was a fraud, then he had to consider that he might be one, too. What's more, Chad's use of Junior to help reframe his own life trajectory—as a series of rebellious choices rather than disappointing failures—required that Junior's participation in gangs, violence, and drill rap remained a willful choice to "be bad," rather than the result of poverty, segregation, or other social disadvantages. Think about it: If Junior's actions were merely survival strategies for someone lacking the safety, comfort, and opportunities provided in places like Beverly Hills, then what, exactly, was Chad's excuse for acting like Junior?

Chad's dilemma sheds light on some of the more troubling implications of this new mode of slumming. Although drill brings privileged white populations into increased social contact with poor black residents, these new social ties don't necessarily help to close the chasm dividing them. In some respects, it makes it even wider and more durable. Chad's embrace has breathed new life into popular conceptions of the black ghetto that permeate the popular imagination and conservative stump speeches. I suspect that Chad will eventually cave to the wishes of his family. One day, he'll put his fascination with street life behind him. When he takes over his father's business and climbs the corporate ladder, he and his friends are likely to look back on his flirtations with the drill world as merely a youthful phase that he was destined to outgrow. The problem, of course, is that they are likely to wonder why Junior didn't do the same. They'll question why the Corner Boys and their peers continue to "choose" to live violent and criminal lives.

These dynamics aren't lost on the Corner Boys. Although these interactions are exhilarating and financially beneficial, they're also tiring and sometimes humiliating. But if drillers hope to walk away with money, clothes, and other rewards, they have to bite their tongues in the face of essentializing and disrespectful treatment that, back in Taylor Park, might have been grounds for violent recourse.

Of course, the Corner Boys didn't view *every* consumer's demand on their time so resentfully. Some of their patrons provided far more enjoyment. There was no request they looked forward to more than those coming from women soliciting them for sexual rendezvous.

DRILLERS AS SEXUAL TOURIST ATTRACTIONS

Chicago summers are nothing short of magical. The city hums with visitors from all over the world. They're lured by Chicago's signature music festivals, culinary scene, ivy-lined baseball stadium, and, more recently, the transgressive thrill of bedding down "real gangbangers." During my first year with the Corner Boys, as the sidewalks began to thaw from the city's long winter, I received the first of several early morning text messages from AJ, asking me to give him a ride from downtown back to Taylor Park. Aware of the danger the young man faced riding public transit through dozens of rival gang territories along the way, I quickly agreed. Thirty minutes later, I arrived at the intersection he had specified. There he stood, clad in a fresh new outfit, holding a shopping bag with one arm, and the hand of a thirty-something white woman in the other. I sat in my car, trying to look busy as they kissed goodbye and parted ways. As the woman climbed into her gray Toyota Corolla, AJ opened my car door and tossed himself into my passenger seat. He smiled from ear to ear.

Over the next forty-five minutes, he filled me in on his past twenty-four hours. After meeting the woman on Instagram a couple of months earlier, he convinced her to make the two-hour drive from her home in the suburbs of Milwaukee. They spent the day walking along the famed Magnificent Mile, where she spoiled AJ with lunch and new clothes. Afterward, they retreated to a hotel near Michigan Avenue for an intimate evening. Over the next couple of months, the woman returned to Chicago for more of these twenty-four-hour liaisons. I received more morning-after text messages from AJ and two additional Corner Boys following similar rendezvous. These women included AJ's dental assistant from Wisconsin, a retail store manager from Minneapolis, and an administrative assistant from Toronto.

On our drives back to Taylor Park, I peppered my passengers with questions about the origins and dynamics of these relationships. Over the following two summers, they kept me abreast of their out-of-town lovers. As I watched these relationships begin, peak, and fizzle, I gained a rare window into an emerging form of sex tourism. I'll admit: Of all my discoveries in the drill world, this was by far the most unexpected. However, if we put these relationships in historical perspective, it's not nearly as remarkable as it first seems. As Chad Heap reminds us, it's impossible to talk about slumming—whether a century ago or today—without talking about sex.[15] Then as now, women—particularly white, middle-class women—have long used sexual expeditions into black Chicago as a means of resisting conventional sexual roles and reconfiguring gender norms. To borrow once more from hooks, slumming allows its participants to "leave behind white 'innocence' and enter the world of 'experience.'"[16]

In fact, the demand is so prevalent that a transnational sex tourism industry now stretches from Thailand to Costa Rica, providing predominantly white, Western consumers with sexual encounters that cut across race, class, and nation.[17] But what happens when gang-associated young men become the objects of desire? What does it mean when privileged women consume the company and intimacy of stigmatized ghetto residents? We have to remember that, at its core, sex tourism is always about more than just sex; intercourse is rarely the primary commodity being exchanged.[18] Rather, it's about providing authentic and otherwise "forbidden" experiences. It's about offering clients the emotions, identities, and roles they desire.[19] In Jamaica, for example, male sex workers—known as "rent-a-dreads"—act out stereotypes of hypermasculine Rastafarians for European vacationers.[20] In Vietnam, sex workers perform dramatic caricatures of rural poverty and third world dependency to appeal to Western backpackers' benevolent yearnings.[21] In the Dominican Republic, it's about pretending to be in "real love" with German tourists looking to couple up and relocate to the Caribbean.[22] No matter the location or precise strategy for commodifying the exotic, these performances are *always* informed by, and play on, existing racial and class hierarchies.

As young men who devote their online lives to performing exaggerated stereotypes of ghetto outlaws, it wasn't long before the Corner Boys discovered, and then learned to satisfy, slummers' appetites. For the Corner Boys, these exchanges began on social media, as they started "sexting" and video chatting with women they met online. Months before AJ sent me the morning-after text message, we spoke about his favorite aspects of micro-celebrity. He mentioned that one of the best parts about YouTube and Instagram popularity was the newfound sexual attention he received from white women—a group that he hadn't had any romantic experience with previously.

"Bro," he said in a serious tone, preparing me for his next statement. "I got *white* bitches all up on me now. *White* bitches. That's how much love we gettin' now."

"What do you mean?" I asked, hoping he'd elaborate.

"No lie, bro," he continued. "They be hittin' me up on FaceTime. Gettin' naked and shit."

"No way."

"I'm tellin' you. No lie, bro." AJ beamed. He pulled out his iPhone. "Watch this."

I sat down next to AJ on the couch and watched him go through what had become a regular routine. He opened up Twitter and composed a new tweet. He typed out his cell phone number, along with succinct instructions:

im on FT 4 da next hour. fans hml

The words were an invitation to his Twitter followers. He'd be taking calls via the iPhone FaceTime (FT) application for the next hour. He was telling them to "hit my line" (hml) if they wanted to chat.

"Watch," AJ repeated as he sent out the message. He held the iPhone in front of us, urging me to keep my eye on it, as if performing a magic trick. Less than thirty seconds later, it started vibrating. The familiar FaceTime ringtone echoed off the bare walls of his apartment. He looked at me and smiled. "See!"

Over the next five minutes, AJ quickly answered what I counted to be fifteen different calls. It was hard to keep track of the exact number because they were coming at such a rapid pace. The repeated notifications for incoming calls made it hard to hear much of what was said on the other end of the line. At one point, AJ has so many simultaneous calls that his phone froze and crashed. After restarting it, he continued jumping from one call to the next, spending only a couple of seconds saying hello to each caller. I did my best to read callers' locations off the screen before AJ answered. The first few were from black teens in Indiana, New York, and downstate Illinois. One call came from a couple of white men, sitting on a couch in what looked to be a college fraternity house. AJ immediately hung up. He was cycling through callers even more quickly now, still intent on proving his earlier point to me. Roughly fifteen minutes into the process, he found what he was looking for. A call came in from a white woman from Ontario, Canada, who appeared to be in her mid-twenties. AJ glanced up at me from the screen. He lifted a single eyebrow as if to say, "I told you so."

He spent the next five minutes flirting with the woman, giving her a taste of desire on the part of a micro-celebrity. He asked her questions about herself. He teased her lightly, quizzing her on the names of his songs, the names of his shooters, and other recent news of the drill world. She was bashful in her responses, but was clearly familiar with AJ and these topics. With another sly glance in my direction, AJ launched into what I would come to learn was his standard strategy. He began by complimenting her, calling her beautiful. He asked to "see" her, requesting that she stand up in front of a mirror so that he could inspect her body. She eventually did. AJ showed his gratitude with even more compliments. At this point, it was clear that he was slowly working his way to getting her undressed. However, before he was able to make the request, she said she had to get off the phone and go to work. They scheduled a FaceTime call for the next day. He told her he wanted to see "all" of her. She agreed that she wanted to see more of him too.

"I told you, bro!" he yelled as he ended the call and deleted his earlier tweet. The calls kept coming in for the next half hour or so, but he declined them all. "It's so *easy*," he continued. "They be lovin' us. They be *lovin'* this Chiraq shit. They ain't never been to the hood, but they *love* the hood. Especially the ones that be livin' out in the suburbs. They feel some type of way when you tell 'em 'bout some hood shit!"

From that point on, AJ made a continual effort to prove to me just how enthralled these women were with gang life. A week after the FaceTime session, a group of us were playing dice behind Charmain's apartment when AJ got a call from one of the out-of-town women he had been speaking with lately on FaceTime. After a quick greeting, she asked him what he was doing.

"We out here on the block," he replied. "Gang shit, you know."

"Let me see," the voice on the phone requested.

AJ indulged her. He flipped the camera toward the dice game. "See," he said. "This is how we do out here. Rollin' dice and shit. Out here on the block. I'm out here takin' niggas for all their money."

"Who's that?" the woman asked.

"You ain't know about the guys," he teased. He pointed the phone at one of his shooters, Poo. He walked closer to zoom in on the prison tattoos lining Poo's face. "This is that savage nigga, Poo. You better learn about this nigga."

Well aware of AJ's routine, Poo played along. He bent his fingers to form the CBE gang sign. "Gang gang gang gang," he yelled loudly, bouncing his hands in the air in front of the camera.

"Alright, girl," AJ said, "I showed you. Now you finna show *me* somethin', right?"

Over the next five minutes, AJ coaxed her down to her underwear. By this point, the dice game had stopped completely. Poo, Zebo, and two others crowded around AJ's phone. They giggled quietly, taking care to stand just out of view of the camera.

"Let me see some more," she demanded of AJ. The vague request left it open as to whether she was asking to see more of the neighborhood street scene, or asking for AJ to get naked too. He obliged, providing both. He walked away from the group toward Charmain's apartment. He turned the camera once more, giving a panoramic view of the surrounding block. I heard him narrate a bit more about "the guys" and "the opps" before ducking inside. He emerged twenty minutes later, bragging about how much the woman enjoyed the phone sex session. The others begged him for details, which he gladly provided. He was the center of attention for the rest of the afternoon.

Beyond his own sexual enjoyment and bragging rights, AJ learned to leverage these exchanges for cash and other gifts. It isn't long before he begins asking women for favors. Every once in a while, he persuades them to travel to Chicago, where they can see him, and "the block," in person.[23] I witnessed AJ successfully apply his system on Breanne, a white woman in her mid-twenties, who had recently moved to Chicago to attend law school. Breanne grabbed my attention more than any of AJ's other lovers because she had moved into an apartment only a few blocks away from my office at the University of Chicago. Shortly after their first online interaction, Breanne began using the Uber ridesharing application on her phone to shuttle AJ from Taylor Park to her home. I sometimes gave AJ rides back to Taylor Park in the early evenings once I wrapped up my day's work at the university. I followed their relationship from beginning to end. What I learned about Breanne was mostly from AJ. She had grown up in a predominantly white suburb on the East Coast. Pushing back against her upbringing, she intended to become a trial lawyer, perhaps a public defender. Now, living on Chicago's South Side, the topics she first discovered in college—urban poverty, race, violent crime—were literally at her doorstep. She was enthralled. Having discovered drill music before her arrival, she reached out to her favorite driller.

AJ capitalized on Breanne's fascination with gangland Chicago. The two of them spent most of their time together lounging in her apartment, smoking weed, while she quizzed him about drugs, violence, and the drill world. Although he often found her questions annoying and repetitive, he knew that it aroused her. He realized that he could ensure future interactions and extract ever more favors by offering her sensationalized impressions about his life in Taylor Park. Whenever she seemed to be losing interest, he pulled her back in with small kernels of information about something "going down on the block."

Once, I stood with AJ in one of the neighborhood's back alleys as he spoke to Breanne on FaceTime. A half dozen others played dice nearby. AJ had already lost all of his money. He was now working up to ask Breanne to let him "hold" some cash. In recent days, he had begun to worry that their arrangement had run its course. So on the call, he insinuated that he was in danger and needed to get out of the neighborhood for a few hours.

"Shit's crazy 'round here right now," he said, only a couple of minutes into their call.

"What do you mean?" she asked in response, her voice sounding hollow in the small iPhone speakers.

"Shit's fucked up," he answered. "I can't be here right now. Can I roll over to your crib?"

"What do you mean?"

"The opps," he answered succinctly. "They slidin' through." I immediately knew this to be a lie. I had been in the neighborhood all day. No one had seen any rivals. There was no word of pending shootings.

"Oh my god," she said in a concerned tone. "Are you OK? Are they shooting now? Is anybody hurt? What's going on?"

"I'm OK for right now." AJ adopted a dramatic voice, though offering no further details.

Meanwhile, Breanne seemed to be growing more concerned by the moment. "What's going on?"

It was time for AJ to make his request. "Yo, um, can you, um, can you send the Uber to come grab me? I can tell you when I get there. I can tell you everything when I see you. I just can't talk about it right now. Can you just call the Uber for me?"

Breanne pressed for more information, but AJ continued to skirt her questions. The two went back and forth for a couple more minutes before Breanne caved and agreed to send a car for him. When he finally hung up the call, he did a victory dance, gyrating and thrusting his hips. His tone, which had grown more sympathetic and vulnerable as he spoke with Breanne, grew more brazen as he bragged to the other young men at the dice game. He announced that he would return with more cash, which he would use to re-enter the game and win back the money he had lost earlier.

Slummers' captivation with the ghetto, and drillers' subsequent manipulation of that fascination, was particularly visible when AJ invited Breanne to come visit Taylor Park. As autumn arrived, it seemed that Breanne had decided to end the relationship. She called AJ less frequently and seldom returned his texts. In the hope of reigniting her interest, AJ decided to play his trump card. He granted her long-standing request to see CBE's gang turf with her own eyes. It happened following the shooting death of a fellow Taylor Park resident, during the repast, when residents gathered in the streets for a memorial block party. From the moment Breanne arrived, AJ acted as tour guide and ambassador.

The ensuing tour had a clear theme: AJ presented the neighborhood as a world apart—a place where the looming threats of drive-bys and police raids forced the residents to develop an alternative social world. AJ introduced Breanne to the woman who sold cigarettes, cigars, and snacks out of the "store" in her apartment. He introduced her to the "big homies" and resident drug dealers. She met the elderly men who barbeque at all the memorials for slain residents. Throughout, AJ portrayed the neighborhood as a Darwinian battle where only the strong survive.

"In the projects," he confided at one point, "you hustle, or you die." I was shocked to hear him use this term. During my time in the neighborhood, this was the first and only time I heard AJ, or any resident, refer to the area as "the projects." They called it "the Park," "the block," even "the low-incomes," but *never* "the projects." For most Taylor Park residents, *the projects* was a term reserved for the city's infamous high-rise public housing complexes—places like Cabrini Green and the Henry Horner Homes.

For them, those were immoral places, where the "bad" segments of the urban poor lived. In community meetings and daily conversations, residents were quick to trace Taylor Park's problems—from litter to gangs—to the influx of "project people." And yet, here was AJ, referring to his own community with this pejorative term. It seemed to have the intended effect on Breanne. As if the tour couldn't get any more sensational, AJ and his fellow Corner Boys decided to record a new music video, capitalizing on the high turnout at the repast. More than a dozen young men amassed in one of the parking lots alongside their neighbors. As the camera began to roll, one of them pulled out a pistol, waving it threateningly in the air.

The notion of "eating the Other" is helpful for understanding why AJ approaches these cross-racial and cross-class exchanges with such exhilaration and pride. It helps explain why he would so forcefully denigrate his neighborhood and lifelong neighbors. As hooks writes, "marginalized groups, deemed Other, who have been ignored, rendered invisible, can be seduced by the emphasis on Otherness, by its commodification, because it offers the promise of recognition and reconciliation."[24] Simply stated, AJ's relationship with Breanne didn't just make him *feel* special, it was proof that he *is* special. AJ reminded me that few of his neighbors and peers had ever been courted by someone like Breanne.

"Ain't none of these goofy ass niggas out here stayin' up in hotels and goin' shoppin' DT [downtown]," he bragged. "Ordinary ass hood niggas ain't out here fuckin' white bitches. I'm fucking *white* bitches. These is like *real* women. Like, professional. Not like these thots [promiscuous women] we got on the block. These ones got jobs, they got cribs, they clean. Ain't no bugs up in their cribs."

We shouldn't forget the fact that young men like AJ live in a city that is hypersegregated along racial and class lines. In most neighborhoods, interracial friendship, much less interracial romance, is exceedingly rare. But thanks to his micro-celebrity—built through online displays of street life and gang violence—AJ feels as though he has overcome Chicago's urban apartheid.

DRILLERS AS PROPS FOR MIDDLE-CLASS RESPECTABILITY

The gulf dividing drillers and their more privileged white audiences is admittedly large. However, the slumming character of these exchanges isn't solely due to geographic or racial distance. Ironically, their success at forging violent and criminal personas catalyzed new ties with local black churches. This occurred as middle-class pastors and their congregations engaged in what historian Evelyn Brooks Higginbotham famously termed "the politics of respectability."[25] Given the durability of racial segregation, combined with the blanket stigma cast over the entire population of black neighborhoods, the black middle class faces challenges distancing themselves from their poorer, even more stigmatized neighbors. The latest tactic for overcoming this dilemma involves enlisting drillers to help affirm their own decency and difference. As Mary Pattillo documents in her extensive research throughout Chicago's South Side, "the virtuous behavior of the black middle class require[s] the depravity of the black poor as its counterpoint."[26]

When one of Chicago's large black churches reached out to the Corner Boys, the young men had no idea of the extensive role they'd play in the church's respectability politics. They were unaware that the church's leader, a fiery orator named Steven Wilkins, intended to leverage CBE's online persona to help him address his own organizational dilemmas. Through my own conversations with members of his congregation, I learned that Wilkins had recently come under criticism for his church's diminishing participation in local social justice campaigns, including several recent protests decrying the deaths of young black men at the hands of Chicago police officers. The church's waning activity was largely a result of demographic shifts. The congregation was growing older and, as a result, was less active in controversial community issues. As the church grew more conservative, Wilkins was also having difficulty attracting and retaining younger members. This led Wilkins and other church leadership to develop new outreach and community-engagement strategies designed to bring a younger and more socially active demographic through its doors. In the words of one senior member, the plan was to "meet young people where they are." In practice, this meant embracing digital social media, rap music, and local youth culture to make church involvement and activism seem "cool." It was time to embrace the future.

Enter the Corner Boys.

Wilkins's son-in-law—a church-raised forty-something named Kevin—spearheaded the outreach and rebranding campaign. If successful, it would solidify his own position in the church's future, perhaps even as his father-in-law's successor. Kevin told me that he discovered CBE serendipitously. He had been visiting a friend in Taylor Park when he noticed a group of teens excitedly bobbing their heads to a song blaring out of the speakers of a nearby car. Seeing how much love these youth had for the Corner Boys' music, Kevin enlisted his friend to set up a meeting with the drillers. He propositioned them to make a song on behalf of his church. Instead of their typical lyrics about gunplay and drug profits, however, this song would describe the problems facing the black community. If all went according to plan, the song would not only attract a younger demographic but also signal the church's renewed commitment to social justice. They never ended up making the song or video, but contributed to the church's rebranding nonetheless.

The church's evolving partnership with popular drillers revealed deep fault lines in Wilkins's congregation. A group of prominent and elderly members criticized the plan to associate so publicly with violent, gang-associated, and seemingly unrepentant youth. They also expressed concern about taking a relatively contentious stand in regard to the Chicago Police Department and the broader city administration. Such dissention is not without precedent. As Higginbotham notes, the politics of respectability undertaken by middle-class and religious blacks frequently split along radical and conservative lines.[27] As Wilkins endeavored to move his church toward the former, church elders attempted to uphold their more reserved stance. Facing dissention, Wilkins called on CBE once more: He invited them to attend a large Sunday service as his personal guests of honor. I accompanied a group of five Corner Boys that included AJ, Xavier, Dominik, and Adam. Clad in their sagging jeans and t-shirts, they stuck out among the finely pressed suits and pastel-colored dresses. I felt the room full of eyes watch the young men with suspicion. They felt it too, fidgeting in the seats Wilkins had reserved for them in front of the pulpit.

From the opening minutes of the sermon, it was clear that Wilkins was intent on using the Corner Boys to help him shift his church's public identity. He took full advantage of their attendance. First, he used the upcoming collaboration with CBE to defend his new youth recruitment and engagement strategy. He asked CBE to stand up, leading the room in a prolonged round of applause. Wilkins thanked them for agreeing to work with the church. He introduced several new social media campaigns designed to appeal to a younger, more internet-savvy demographic. As if to silence any future criticism from what Wilkins referred to as the "old guard," he insisted that rather than turn their noses up at seemingly wayward youth, the church needed to embrace them. Not because *he* demanded it as their spiritual leader, but because it was God's will—a will that Wilkins said he was merely honoring in earthly form.

Second, Wilkins used CBE's presence to reinforce his own position as the church's rightful spiritual leader. He suggested that despite the fact that young men like the Corner Boys frequently engage in violent crime—as clearly illustrated by their violent online videos—he had been able to convince them to temporarily put down their guns and redirect their anger toward the larger forces of racism and oppression. Although they were once "lost to the streets," Wilkins had saved them, putting them on the path to redemption. He called on the congregation to forgive their past transgressions.

Finally, and adopting a more confrontational tone, Wilkins lectured the congregation that the Corner Boys had valuable lessons to teach *them*. He exalted CBE's fearlessness. "Because they grew up in the hood," he said in a time-honored call-and-response style, "they don't fear *nothing*!" He admitted that their fearlessness had led them to violent behaviors. Yet, he preached, if the racism and oppression are ruinous enough, violence may actually be appropriate. As if to further reprimand the conservative and more passive members of his flock, he told a brief story about how he himself had forcibly defended his family against racist white neighbors that once tried to run them out of their middle-class neighborhood. Sometimes, he schooled, it was necessary to be a little "street."

I felt the energy in the room building as Wilkins moved through each piece of the sermon. This began with calls of "Amen!" and "Preach!" from a group of sympathetic middle-aged men seated with Kevin. The section of elders, who had begun the day with brows furrowed in disapproval and suspicion, began nodding their heads in agreement. Like the conductor of a symphony, Wilkins brought his sermon to a final crescendo and call to righteous action. The entire church, including the group of elders, rose to their feet in a standing ovation. The congregation seemed won over as they shouted and whistled in approval. The excitement was infectious. The Corner Boys stood with the crowd, clapping. They beamed with a pride that I had seen on only the rarest, most jubilant occasions. I joined the roaring applause. None of us were immune to the collective effervescence.

On the ride back to Taylor Park, Xavier and AJ could hardly sit still as they launched into minute-by-minute recaps of the past two hours. Their careers were on the rise. They were *really* "on."

I was excited as well. I had been gently encouraging CBE to try their hand at making more "socially conscious" content, without all the hyperbolic talk of murder. Surely, I thought to myself, their reception in the church would help prove that they could still receive praise and recognition without violent personas and images.

"See," I said, once again walking the line between researcher and violence-prevention worker. "I told you that you don't need to be waving your guns around to get views! You've got all these new fans. You guys were the stars today! And they want you to make music for the church. This is huge for you!"

The car suddenly fell silent.

Xavier dashed my hopes. "Bro," he said, "that shit's dead. We make gang music. Plain and simple. We ain't tryna make no soft shit like that." Xavier, who had always been the most receptive to my ideas of branching out from the violent content of the drill world, described the costs associated with my suggestions. Moving away from violent content would not only alienate their existing fans, who had come to expect talk of gunplay, but also allow their rivals to portray them as weak. This might result in increased attacks and even more efforts to catch them lacking.

As if to deal a final blow to my suggestion of moving beyond drill music, AJ walked me back through the origins of their relationship with Wilkins and the underlying message of the sermon: Their violence and gang affiliation was precisely what made them so attractive in the first place.

"Tell me this, bro," AJ said, chiming in, "you really think we woulda been up in there if all we did was rap about peace and shit? Hell naw! They reached out to *us*, bro! You heard him, talking 'bout 'These is some real ass niggas, with some real ass guns, doing some real ass shit.' We real, bro. He talkin' 'bout we don't fear *nobody*. You heard his ass. He said he needs niggas like us to keep keepin' it real. Those people need to act more like *us*! So we *definitely* can't change it up now." AJ, always one of the most strategic of the bunch, had fixated on Wilkins's argument that young men like the Corner Boys should be seen as models of the kind of righteous indignation that he was trying to instill in the church's elderly, conservative members.

Xavier and AJ were right. Just as the Corner Boys exchanged their hard-earned clout for material and social rewards among peers and fans, Wilkins capitalized on these same images and reputations to buttress his authority over the congregation.

I felt oddly relieved when CBE's relationship with Wilkins turned out to be short-lived. Despite his promises, Wilkins didn't follow through on further partnerships. He didn't invite them to any more sermons. They had served their purpose, it seemed. And yet, their brief collaboration lingered well into the future. If anything, the Corner Boys' experience in Wilkins's church only *renewed* their commitment to producing controversial and violent content. It confirmed these young men's long-standing belief that, deep down, even middle-class blacks envy their fearless, outlaw ways.

■■■

The unexpected relationship between drillers and their more privileged patrons is yet one more example of social media's power to bring distant groups into contact. Through their digital production practices, the Corner Boys forged new relationships with more privileged consumers beyond Taylor Park. For many observers, this is grounds for real optimism. In one of the most influential writings of the past half century, the sociologist William Julius Wilson argued that the lack of contact between urban poor residents and "mainstream" individuals and institutions is one of the most powerful engines driving urban poverty and its associated problems.[28] Living in such social isolation, Wilson wrote, impoverished residents aren't able to develop the "mainstream role models" that might otherwise "keep alive the perception that education is meaningful, that steady employment is a viable alternative to welfare, and that family stability is the norm, not the exception."[29] Youth enter into a "vicious cycle," developing cognitive, linguistic, and social dispositions that push them further toward crime, gangs, and drugs.[30]

Since Wilson's writings, many policy makers have come to assume that we could alleviate poverty if we created more ties between poor residents and their middle-class counterparts. But as the Corner Boys' interactions with people like Chad, Breanne, and Pastor Wilkins reveal, these exchanges are no panacea. Amid all the talk of mainstream role models, we tend to forget that these so-called mainstream individuals enter these relationships with their own desires, interests, and requests. Given the power differential between the parties involved, the concerns of disadvantaged residents are the ones most likely to be ignored, silenced, or exploited in the process. As I saw firsthand, the Corner Boys' relationships with well-to-do patrons didn't produce much meaningful upward mobility. Sure, these ties provided some of the resources drillers need for daily survival. They also provided a great deal of hope and optimism. But once the exhilaration of quick cash, praise, and new clothing faded away, these young men were typically right back where they started, sometimes in even more perilous circumstances. These momentary glimpses of the good life leave them wanting more, hunting for the next potential benefactor. Drillers know full well that one of the best ways to attract patrons is to continue producing extreme content. These young men come away from these exchanges resolved to "go harder"—to do whatever it takes to cut through the noise of the internet.

Of course, privileged, out-of-town consumers aren't the only ones driving the market for online violence and criminality. There is an equally hungry audience back home on the South Side. Local teens make up the last piece of the drill world left to consider. Like wealthier consumers, drillers' neighbors and classmates help drive the broader demand for authentic content, though for very different reasons.

7

...

Hometown Heroes or Local Menace?

On a dark Chicago evening, I stood arm in arm with nearly a hundred residents on one of Taylor Park's main streets. We had assembled for a candlelight vigil in memory of a young woman killed in a recent shooting. The teen's closest friends used small, flickering tea lights to spell out her name on the sidewalk. In the parking lot behind us sat a car, engine running, doors propped open, playing one of the Corner Boys' most popular songs. I found it odd to hear such explicit talk of crime and murder amid heartfelt words of remembrance, prayer, and community solidarity. If anyone else noticed the peculiar juxtaposition, they certainly didn't show it. Most bobbed their head quietly to the beat. As the event wrapped up, a distraught young woman approached Dominik and two other CBE members in attendance. Holding back sobs, she made a plea. She asked them to scour their online connections to find out who was responsible for the murder, and to get justice. Like most Taylor Park residents, she knew that the Corner Boys were tapped into the local online gang networks. They're the ones most likely to see the killers boasting about their deeds online. Dominik and the others agreed to her request.

Fast forward to later in the year. I sat next to Junior at Javon's funeral service. We had been lucky to find a seat as the small church quickly reached capacity. AJ, Xavier, and the rest of the Corner Boys were also there. Each of them sat quietly on the hard pews, hoodies covering their faces, staring down at their feet. They were hoping to avoid the angry stares of their neighbors, who blamed them for the death of the young man who lay in a casket at the front of the room. Tensions rose as Javon's family members took turns at the microphone, eulogizing the slain teen. Their sweet words about Javon turned to scorn, directed squarely at Junior and the others. The sentiment was reinforced by the pastor.

"This boy was sacrificed for their rap music," he yelled across the room, staring directly at AJ and Xavier. "They're going to hell." After the service, a small fight broke out when one of Javon's relatives took a swing at one of the Corner Boys.

These two different, but equally emotional, scenes capture the contradictory ways that South Side residents—particularly young people—interact with drillers and consume their products. In one moment, drillers and their uploads are a symbol of collective struggle, solidarity, and even hope. In another moment, they're the object of contempt, blamed for the violence and other problems that plague the community.

For local audiences, drill carries very different meanings than it does for more privileged consumers, like Chad, who obsesses over drill from the safety of his Beverly Hills townhouse. Those living outside of Chicago, beyond drillers' immediate neighborhoods, can avoid the drill world by merely shutting their laptops or turning off their phones. The Corner Boys' neighbors, in contrast, have no such option. They attend the same schools, ride the same buses, and walk the same streets as drillers. They are a part of the drill world, whether they like it or not. They can reduce some of its influence, but they can never escape it completely. It's woven too tightly into the fabric of daily life.

In some respects, young Chicagoans consume drill for the same reasons as well-to-do, out-of-town audiences. It's a thrilling, evocative genre that local residents use to conjure desired emotional states, interactions, and identities. But the similarities stop there. Throughout the course of their days, local youth increasingly rely on drill as a resource for navigating the myriad obstacles they face in their impoverished, violent neighborhoods. They draw on it for motivation in their efforts to pursue conventional pathways; they tap into it as a means of self-regulation, allowing them to avoid and cope with victimization without engaging in retaliatory violence; and they use it to develop peer bonds outside of the local gang networks. Of course, these benefits are not cost-free. When local teens consume drill content in careless and uninformed ways, they open themselves up to the potential of attack. If they cue up the wrong song, in the wrong place, at the wrong time, nearby gangs may misinterpret their behavior as a sign of affiliation or even as a direct challenge. Teens typically respond to this dilemma by *deepening* their dedication to the drill world, becoming smarter, more careful consumers. By staying closely connected to drillers online, Chicago youth are better positioned to sidestep drill-related violence offline. Ironically, this ends up increasing the clicks, views, and other metrics that support drillers' sensational displays of violence. In their hope of reducing the negative effects of drill, local audiences unwittingly fan the flames, making their daily consumption habits even more necessary.

DRILL'S UNEXPECTED AFFORDANCES

Working in youth after-school programs, I was forced to reckon with drill's central role in local teens' lives long before I ever met the Corner Boys. Given the explicit goal of these programs—to provide teens with safe spaces for processing trauma, building confidence, and avoiding violence—we worried about the constant presence of such hyperviolent media. We feared it might be counteracting our work. Over time, however, we realized that we hadn't fully understood what drill meant to youngsters. In fact, despite their gleeful fascination with the guns and drugs, youth consistently increased their commitment to personal, academic, and professional achievement over the course of the program. In her extensive research on middle-class black youth, Mary Pattillo similarly documents that even the most high-achieving, non-delinquent teens routinely capitalize on safe spaces like churches and community centers to play out their street hustler fantasies.[1] As Pattillo notes, the act of consuming transgressive content can be highly pleasurable. Neither middle-class nor poor black teens are immune to the delight that comes from the stylistic affectations of "real gangstas," even though they themselves infrequently, if ever, cross that line.

Understanding drill's affordances in teens' lives requires that we recognize how it provides what the sociologist Tia DeNora refers to as a "technology of the self." In other words, drill offers "a means for creating, enhancing, sustaining, and changing subjective, cognitive, bodily and self-conceptual states."[2] When teens consume drill, they appropriate the sounds, lyrics, visuals, and biographies of drillers as referents for where they wish to go mentally, physically, and in their broader life course.

Gettin' T'd

Consider the following scenes. Over the course of several months, a half dozen teens in our program regularly assembled around the center's plastic folding tables, listening to their favorite songs as they completed the day's homework assignments. I recall one afternoon when the group sat for about an hour in near silence, their phones positioned to the side of their worksheets as they streamed local drill music videos on YouTube. Headphones seemingly glued to their ears, they each gyrated and shimmied in their seats to the beat. Every few minutes, one of them would form an imaginary gun with his fingers, point this weapon at the page in front of them, and fire an imaginary bullet at a recently completed math problem or essay assignment. After watching this odd juxtaposition of drill music, simulated gun violence, and scholastic diligence, I pulled a few of the teens aside to ask about this unexpected homework ritual. Their responses were surprisingly uniform.

As a fifteen-year-old named Reggie described, "It helps me when I gotta get T'd for math." In slang terms, getting "T'd" or "turnt" means becoming excited, motivated, and confident.[3] "I hate math," Reggie continued. "I suck at math. It's really hard. But I gotta do it." This difficulty is particularly troublesome for Reggie, who dreams of pursuing a career in the medical field, which demands high marks in math and science. "I gotta find a way I can do it. But this music. I dunno, it's like, it gets me feelin' like, like I'm unstoppable or something. Like I can do anything." Reggie laughed to himself as though saying this out loud for the first time.[4]

"Tell me more about that," I probed.

Reggie responded immediately, echoing the ways drillers often described their songs. "You could just hear it." He invited me to listen to the YouTube video currently playing in his headphones, titled "Chiraq Remix," by a prominent South Side driller named "Montana of 300." At that time, the video had already amassed more than ten million YouTube views. I shoved the earbuds into my ears as Reggie hit the play button on his phone's YouTube application. It didn't take long before I began to understand what Reggie was talking about.

The beat began rather simply. Just three or four piano notes playing over and over in a repeating loop. The dissonant, minor keys began to put me on edge. It bore a remarkable resemblance to the theme music of John Carpenter's classic slasher film *Halloween*. The foreboding quality was only amplified by the steady march of a deep kick drum. The low frequencies clipped and distorted as they pounded through the cheap headphones. Without warning, the sound of gritty, computer-generated snare drums pierced the melody. Arranged in rapid succession, they mimicked the fire of gunshots ringing out on a city street. Montana's frenetic, high-paced rapping added to the mood of urgency. The beat continued to build like this for a minute or so, adding one element after another. Montana ramped up his pace and volume, until the song reached its climax. For me, the sound felt overwhelming and inescapable. Relentless. When the beat finally ended, I felt myself let out an unconscious sigh.

"Dang," I said, pulling out the earbuds. My heart was beating notably faster. "That's so intense!"

"See!" Reggie responded, a broad grin across his face. "You're getting T'd, right? You could just feel it in your chest. You feel unstoppable, right?" He pointed back to his phone sitting on the table. "I'm drillin' on this school stuff. Montana got *his* enemies, I got *mine*." Reggie smiled widely—a silent acknowledgment of the unlikeliness of his analogy.

Teens like Reggie actively use drill's stirring, emotive beats to put themselves into a particular mental and bodily state. Without prompting from me, Reggie explicitly noted the images of street hustling and gangbanging summoned by Montana's song. As Reggie confronts the obstacles in his own life, he imagines himself in the drillers' shoes, as if he too were "posted on the block," facing down rivals in a life-or-death struggle.

But drill's unique affordances are only partly explained by its sonic qualities and lyrical content. Equally, if not more, important for teens' consumption practices is the fact that they're deeply versed in the details surrounding drillers' backstories and daily travails. Every drill song and video is supplemented by hundreds of posts, updates, and comments that allow consumers to piece together the circumstances surrounding a particular scene, verse, or lyric. The fact that drillers come from many of the same neighborhoods, know the same people, and experience some of the same traumatic events as their young consumers allows this audience to deploy drillers' biographies for their own purposes. This process was readily apparent in the case of Will, another one of the teens who was fond of firing imaginary bullets at his daily school assignments. Will was among those who were most up-to-date on all news—good and bad—about drillers and their gangs. He was particularly fond of one local driller, known as "Rondo Numba Nine," whose micro-celebrity soared after posting a picture of himself on Instagram holding a large, military-grade rocket launcher. Rondo's popularity continued to rise after police accused him of driving into rival gang territory and shooting a man to death. In the summer of 2016, Rondo was found guilty of the shooting death, and was sentenced to thirty-nine years in prison. As tends to happen in the drill world, the conviction led to an even bigger spike in Rondo's popularity. Though he hasn't created any new music, he provides interviews for YouTube channels and drill music blogs from prison.[5]

Although Will had initially begun researching and listening to Rondo following the rocket launcher incident, he became a devoted fan after learning how much Rondo's biography resonated with his own. Both Will and Rondo had lost close friends to gun violence. Rondo's songs, videos, and social media updates are steeped in tributes to his slain friend and fellow gang member. He continually expressed his mourning, as well as his desire to honor the deceased by seeking revenge and making enough drug money to lift himself and his surviving friends out of poverty.

"Rondo's best friend got shot too," Will explained. "That's why I been messing with his music. He knows what it's like." In the months after his friend's death, Will was struggling to cope. He was having trouble sleeping and found it difficult to concentrate in school. Will described it as a "cloud" of depression that made it nearly impossible to think about anything else. Yet, Rondo's resilience inspired Will to, in his words, "cut through the cloud." Seeing himself in Rondo, he decided that the best way to honor his friend was by overcoming all the obstacles in his way. And this began by conquering his homework.

Coping with Feelings of Powerlessness

In addition to using drill music as a resource for generating inspiration and coping with loss, youth routinely appropriate drill content as a means for rechanneling their energies and emotions *away* from physical violence. I learned of this particular usage over the course of a summer that I spent with an informal weightlifting "club" that I formed with a group of Taylor Park residents. Besides me, the group was made up of a half dozen men between the ages of eighteen and twenty-one. Although they were closely linked to the Corner Boys—as cousins, former classmates, and neighbors—they were attempting to walk entirely legal, nonviolent paths. Three were sporadically enrolled in vocational and community college classes. Two of the men, who had excelled at basketball in high school, were now playing on teams at small Division III colleges in downstate Illinois and Indiana. Friends since adolescence, they spent their days together playing video games, babysitting younger siblings, and slowly walking laps through Taylor Park in search of young women to flirt with. Facing the potential of a long, hot, and boring summer, two of them asked if I could help them improve their workouts. Roughly three times per week, we packed into my car and drove to a community center a few miles away to lift weights.

Over the course of our workouts, drill music—including a steady wave of CBE songs—filled the space between conversations about school, weightlifting technique, and life more generally. Throughout our time, one particular consumption practice stuck out more than any other. In the seconds before picking up a particularly heavy weight, the young men cued up notably violent songs. They maxed out the volume, stuffing their earbuds even deeper into their ears. Those without earbuds positioned their phones on the exercise equipment just inches from their ears. With a scowl and a heavy exhale, they executed the exercises with a determined intensity. They repeated this ritual over and over for the duration of our workouts, until their white tank tops were stained with sweat and their legs shook with fatigue. At first, it seemed that these young men were using drill much like Reggie and other young people, as a means of conjuring particular mental and physical states. Drill certainly helped them get "T'd up" for our taxing and difficult sessions. Over time, however, it became clear that they were conjuring far more than just motivation.

During one session, I noticed Allen, a long-limbed and soft-spoken young man, exercising with a notable level of ferocity. He danced slightly between exercises waving an imaginary gun in front of him. He mouthed the words of the song playing in his headphones, as if speaking to someone in anger. I immediately recognized the tune, called "Michael Jordan." It had been made by one of the most popular local drillers, known as "King Louie." I listened to Allen repeat four particular lines:

> Niggas ain't on nothin',
> Gon' make me shoot somethin',
> Doing that gum bumpin',
> Now they Forrest Gumpin'.

In this particular verse, King Louie calls out his rivals as weak (They "ain't on nothin'"). He goes on to describe how, when he pulls out his gun and starts shooting at them, his rivals run away in fear rather than retaliate ("Now they Forrest Gumpin'").[6]

After the workout, I pulled Allen aside to check in with him. I asked about his behavior from earlier. After a bit of prodding, he confessed that he had been robbed at gunpoint the night before by several men associated with the Murderville gang faction. They had recognized Allen as a cousin of one of the Corner Boys and decided to capitalize on the chance to catch him lacking. Staring into the barrel of their gun, Allen gave up his wallet without a fight. In the wake of the traumatic experience, he found himself so distraught that he couldn't tell anyone about the robbery. He knew that if his cousin and the other Corner Boys found out, they would feel forced to retaliate. They had their reputations to protect, after all. Allen knew what the potential consequences were for his cousin, who could be shot, killed, or arrested while attempting to avenge his family member. Now, in the gym, and with the help of drill music, Allen was taking out his anger and frustration on the weights.

"I just kept playing last night over and over," Allen said, describing his mental state as he listened to King Louie's song. "It's like a movie. I just kept thinking 'bout what I wish I coulda' done to them. I want *them* to feel how *I* was feeling, you know? Like, if *I* had a pole [gun]. They'll see they can't do me like that. Like, how it would be if *I* started shootin'. They wouldn't be acting so savage." I noticed Allen's facial expression change as these words came out of his mouth. As if suddenly ashamed of his statement, he took a deep, calming breath. "Naw, I ain't like that. I ain't tryna' be doing that for real. That's CBE and them. They're 'bout that life. I just wanna hoop and do school and stuff."

Allen described a coping strategy that every one of the young men in our group utilized at least once during the summer: After experiencing violent victimization, they intensified both their listening and their workouts in the following days. In doing so, they effectively used drill music to help them recapture virtually what they had been forced to concede interactionally—namely, their feelings of masculinity, power, and control.[7] In the weight room, with drill music blasting in their ears, they transported themselves back to these frightening encounters. They worked themselves up, recreating the adrenaline, rapid heartbeat, quickened breathing, and sweaty palms that marked those difficult moments. They imagined themselves acting differently—this time with fearless defiance. They replayed and revised the scene as if they were a driller, like King Louie, who (they believed) would have pulled out a gun and punished his assailants rather than give up his wallet. Allen and his close peers are well aware that their lives, as well as their continued success in school, sports, and noncriminal pursuits, require their constant and quiet submission in the face of violent assaults. Unable to fight back, they feel powerless and beaten down. By consuming drill music in this manner—by creating a virtual reality where *they* are the aggressor—they weather repeated degradation and emasculation without retaliating.

Surrogate Drillers

At other times, local youth appropriate drill content as a means for forming and regulating friendship groups. It's yet another counterintuitive strategy they rely on to chart non-delinquent pathways. The past century of sociological and criminological research shows that peer groups are among the most powerful sources of young people's attitudes and behaviors.[8] When adolescents form friendships with older, delinquent peers, they're more likely to commit crimes. They're also more likely to affiliate with gangs, abuse drugs and alcohol, and perform poorly in school. According to the sociologist David Harding, peer selection is often influenced by broader neighborhood conditions.[9] In disadvantaged and violent areas, where youth feel unsafe traveling too far from home, they tend to associate with older men from their immediate neighborhood. In contrast, youth who are less fearful traveling across the city have far more opportunities to form friendships with same-age, non-delinquent peers. These findings have inspired decades of after-school programs, like my own, that build safe spaces where teens can more easily bond with youth their age, from a variety of residential neighborhoods, as they engage in non-delinquent activities. There is just one issue. The fact that a youngster *can* associate with same-age peers doesn't mean they will. And if they don't form strong ties, they're more likely to stop frequenting these spaces altogether. They're more likely to seek community with the older residents waiting back home. So although neighborhood conditions certainly matter, we also have to pay attention to the actual content and quality of peer interactions. Teens are far more likely to remain in peer groups that offer stimulating and fulfilling exchanges.

As one of the most popular and easily accessible cultural products in Chicago teens' lives, drill music provides youth with a powerful medium for organizing friendships, building solidarity, and ensuring inexpensive entertainment.[10] Reflecting a popular form of "competitive sociability," community center teens constantly jockeyed for intra-group status and campaigned for respect from their peers by displaying their intimate and up-to-date knowledge of drillers' exploits, conflicts, and deaths.[11] Teens spent considerable time debating the authenticity and clout of their favorite drillers.

These interactions typically begin with one teen sharing an opinion, news update, or newly released video from one of his favorite drillers. Debate ensues with one or more of the others belittling the driller in question while proclaiming the superiority of a different, often rival driller. Their claims and counterclaims drift seamlessly between criticisms of an individual driller's musical talent and their perceptions of whether he "really does the stuff he raps about." As they debate, they draw on any and all information available online. After a few minutes of back-and-forth, when they run out of readily available information, they dive back into their phones for more ammunition for their respective arguments. When one of the young men stumbles onto new evidence—an old YouTube video or a previous tweet, for example—he brings it to the group's attention. The group spends the next few minutes huddled around the phone, examining the discovery. Before long, one of them will offer a new controversial comment, starting the entire process over again.

I watched this process unfold one afternoon as I walked with four teens to the local basketball court. The exchange kicked off innocently. One of the young men, a stocky fifteen-year-old named Antwan, started singing a few lines from a song called "Money Counter," by a local driller known as "Tay 600." Antwan melodically rapped:

> I need a money counter,
> I got my gun around me.
> I catch a opp up in the streets,
> he better run from 'round me.

As Antwan finished this last line, he cracked a huge smile. "Bro!" he exclaimed, turning to the rest of us. "Tay 600 is raw as hell. He's talkin' 'bout stacking so hard [making so much money] he needs a money counter. I'm messing with him right now. He's on."

Before Antwan even finished his statement, two of the other teens interrupted with a verbal takedown. Devan, a confident seventeen-year-old with a love for Nike high-tops, spared no time in dismissing Tay 600 as an inauthentic driller. "He's a lame," Devan began. "He ain't really out there in the field. He a snitch!"

"He ain't a snitch," Antwan countered. "You don't know what you're talking 'bout."

A tall seventeen-year-old named Shaquir joined Devan in the argument. "Ya huh!" Shaquir yelled. "He *is* a snitch. He snitched on his own gang. He's the one who got Rondo locked up! He ain't stackin'. He ain't even gang no more. They're after him."

As Shaquir spoke, Devan furiously typed on his phone, searching the internet for evidence for his earlier claims. In less than twenty seconds, he had pulled up a relevant blog post. It presented a series of videos and tweets made by members of Tay's own gang, known locally as "Team 600." The blog claimed that Tay had provided testimony that led to the prosecution in Rondo's murder case. Shaquir was right: Team 600 had indeed ostracized Tay 600, publicly disowning the maligned driller.

"I told you," Devan bragged as he held his phone up for the group to see.

"Rondo. That's the *real* savage," Shaquir said, pivoting to praise *his* favorite driller. "He's *really* in the field. He's got that rocket launcher, too. If Tay's out there snitching, then Rondo gon' find a way to shut him up, even if he *is* locked up."

"Naw," Antwan replied quietly, though offered no further argument. He ceded the debate for now.

As if to finally settle any questions about Tay 600's authenticity, the fourth young man present, a high-school sophomore named Kenyon, added one last piece of information. Kenyon frequently bragged that he had family connections to Team 600, which he brought up once again. "My cousin says they never really wanted Tay in 600 anyway. They only let him in 'cause he was good at rappin'. My cousin says he *is* a lame! He can't even come 'round there no more."

As they stood at the edge of the basketball court, Devan and Shaquir spent the next few minutes pressing Kenyon for more information about Team 600's intra-gang conflict, and about life more generally in their territory. Antwan eventually joined back in, and the four continued comparing their favorite drillers until joining the next basketball game.

Two aspects of this exchange are worth noting. First, each young man has adopted a "surrogate" driller, whose biography and content resonates with him on a personal level.[12] Competing through surrogates allows them to jockey for status, hipness, and masculinity without ever engaging in violence or crime themselves. It also allows them to keep these contests confined to a friendly, depersonalized register. Although Devan's, Shaquir's, and Kenyon's harsh criticism of Tay 600 is also an indirect criticism of Antwan (as someone who has difficulty distinguishing a "real" driller from a "lame" one), its indirectness ensured that Antwan never completely fell out of community.[13]

Second, Chicago teens use their detailed knowledge about drillers and related events in the local gang world as a form of social currency, or "cultural capital."[14] Knowledge about drillers is the price of admission. It also allows teens to create and reinforce group hierarchies, boundaries, and status.[15] Meanwhile, the inability to adequately adopt, defend, and discuss surrogate drillers effectively locks them out of such company. When Kevin, a studious fifteen-year-old moved to the area, he had a difficult time integrating himself into Antwan's friendship group. During his first few weeks, Kevin tended to stand quietly on the outside of their spirited debates about the latest drill music and gang gossip. The young man's slight speech impediment made him hesitant to interact with new people. Fortunately, Antwan routinely reached out to Kevin, usually asking his opinion on recent drill-related events as a way of breaking the ice. But Kevin repeatedly came up empty, confessing that he didn't know who or what Antwan was talking about. It didn't take long before the others in Antwan's group started making fun of Kevin. They called him a "bruford" and a "lame." These insults ceased, however, once Kevin increased his daily consumption of drill content. For several weeks, he meticulously studied local drillers and their conflicts via YouTube and Twitter. He pieced together the origins and outcomes of gang wars. He even adopted a surrogate. It wasn't long before Antwan's group changed their stance toward him. Within a short time, Kevin had moved closer to the center of the daily drill debates. In one of my conversations with Kevin, I remarked on his new love for drill music, along with the friendships that resulted.

"When I first came here," Kevin excitedly shared, "I didn't know none of the rappers. I only used to listen to what my mom played in the car. Everybody kept talkin' 'bout Chief Keef and JoJo and everybody else. I wanted to see what they were talking about, so I started watching the videos." Kevin now watches with satisfaction each time his favorite driller gains in popularity. "He's really good," Kevin bragged. "He's gonna make it. Watch. Other people don't like him, but I do."

I was relieved when Kevin successfully integrated himself into one of the center's most popular friendship groups. I had worried that this socially awkward teen might come to feel out of place. I was afraid he might seek friendships elsewhere, perhaps with residents who were less committed to their educational and professional success than Antwan's group. Counterintuitively, Kevin's newfound obsession with violent, gang-related content online paved a way for him to integrate himself in a peer network that actively avoided gang-related violence offline.

THE PERILS OF INAPPROPRIATE CONSUMPTION

Despite the powerful, if unexpected benefits of drill content, young people aren't free to enjoy it anywhere or anytime they please. For South Side teens, inappropriate consumption can lead to serious trouble. For decades, young residents have risked appearing like rivals, potential threats, and easy targets when they adorn themselves with the cultural products, styles, and symbols associated with local gangs. "Youth," Mary Pattillo observed in the 1990s, "can be consumed as victims, their innocent stylistic signs misread by some real gangsta."[16] These instances of mistaken identity are even more likely today as gangs increasingly use drill music as a tool for broadcasting their affiliation and challenging rivals. Sometimes, when drillers and their gangs travel through neutral public spaces, they play their own songs from their phones or rap a few lyrics loud enough for others to hear. This new mode of sonic identification is a direct result of the broader shifts in gang organization over the past two decades. As corporate gangs continue to splinter into smaller, block-based factions, their members are less likely to identify themselves using the official gang colors. Today, it's mostly just black t-shirts and jeans. This sartorial shift makes it harder for young people to determine the affiliation (or lack of affiliation) of the person sitting next to them on the bus, at the stoplight, or at the movie theater. By closely monitoring a stranger's choice in drill content, however, young people have learned to quickly identify those around them, their likely affiliations, and the potential threats they pose.

In a social world where young people constantly monitor each other's consumption habits, non-gang-associated youth risk being misrecognized and attacked. As an outgoing nineteen-year-old named Ray expressed, when gangs hear someone listening to their rivals' music, they may opt to "shoot first and ask questions later."

"Can't nobody stop you from listenin' to what you want to," Ray said, "but at the same time, you can't . . . listen to CBE music and ride through Murderville. You can't do that. . . . They hear, then they gonna automatically think it's them [CBE], so they just gonna shoot the car. There ain't no tellin' who in the car. Mama could be in the car!"

A Taylor Park teen named Antonio shared a frightening instance of misrecognition. Unlike most of the young people from the neighborhood, Antonio seldom listens to CBE's music. It's an intentional choice. He's determined to separate himself from the local gang faction. Instead, he gravitates toward other Chicago drillers, like Chief Keef, who have reached mainstream status and are relatively less embroiled in ongoing gang warfare. But even this strategy isn't failproof. Antonio told me that he had been riding the train home from downtown one afternoon when he was misrecognized on account of his music choices. He stood holding the handrail, engrossed in the song blasting in his headphones. It was a Chief Keef tune called "Off the Tooka," written initially as a "diss track" insulting a member of the rival St. Lawrence Boys gang, named Tooka. In the chorus, Chief Keef repeatedly brags that he is "smokin' Tooka"—that is, celebrating the murder by smoking Tooka's ashes in his weed blunt. In the years since its release, listeners like Antonio have gravitated to the song with only passing regard for its original, antagonistic purpose. According to Antonio, he had gotten so "carried away" by the chorus that he began absentmindedly singing along on the train. Suddenly, another passenger stood up and got in Antonio's face. Antonio immediately realized that the man was a member of the St. Lawrence Boys, which had renamed their territory "Tookaville" following the death of their close friend.

"He thought I was one of the opps," Antonio recalled in shock. "He heard me singing that, and he was asking me what gang I was in. He was mad as hell. I kept sayin' I don't gangbang. He didn't believe me 'cause then he tried to punch me, and that's when I ran off the train and got to runnin' down the stairs." Antonio rapidly patted his thighs with his hands, mimicking the sound of his feet hitting the ground as he sprinted. "I looked back and he was right behind me, coming fast. I just kept thinking he was gonna shoot me." Once Antonio was off the train platform, he ducked into a busy store. The man waited outside, watching him through the windows. Antonio feared that the man would call his fellow gang members, but the man walked away after a few minutes. Antonio finally left the store and reboarded the train. Following the incident, he avoids singing along to *any* drill songs in public, and is mindful to keep the volume of his music low, even when listening on his headphones. "You don't know who's standing next to you," Antonio warned. "You could be listening to a song talkin' 'bout F his cousin' or smokin' his brother and stuff, because it's in the music. But the music is about his gang! Now he wants to get on that with you."[17]

I was surprised at how young some residents were when they were first misrecognized on account of their listening habits. Even elementary and middle-school age kids have to be mindful of their public music choices. Across multiple interviews with Taylor Park residents, I heard the story of a thirteen-year-old resident who walked to the McDonald's located on the edge of nearby Murderville territory. As he sat eating his meal, his phone began to ring. Like many local residents, he had reset his cell phone ringer to play his favorite CBE song. It played for only a few seconds, but long enough to catch the attention of nearby customers. This included a group of teens associated with Murderville, seated only a few tables away. Interpreting the boy's choice of ringtone as a sign of potential membership in CBE, they chased him out of the restaurant and back into the Corner Boys' territory.

At times, even the slightest, seemingly innocuous association with a local gang's songs, videos, and supplemental online content can lead to misrecognition and attack. Chris, a fifteen-year-old Taylor Park resident, learned this lesson the hard way. Given his enviable athleticism, Chris devotes most of his time to playing sports. As a freshman, he was named starting linebacker for his high school football team. His dedication to football and school led Chris to limit the time he spends hanging out with the Corner Boys. Keeping his distance from the group has been vital for his safety, as he's forced to walk through Murderville territory to get to school every day. He did so safely for the first few months of the school year. This changed, however, when Murderville misidentified him as a member of CBE. Within twenty-four hours, they publicly declared war on Chris, and orchestrated ambushes along his walk to school.

This misunderstanding originated rather innocently. Like many his age, Chris started spending significant time with young women, bouncing from one teenage love interest to the next. One afternoon, he and a young woman snapped a selfie photo together in front of AJ's apartment building. Eager to show off her new beau to her online networks, the young woman uploaded the photo to Facebook. There, it was noticed by a member of Murderville, who had a crush on the young woman, and had been scrolling through her photos. He immediately recognized the distinctive brick façade of the apartment building, which is a common background in CBE's music videos. It was enough for the Murderville member to assume that Chris was one of the Corner Boys. The news quickly circulated to other Murderville members, who began threatening Chris on social media. Chris was justifiably terrified. Fortunately, one of the older players on Chris's football team had a familial connection to Murderville. He saw the online threats and assured them that Chris wasn't actually a member of CBE. Chris's teammate facilitated a conversation among all the parties. They cleared up the misunderstanding, but it was another two weeks before Chris felt safe enough to walk to school again.

Unfortunately, not all teens have access to friends and family who can effectively broker peace in the event of misrecognition. Unlike Chris, many young people must find alternative means for avoiding the consequences of their associations with local drillers (whether real or perceived).

USING DRILL CONTENT TO STAY SAFE

Some of the savviest teens have developed innovative ways of using drill-related content to sidestep potential victimization. Earlier, I detailed how drillers and their gangs monitor rivals' online activity to gain intelligence about their current whereabouts and activities. Non-gang-associated youth similarly engage in intelligence gathering. However, rather than use it to ambush enemies, they collect this information to better avoid those who might do them harm. By consuming the music, videos, and other content, teens create and refine cognitive maps of the city. According to the urban sociologist Gerald Suttles, cognitive maps are the "creative impositions" that residents overlay on physical maps for the sake of "regulating spatial movement to avoid conflict between antagonistic groups."[18] These maps "provide a set of social categories for differentiating between those people with whom one can or cannot safely associate."[19]

With the recent balkanization of large corporate gangs into smaller, drill-centered gang factions, young Chicagoans have become even more pressed to develop cognitive maps. Throughout my time with South Side teens, I enlisted them to participate in a mapping exercise I had developed. Placing a blank, physical map of the South Side in front of them, I asked them to draw the boundaries of all the gang territories they were aware of. I was continually impressed by their ability to account for the dense mosaic of gang turf not only in the blocks surrounding their homes but even in distant neighborhoods that they had never personally visited. Although some teens first learned some of this information from uncles, brothers, and other adults with firsthand experiences, teens' spatialized knowledge of gang activity derived mostly from their daily consumption of drill content.

Consider the cognitive map of a fourteen-year-old Taylor Park resident named Markell. Although he's not associated, even peripherally, with the Corner Boys or any other gang, Markell detailed the boundaries of nine different gang factions within a three-mile radius surrounding his neighborhood. I asked Markell how he came to learn such precise boundaries. He told me that once he started attending a high school located several miles outside of Corner Boys territory, he made a conscious effort to consume drill content, hoping to discover the most relevant gang boundaries.

"I just started watching all the videos," Markell instructed. "If you watch, you could tell where they [different gang factions] be at and what they on. I just kept looking for the streets they be on and what signs they be droppin'. I hear them talking 'bout their opps and then I go watch their opps' videos. That's how I know where I can't go. They into it [at war], so if I'm walkin' in one of their hoods, they might think I'm a opp."

Teens like Markell reappropriate a number of ubiquitous elements found in drill music videos. As drillers demonstrate their authenticity, they emphasize their connection to particular South Side neighborhoods. To do so, they often record their music videos standing underneath notable street signs, in front of low-income housing units, and near other recognizable landmarks. These genre-defining visuals allow teens like Markell to quickly link drillers and their gangs with particular city blocks.

Some teens take their intelligence gathering even further. In addition to deciphering physical territories and potential rivalries, they monitor music videos and other social media uploads to gain knowledge of a gang's violent capacities. When another teen, named Scotty, mapped the surrounding gang territories, I asked him where he felt the least safe. He immediately pointed to the nearby Pharaohs' gang territory.

"Why don't you feel safe going over there?" I asked.

"They got them big guns," Scotty answered with a seriousness in his voice. "AKs [AK-47 assault rifles], extendos [extended magazines], big guns."

"How do you know?"

"I seen 'em right there in their new video," he replied. "They're piped up [heavily armed]. Hell naw, I ain't goin' over there!"

"What about over here?" I asked, pointing to a different area of the map that Scotty had identified as Crown Town territory.

"Eh," Scotty began, resuming his typical nonchalance. "I ain't really tweakin' 'bout them over there. It's kinda quiet over there now. All their shooters is locked up. They ain't really on nothing right now. They rebuilding."

"How do you know?" I asked.

"I seen it on Facebook," he answered immediately. "They keep talking about 'Free the shooters' and stuff. That means they don't have no muscle right now. They ain't about to do nothin' with all their shooters is locked up. So their block is real quiet"

I spent the next fifteen minutes pointing to the various gang boundaries Scotty had drawn on the map sitting in front of us. For each, he mentioned a particular YouTube video, Facebook exchange, Twitter conversation, or drill-related blog that had revealed key information about the gangs in each area.[20] By consuming drill-related content, Scotty was able to generate enough information to feel as though he could stay safe if or when he visited the surrounding neighborhoods.

For teens who cross multiple gang territories on a regular basis—to simply get to school, for instance—general knowledge about different gangs' turf boundaries and violent capacities may not be enough.[21] Consulting drill-related content on a near-hourly basis, they compile finer-grained details on the current whereabouts and mental states of the individuals who might do them harm. For many teens, this begins the moment that they wake up in the morning. They reach for their smartphones and open up their social media apps. Like Chris, sixteen-year-old Evan has to walk through Murderville territory at least twice a day to get to and from school. Although Evan isn't a member of CBE, his family ties and online connections to the Corner Boys have put him in Murderville's crosshairs. They've threatened, chased, and robbed him on multiple occasions. Determined to reduce the chances of victimization, Evan began following nearly every Murderville driller, shooter, and member on Instagram and Twitter, and even became "friends" with them on Facebook. As part of his morning routine, Evan pulls up their online profiles so that he can chart the safest course possible through their turf.

One morning, for example, as Evan prepared to leave his house around 7 AM, he reviewed the Twitter activity of a Murderville member who lives along the most direct route to school. Evan saw that, only minutes earlier, the young man had posted a photo that displayed several handguns neatly arranged on a coffee table. A startling caption accompanied the photo:

IM HUNTIN OPPS TDAY CATCHIN SWEET NIGGAS LACKIN

Fearing that this young man was armed and looking for a suitable target, Evan decided to steer clear of his street and make a two-block detour to the north. Before he could do so, however, he needed to check on the Twitter activity of the two Murderville members who lived along the new route. Evan was relieved to see that, at least according to their Twitter activity, both were indisposed. One of them had posted a tweet the night before, indicating that he was stuck in the suburbs. The other had tweeted in the early hours of the morning, indicating that he was finally going to bed after partying all night. Although Evan's new route added five extra minutes to his walk to school, he arrived safely to his first-period class. After his final class period, Evan consulted Murderville's online activity once more, charting the safest route possible back home.

Although this strategy is common among teens living in and around warring gang territories, it's difficult to calculate just how much danger it helps them avoid. As I've emphasized throughout this book, much of the content uploaded by drillers and their gangs is hyperbole, sometimes complete fabrications. The information Evan discovered on Murderville's various social media profiles—about guns, partying, and physical locations, for example—may misrepresent reality. However, if past research holds true, teens like Evan are safer nonetheless, even if some of their information is inaccurate. In their efforts to build cognitive maps and chart safe passage, teens like Evan develop "street efficacy"—the sociologist Patrick Sharkey's term to describe the "perceived ability to avoid violent confrontations and find ways to be safe in one's neighborhood."[22] *Perceived* is the operative word here. Teens who believe they have the skills to navigate around violence—even if that violence feels ubiquitous—are far less likely to seek protection via local gangs, engage in preemptive violence, or resort to other delinquent forms of status-building.[23]

■ ■ ■

Evan, Reggie, and other local teens may experience a transgressive thrill as they watch violent videos, listen to aggressive songs, and swipe through gang-related images. But they simultaneously consume this content for additional and more complicated reasons. As it turns out, many of the same neighborhood conditions that initially compelled drillers to engage in digital production—physical insecurity, lack of upward mobility, and a desire for recognition—also drive local consumption practices. Among other things, drill content provides South Side teens with valuable resources for coping with loss, motivating scholarship, organizing peer groups, and staying safe.

Drill's counterintuitive affordances challenge many of the assumptions we tend to hold about media consumption more generally. In both the academic and public imagination, there's a tendency to treat young audiences as passive and powerless consumers, unwittingly blown by the winds of popular culture toward mindless, self-destructive behavior. Throughout history, moral panics about youth delinquency tend to feature a musical scapegoat. In the 1960s and 1970s, adults blamed musicians like Jimi Hendrix and the Grateful Dead for what many saw as a drug-fueled counterculture. Later, in the 1980s and 1990s, they blamed NWA, Ice Cube, and other pioneering gangsta rappers for urban unrest and anti-police sentiment. Following the shooting massacre at Columbine, parents pointed to goth rocker Marilyn Manson for his supposed promotion of teen suicide pacts and Satan worshipping. Beginning in 2012, they found a new bogey man—drillers. I hear panicked pleas in community meetings, barbershops, and just about every other public forum. According to the loudest critics, this new cultural product is corrupting virtually anyone who hears it, convincing them to quit school, pick up guns, and seek their fortunes in the street.

Yet, as the behaviors of South Side teens suggest, this narrative misunderstands why and how young residents *actually* consume controversial music such as drill. We need to remember that drill and its related social media content doesn't simply "act" on people. Rather, as the sociologist Tia DeNora reminds us, the effects of cultural products—whether it's drill or country western music—"emerge from the ways in which individuals orient to it, how they interpret it and how they place it within their personal musical maps, within the semiotic web of music and extra musical associations."[24] In other words, if we want to understand the true influence that drill is having on local youth, we have to ask what *else* is going on in their lives. We need to actually talk to young people and find out what's going on in their worlds. What are their daily dilemmas and concerns, and how might consumption fit into their repertoire of solutions?

When we start with this question, we arrive at a far more complex, but accurate account of how, exactly, consumption influences future violence and criminality. As I came to discover, it unfolds in a feedback process: Living in dangerous neighborhoods, teens like Scotty and Evan consume drill content to more safely navigate their physical and social surroundings. The more violent a particular driller, the more attention these teens pay him, the more they click on his content and follow his social media accounts. In doing so, these young consumers unwittingly provide the exact metrics—the clicks and views—that drillers work so hard to attract. In doing so, local audiences spur drillers to additional and more intense digital production practices, which embroils drillers in even more disputes over their authenticity. This, in turn, makes the surrounding streets feel even more dangerous. Hoping to avoid that danger, local teens feel even *more* compelled to consume drill content. When they do, they close the feedback loop and begin the cycle all over again.

Conclusion

■ ■ ■

Chicago's South Side may be the birthplace and epicenter of the drill world, but arguably the most successful drill music video to date was created by a teen living roughly a thousand miles away, just outside of Dallas, Texas. The video's popularity is a testament to the global demand for drill's garish displays of violent criminality. In an online attention economy that covets authenticity, it's hard to imagine a piece of content that more powerfully erases the line between art and reality.

The story begins on the evening of July 25, 2016. Sixteen-year-old Taymor MacIntyre and four friends broke into the home of twenty-one-year-old Ethan Walker. The plan was simple: rob Walker of his drugs and money. But something went wrong, leaving Walker dead of a gunshot wound. It didn't take long for the police to identify and arrest MacIntyre. He was released on house arrest while the court decided whether to charge him as an adult.

In the past, it might have been hard for someone like MacIntyre to find the silver lining in a capital murder charge and potential death sentence. But times have changed. A year before his arrest, MacIntyre had followed in the footsteps of Chief Keef, the Corner Boys, and the throngs of other aspiring drillers. Using the moniker "Tay-K47"—a nod to the durable Soviet assault rifle—MacIntyre uploaded his first homemade song to social media. Despite his boisterous claims of drug dealing and homicide, the song hardly moved the needle. With so much similar content saturating the internet, MacIntyre's music seemed destined for obscurity. That is, until news of the deadly home invasion went public. Practically overnight, MacIntyre's clicks and views skyrocketed. He had finally gotten the attention he was hoping for. The pending murder charge was just what the aspiring driller needed to convince audiences of his street authenticity, that he was someone who *truly* did the violent deeds he rapped about.[1]

After spending so much time with the Corner Boys, I wasn't surprised by MacIntyre's next move. On March 27, 2017, he cut off his ankle monitor and went on the run. He announced it to the world via Twitter:

Fuck dis house arrest shit fuck 12 they gn hav 2 catch me on hood

And like that, MacIntyre was in the wind. As his escape picked up steam, so too did his micro-celebrity. Fans flooded social media with words of support, along with impassioned pleas for more music. MacIntyre gave them what they asked for. On June 30, 2017, he partnered with popular videographers and a well-trafficked YouTube channel to release a music video chronicling his life on the run, appropriately titled "The Race." The opening scene shows MacIntyre standing next to his own wanted poster, lighting a blunt, seemingly unafraid to show his face in public. The rest of the video features the young man waving high-powered pistols and flashing gang signs at the camera. These images confirm the message in his lyrics, which paint a picture of his days as a fugitive:

> Fuck a beat, I was tryna beat a case.
> But I ain't beat a case, bitch I did the race.
> I'm gon' shoot bitch, without debate.
> I'm gon' shoot, you can see it in my face.

Despite his apprehension mere hours after the video appeared on social media, "The Race" went on to become the most watched drill music video *ever*, tallying nearly two hundred million views on YouTube alone. The song, barely two minutes long, debuted at number 70 on the Billboard charts, eventually peaking at number 44. Mainstream hip-hop artists—including some of Chicago's drill pioneers—scrambled to capitalize on MacIntyre's street cred and popularity by releasing their own remixes of the song. J Grand, the senior vice president of A&R and marketing at RCA Records, signed MacIntyre to his independent label, 88 Classic. The now nineteen-year-old's Instagram account boasts a staggering 1.4 million followers.

MacIntyre's story is an extreme example of the digital production practices increasingly deployed by young people in America's most dispossessed communities. Most drillers are not engaged in such remarkable levels of crime. And most will never attract as much mainstream attention. But the recipe remains the same: Experiencing few pathways for upward mobility in the formal low-wage service economy and the informal drug economy, these young people are trying their hand in the online attention economy. As social media platforms continue to democratize the means of cultural production, poor black teens like MacIntyre and the Corner Boys are converting their negative stereotypes—as superpredators and willful perpetrators—into profitable online commodities.

Even if most drillers are able to avoid MacIntyre's capital murder charges, they still face a host of negative consequences in their dogged quest for micro-celebrity. From the outside looking in, these costs hardly seem worth it. After all, for every Chief Keef who successfully builds fame and fortune, there are thousands of others who end up in jail, seriously injured, or drawn even further into the streets. A closer view, however, shows that these young people aren't naïve; they know that the odds are stacked against them. This means that their continued participation in digital production is driven by other, more pragmatic concerns. For those already living in grinding poverty, amassing even a little bit of online popularity is often one of the most effective ways to stay fed, clothed, and housed. They might not be able to afford Chief Keef's mansion in LA, but the couple of hundred dollars they earn from a feature in a YouTube video goes a long way toward everyday survival.

But it would also be a mistake to assume that drillers are driven solely by economic needs. Perhaps above all else, these young people are desperately looking for dignity and recognition. One particular interaction I had with AJ underscores this point. The two of us were chatting in his apartment one afternoon early in our relationship. We had gotten onto the topic of role models when AJ shared that he had been actively discouraging his younger neighbors from following in his footsteps and entering the drill world. I was somewhat surprised to hear this. I often marveled at the fact that AJ could hardly walk through the neighborhood without groups of middle-schoolers accosting him, begging to be in his next music video.

"I don't want this life for them," AJ said, a hint of guilt in his voice. He listed a few of the repercussions he was now facing on account of his growing popularity. Murderville had increased their attempts to ambush him. Local detectives had been questioning his neighbors about a gun that appeared in one of his YouTube videos.

"So why do you keep doing it?" I asked.

He didn't say anything at first. He shot me a look of disbelief, as though I should realize the absurdity of my question. "Why am I doing this?" he asked, mostly rhetorically. "If I wasn't doing this, would *you* even be down here in the low-incomes? Would *you* even care that I exist?"

AJ's words hit me hard. My stomach tightened as I searched for an answer. I didn't have one. He had a point. There were hundreds of people living in his neighborhood, but I had sought him out *precisely* because he was creating violent online content. This was his goal, after all: to be noticed and seen by the world at large—by classmates, neighbors, out-of-town fans, and perhaps even curious professors—as a noteworthy and exceptional individual. Like the rest of the Corner Boys, AJ was looking for a way to stand out from the crowd, to distinguish himself from what Junior often referred to as "ordinary hood niggas."

There's something strikingly ordinary about drillers' use of social media to gain praise and feel special. Middle-class white kids on Chicago's North Side do it. America's most powerful politicians do it. Even the pope has a Twitter account, which he uses to demonstrate that he is, quite literally, holier than thou. Spending my days on college campuses filled with tech-savvy millennials, I'm surrounded by social media self-promotion. As I write this, students across the country are in the midst of graduation ceremonies. Instagram, Twitter, and Facebook will soon be overrun with pictures of smiling graduates draped in Stanford cardinal and Harvard crimson. The encouraging comments will pour in. Friends and family will shower graduates with compliments about their intelligence, perseverance, and distinction.

These online displays of love and affection raise one of the most important questions we can ask in our social media age: What can those *without* such privileged opportunities and credentials possibly do to elicit such levels of praise?

For an increasing number of poor youth, the drill world provides the answer. I've witnessed firsthand how the newfound attention provides rare encouragement and optimism amid otherwise dark and difficult days. It feels good to be stopped by an adoring fan while waiting in line at the grocery store; it feels good to be wined, dined, and bedded by rich white women; it feels good to be flown, all-expenses-paid, across the country. But there's a catch. These online performances can ignite violent challenges and entangle young people even deeper into gang rivalries. Meanwhile, across town in safer, economically stable neighborhoods, privileged residents are free to engage in rabid online self-promotion—posting pictures with their diplomas, videos of their European vacations, or status updates from their prestigious internships—without worrying that this content will ever threaten their lives. They reap immense social benefits with few of the costs regularly faced by those in America's poorest neighborhoods. This gap is digital disadvantage. And it's growing by the day.

Although I've focused on the lives of Chicago youth, they're not the only ones capitalizing on the newly democratized means of cultural production. During my time with the Corner Boys, I met teens from across the Midwest, American South, and East Coast who are similarly turning to drill as a strategy for distinction and upward mobility. As I wrapped up my time in Taylor Park, I received an email from Ciaran Thapar, an outstanding London-based journalist and youth worker who has been documenting the rise of what is now being referred to as "UK drill."[2] I recently met up with Thapar in his London neighborhood of Brixton.

There, hundreds of young, marginalized, gang-associated men in one of the city's poorest black neighborhoods are emulating the Corner Boys and other Chicago drillers. In similar fashion, they're using social media platforms to challenge rivals, proclaim violent deeds, and build micro-celebrity. The similarities on either side of the Atlantic are striking. UK drillers use many of the same beats as their Chicago forebearers, and even adopt the same vernacular in their lyrics—for instance, taunting "opps" and even bragging about "poles," despite the relative inaccessibility of guns in England. UK drillers' daily production practices are rooted in the same quest to build and defend authenticity as violent criminals. As Thapar so pointedly wrote in his 2017 article introducing Londoners to the genre, "What artists say, and what they can act on . . . has surfaced as the main currency of musical value."[3]

THE MARKET FOR URBAN POVERTY

Whether we're talking about the South Side of Chicago or the south of London, drill represents just one case of a more general phenomenon, in which urban poor residents use digital social media to commodify their own stigma. Since the early 2000s, there's been a steady increase in opportunities for poor residents to capitalize on middle-class curiosity—to curate and market seemingly authentic glimpses into urban deprivation.[4] An expanding online catalogue of "slum tours," "poverty tours," and "dark tours" offer non-poor, predominantly white tourists with safe and intimate access to seemingly dangerous, off-limits, and foreign neighborhoods.

One of the most striking examples of this trend is currently taking place in Los Angeles—a city "built on tourism and self-promotion for more than 150 years."[5] In 2010, a self-described "former gang member" launched "Los Angeles Gang Tours" in the hope of capitalizing on one of the city's *other* informal designations: "America's gang capital."[6] LA Gang Tours operates a three-hour guided bus tour that stretches through the infamous neighborhoods of South Central Los Angeles. This includes stops at the birth places of notorious gangs, the LA County Jail, and notable crime scenes. According to its founder, LA Gang Tours would have been nearly impossible without the internet; given the company's relatively low budget, its survival depends on its website and social media presence.[7] Even a cursory look at the company's online content reveals an explicit appeal to street authenticity. The company overemphasizes the danger and deterioration of South Central, variously describing the area as a "battleground," the "dark side," and the "gritty mean streets." As the founder boasts, "this gang tour . . . is the only tour in the world that goes into an active war zone."[8] The website goes on to claim that its gang-associated tour guides orchestrated a "Safe Passage" ceasefire among four local gangs to allow the tour bus to drive through the community without being attacked. During tours, these guides keep tourists focused on urban poverty and violence by routinely lifting their shirts to display their gang tattoos and bullet wounds.[9] Like other tours of this sort, LA Gang Tours effectively transforms the conditions of disadvantage into voyeuristic pleasures.

The arrival of content-sharing platforms and mobile applications like YouTube unleashed the newest form of this so-called ghettotainment. Armed with little more than their cell phone cameras, aspiring microcelebrities increasingly upload embellished representations of poverty to build profitable self-brands. Like drillers, they've learned to produce content that draws on as many stereotypes as possible. Consider the online exploits of Felicia O'Dell, a middle-aged black woman from South Central Los Angeles. Better known as "Auntie Fee," O'Dell attracted millions of YouTube views and gained international stardom. She did so on the back of low-budget, profanity-laced instructional videos for dishes that included "ghetto caviar" (a combination of sardines, mayonnaise, and Ritz crackers), "sink chicken" (chicken wings seasoned in the sink rather than a mixing bowl), and "big girls cinnamon rolls" (store-bought pastries stuffed with raisins and fried in butter). With her catchphrase, "Lard is the Lord," O'Dell secured mainstream celebrity, making appearances on *Jimmy Kimmel Live!* and *The Steve Harvey Show*, as well as small acting roles in movies including *Barbershop 3*. Adopting some of the very same production practices as her drill counterparts, O'Dell also created a series of intimate "day-in-the-life" mini-documentaries, and even a rap music video. Following her unexpected death in 2017, media outlets went out of their way to praise O'Dell's authenticity, continually referencing her biography as a teen mother, recovering crack addict, and former felon.[10]

Whether it's drill music, gang tours, or ghetto caviar cooking tutorials, the commodification of urban poverty has far-reaching sociological consequences. On the broadest level, it extends the long shadow of the ghetto over interpersonal interactions, popular imagination, and public policy.

First, these digital production practices neutralize, and perhaps even reverse, the long-theorized benefits of technology. In the twentieth century, urban sociologists predicted that improvements to communication technology would progressively "liberate" urban communities from their spatial boundaries and local problems.[11] As the sociologist Barry Wellman argued in the 1970s, urbanites would form "communities without propinquity"— that is, social networks based on interest and affinity, rather than proximity. This idea became a major source of optimism for poverty scholars and policy makers. If Wellman was correct, poor residents would capitalize on new technologies to form social ties with non-poor and stably employed people. These ties would, in turn, deliver new resources and opportunities, generating a potential springboard for economic, social, and residential mobility.[12]

Unfortunately, reality has fallen short of the predictions of liberation and uplift. In at least some cases, the spread of this technology into America's poorest neighborhoods has had the opposite effect, tethering its residents even more tightly to the people, places, and problems of their surrounding blocks. The Corner Boys have only been able to forge extra-local ties because of their deep and demonstrable connections to their stigmatized neighborhood. The more attention they receive from followers and fans, the deeper their reciprocal obligations to shooters and other members of the local gang. Digital technologies similarly tie non-gang-associated youth to their local neighborhoods. As rival drillers challenge one another, their antagonisms spill over to neighbors and bystanders. Uninvolved youth turn to social media platforms to help them stay safe. This often entails creating cognitive maps that limit their travels and associations beyond their immediate neighborhood. In short, social media often make neighborhood turf, physical boundaries, and spatial divisions even *more* important.

Second, digital production practices reinforce the salience and stain of what the sociologist Elijah Anderson calls the "iconic black ghetto."[13] According to Anderson, the historical association between the ghetto and black people has worked to saddle *all* blacks—regardless of class or neighborhood residence—with a perpetually provisional status. In the eyes of the public, every black person is a *potential* resident of the ghetto. This association renders young black men, in particular, as suspicious, dangerous, and "with something to prove" as they venture into wider social spaces and institutions. "They encounter one white person after another," writes Anderson, "who needs to be impressed anew that they are competent, decent, law-abiding, and normal people."[14] Thanks to online platforms like YouTube and content creators like the Corner Boys, the ghetto (or rather, a particular representation of the ghetto) reaches even deeper into the living rooms, offices, and minds of non-black audiences. Despite the fact that most of these viewers will never set foot in places like Taylor

Park, they're now inundated with a virtually endless stream of up-close, seemingly unadulterated images of lawless, drug-infested, violent communities. Because these portrayals are authored by residents themselves, these distortions carry an extra stamp of credibility.

Hyperbolic representations of urban poverty create a perverse irony. The images that amateur cultural producers commodify in the hope of upward mobility become a source of their continued marginalization.[15] When the Corner Boys travel beyond Taylor Park, they face intense discrimination. Restaurant managers deny them service, security guards follow them through retail stores, and pedestrians clutch their purses as they cross to the opposite side of the street. I routinely listened as AJ, Junior, and the others groaned in response. But these people are doing precisely what the Corner Boys' online content has asked them to do—that is, to view them as violent, cold-hearted delinquents. The more successfully the Corner Boys package and sell negative images of themselves and their communities, the more they solidify these stereotypes in the public imagination. And when their micro-celebrity dreams fail to materialize, they're left to live with the very same representations they helped reinforce.

Third, these production practices inform broader "poverty knowledge"— the "disembodied store of learning about poverty's 'causes' and 'cures'" that guides public policies.[16] In all the time I've spent in urban poor neighborhoods, I've never once bumped into a policy maker (or her staff members) conducting the rigorous, ground-level research required to create sound, compassionate, effective legislation. The sad truth is that most of the policies designed to "help" urban poor communities are based on the same distorted representations of the iconic ghetto that inform the popular imagination. As more homemade, inflated images of willful criminals circulate on social media and the evening news, our political leaders encounter even more evidence that poverty is somehow the result of individual choices, wonton morals, and cultural failings.[17] Rather than produce the outrage necessary to force real policy change, this content turns urban poverty into a sideshow. The grainy YouTube videos produced by the Corner Boys and Auntie Fee become the punchlines of jokes and recurring themes for fraternity Halloween parties.[18]

We shouldn't lose sight of the fact that these digital production practices are, at the end of the day, a *reaction* to America's grossly unequal distribution of wealth, power, and status. They're a response to racial and class oppression. Facing a broader society that has, time and again, demonized them, marginalized residents are appropriating new media technologies to build lives denied to them. Like the Corner Boys, they're willing to risk their lives for the slim hope of a better future. This means that any attempt to curtail this phenomenon requires that we eschew current desires to somehow "cure" these cultural producers. Instead, we need to make a concerted effort to reverse the political disinvestment and economic dislocation long crippling their communities. The Corner Boys' struggle for dignity and survival captures but a handful of the human costs if we refuse this responsibility.

WHERE DO WE GO FROM HERE?

As a sociologist, my time with the Corner Boys strengthened my conviction that meaningful solutions to urban poverty and street violence, even in our social media age, require radical systemic change. This includes a massive reinvestment in affordable housing, viable employment, and other social supports. Yet, as a violence prevention worker, and as a friend and confidante to dozens of gang-associated youth, these years opened my eyes to a number of interventions and policies that will immediately improve lives and reduce bloodshed.

The first takes aim at the obstacles digital production creates for desistance and well-being.[19] By the time drillers come to recognize the steep and uneven price of online micro-celebrity, their public personas have typically grown too large to escape. These sticky reputations follow them into workplaces and other spaces that, before the proliferation of social media, provided the safety, stability, and social networks that facilitated desistance from violence and crime. Unlike those growing up in more privileged neighborhoods, poor youth are seldom able to accumulate enough positive online content to overshadow negative exploits and youthful mistakes. They're less likely to amass content related to school and athletic success, professional promotions, or other newsworthy accomplishments. Moving past youthful online transgressions is made all the more difficult as third-party blogs and websites profit from broadcasting these missteps.

Local organizations can address this dilemma by assisting young people in "scrubbing" their social media profiles and online footprints. This will allow youth to move into their adult lives with a cleaner public identity. This kind of work is already underway in the offline world. For example, the Los Angeles–based organization Homeboy Industries provides tattoo removal services for those trying to leave gang life and its outward signs of affiliation behind. Providing these services in the online context is the next logical step. For-profit companies already offer services designed to remove embarrassing information and redirect search engine results away from potentially damaging content. Community organizations must begin adopting these same techniques. We might also consider the merits of "right-to-be-forgotten" laws, like those currently in place in the European Union, which allow individuals to petition internet platforms and search engines to remove damaging information.

A second intervention targets young people *before* they turn to drill production and similar attention-seeking practices. This begins by creating safe spaces and artistic outlets that provide youth with the respect and self-worth they so badly crave. There is nothing inherently violent, criminal, or anti-social about hip-hop, rap, and other urban styles of music. In fact, as research consistently shows, these genres can be one of the most powerful forces in diverting young people *away* from delinquency.[20] The Chicago YMCA's Story Squad Program, for example, instructs middle- and high-schoolers in digital storytelling, music production, and audio engineering in conjunction with trauma-informed social work. Teens learn how to analyze structural issues in their communities while gaining confidence in expressing their fears, insecurities, and goals through artistic practice.

Third, community organizations have to embrace digital social media as a tool for connecting with local youth and interceding to disrupt violence before it erupts. For the past decade or so, organizations like Ceasefire and the Institute for Non-Violence Chicago have successfully enlisted former gang-associated men and women to function as "violence interrupters." Through long-standing relationships with local communities, interrupters gather vital information about ongoing conflicts and potential retaliation. They contact the aggrieved parties, engage in mediation, and prevent retaliation. As gang conflicts move online, intervention programs have to follow suit. Reports out of New York City show that community members and violence prevention organizations are successfully using social media to de-escalate conflicts.[21] Expanding on these early victories requires a renewed commitment to the individuals and organizations that have been carrying out this lifesaving work despite embarrassingly thin budgets.

Finally, recognizing these young people *as artists*—as innovative, important cultural producers—opens new possibilities for anti-poverty programs. Although the American public and its leaders have proven hesitant to provide much assistance to poor black youth, this country has a rich tradition of supporting cultural producers. In the 1930s and 1940s, as part of the New Deal, the Roosevelt administration created work-relief programs for unemployed artists, musicians, actors, and writers. At its height, Federal Project Number One paid artists weekly wages to beautify public spaces, collect oral histories, produce theatrical performances, and teach community arts classes. These federal programs didn't just keep artists alive; they were an incubator and springboard for some of the most respected names in America's cultural history. This includes such luminaries as the painter Jackson Pollock, the filmmaker and producer Orson Welles, and the writers Ralph Ellison, Richard Wright, and Saul Bellow.[22]

It's time for a twenty-first-century Federal Arts Project—one that embraces and supports people like the Corner Boys. Their controversial content aside, these young men are experts in grassroots digital media and viral marketing. It takes ingenuity to curate coherent brands across multiple online platforms, monitor YouTube analytics, and manipulate Google search algorithms. Why not enlist their skills for the public good? Today, federal, state, and municipal governments are forced to compete in the online attention economy to reach the citizenry. A renewed arts program could employ young men like the Corner Boys to design and oversee social media campaigns to address public health concerns, increase voter turnout, and reinvigorate civic life. These kinds of opportunities will provide young people with income and support, eliminating at least some of the need to commodify stigma for public consumption.

I'm convinced these interventions will immediately benefit disadvantaged urban youth. They're ultimately limited, however, because they focus only on the symptoms of much larger social forces. They don't address the underlying dynamics of structural oppression. They don't eliminate the deep historical injustices that leave young people searching for alternative sources of dignity. As a society, we've allowed economic and social inequality to reach historic levels. We've left urban poor neighborhoods to fend for themselves. And now, digital technologies are revealing the human fallout. Amplified by social media, the voices of marginalized communities are finally loud enough to grab global attention. They're telling the world what they need. It's time to start listening.

Author's Note

■ ■ ■

I was first drawn to ethnographic research because of its power to build bridges, to close the moral distance between opposing social worlds.[1] By offering intimate and humanizing portraits of stigmatized communities, ethnography makes the strange more familiar. More important, though, it makes the familiar strange. It reveals just how inaccurate, incomplete, or unfounded our conventional ideas really are.[2] In this light, it's hard to imagine a timelier bridge than the one I've tried to build here, through a portrait of young, black, gang-associated men. As America's premier urban bogeymen, they've been blamed for urban disorder and hunted by the police for generations. Their recent turn to social media, with their brazen displays of violence, has only amplified public fears. I wrote this book to offer a more careful, sociologically informed account; to give researchers a better understanding of the structural factors driving this new mode of expression; to give policy makers a better understanding of what motivates (and harms) these young people; and to give all of us the tools we need to understand and potentially improve their lives.

In recent years, ethnographies like mine—which highlight the voices and experiences of discredited communities—have come under intense scrutiny. When ethnographers elevate marginalized residents as valuable sources of knowledge, they face two different, but equally stinging, critiques. Against this backdrop, I want to offer a more systematic and candid discussion of my approach to the research found in this book.

The first set of critiques come largely from *outside* the ethnographic community.[3] As ethnography's public profile and readership grow, so do concerns about *accuracy* and *transparency*. Ethnography departs from other modes of social science that often involve large research teams, publicly available datasets, and standardized methods for replication. Ethnographies are typically conducted by lone researchers, who are singularly empowered to collect data, analyze patterns, and write up findings. Because there are relatively fewer opportunities in ethnographic research for peer oversight and verification, critics are now calling on ethnographers to take more steps to ensure accuracy. This requires distinguishing between events directly witnessed versus the statements and opinions of research participants. It also means treating participants' words with more skepticism, checking them with additional direct observations, documentary sources, and other forms of external verification. Failing this, ethnographers risk building their analyses on foundations of rumor, shaky recollections, and half-truths. This risk is further compounded by anonymization. Masking participant identities and field sites makes fact-checking and replication more difficult.

These risks weighed heavily on my mind throughout my time in Taylor Park. From my first days alongside the Corner Boys, I made a commitment to increase the accuracy of my research. Not only do I take seriously the wide gap between participants' statements and actions, I've made that gap a primary object of my analysis.[4] Consider one of the central points running through this book: Drillers (and even some of the most active "shooters") *do not* engage in violent criminality at the rate and intensity that they claim on social media. Across the chapters, I explain why and how these young men so convincingly *say* one thing online yet often *do* something quite different offline. From there, I describe the range of consequences (both positive and negative) that result from these embellishments, as well as the meanings and uses these caricatures hold for consumers. I've also prioritized accuracy on a more fine-grained level. I take care to alert readers when I witnessed interactions directly versus those events I heard about secondhand. I also detail my efforts to triangulate the latter (as in Blue's attack on AJ during the dice game) while noting those events I couldn't fully confirm (the Corner Boys' shooting of Smoky-P and community center teens' stories of victimization, for example).

If my commitment to accuracy structured the book, answering the call for greater transparency proved more complicated. This is due to the specific topics and populations I'm concerned with. I'm not being hyperbolic when I say that maintaining confidentiality is a matter of life and death for many of the people involved in this research. They divulged information to me that, if ever disclosed, could land them in prison, open them up to attack by rivals, and even lead to serious punishment at the hands of their peers. From early on, I assured my participants (as well as my university's institutional review board) that I would mask their identities. I employed measures that should be familiar to most fieldworkers. I changed the individual names of CBE members, other gangs, neighborhoods, and residents. I altered personal identifiers, as well as smaller details of events. My underlying goal was to allow my participants plausible deniability.[5]

But as I read through early drafts, I realized that the standard masking techniques weren't enough to uphold my commitments. Given the easily searchable nature of online content, I had to make hard choices about what kinds of data I could and could not use. For example, I could have strengthened numerous arguments about drillers' lives—from their relationship with shooters to their evolving methods of conveying authenticity—by introducing verbatim tweets, song titles, and lyrics. I also could have provided far more detail and analysis regarding the ways offline violence does and does not escalate via back-and-forth exchanges on platforms such as Twitter. As much as it pained me, I had to limit my use of such textual data, which would have made my participants easily identifiable through a standard Google search. When I do mobilize participants' social media activity, I follow the model provided by the new media researchers Jeff Lane, Irina Shklovski, and Janet Vertesi by "un-Googling" where necessary.[6] This consisted of performing a Google search of any social media text I considered quoting, and making minor changes to neutralize future searches. To help preserve the social meanings of anonymized data, I occasionally enlisted participants to do the anonymization for me. In certain places where I knew readers would benefit from seeing finer-grained details of online content, I've offered illustrative tweets, images, and other social media data from public individuals—people like Joseph Coleman and Keith Cozart—who weren't directly involved in my fieldwork.

For ethnographers writing about gang-associated youth and other demonized populations, internet search engines, message boards, and online forums present a new kind of challenge. The democratization of digital production creates the need for even heavier masking at a time when some ethnographers—typically those who *don't* study criminalized, vulnerable communities—are advocating for even less masking, and perhaps even an end to the practice altogether.[7] However, when it comes to protecting my participants, I'm unwilling to compromise. Rather than jeopardize their safety by unmasking their identities, I've instead taken steps to strengthen external verification and future replication. Taylor Park is certainly a pseudonym, but I don't mask the fact that I carried out my fieldwork on Chicago's South Side. As I noted in the very first pages, South Side neighborhoods were *already* saturated with digital production by the time I arrived—sometimes to the tune of one drill-producing-gang for every two blocks. Since then, it's become virtually impossible to spend much time in Chicago public schools, community centers, public basketball courts, and other youth spaces without encountering some of the drill world's most active producers and consumers. More recent fieldwork in community centers and high schools in south London and east San Jose confirmed that drill music and its associated social media practices dominate teen culture in those places as well. This is all to say that anyone serious about replicating my findings need only spend a few hours in an urban poor community, interacting with teens, listening to their concerns, and documenting their social media use. It won't be long before they're inundated with data about the local drill world. If I've done my job well, the sociological processes I describe should be relatively consistent across locales. Any differences will help us to better understand how these processes are remade and reworked as they diffuse beyond the streets of Chicago. This, after all, is precisely how ethnographic researchers work to refine existing theories and generate new ones.[8]

I'm fully aware that some of the stories I've shared will strike some readers—particularly those who haven't spent much time in the drill world or in urban poor communities—as surprising, perhaps even straining credulity. To help temper these reactions, I include numerous unmasked, publicly reported examples that corroborate my own observations. For instance, I turn to *Los Angeles Times* coverage to supplement fieldwork alongside wealthy white consumers. I verify the profits of videographers and bloggers with *Associated Press* articles. I introduce reporting from *The Atlantic* to confirm law enforcement's misinterpretations of social media content. I establish the spread of the drill beyond Chicago through news stories from California, Texas, and the United Kingdom.

To further increase external verification, I returned to Chicago twice in 2019 to fact-check the details of the book with the Corner Boys and their Taylor Park neighbors. We sat together, my laptop open in front of us, reading over every page where I mentioned them. I paused after each paragraph to ask if I had captured the dialogue, details, and mood of the scene accurately. These sessions, which typically lasted an hour or two, were far more enjoyable than I anticipated. It gave us an opportunity to reminisce about our time together and to wrap up that chapter in our lives. The corrections they offered were generally minor. Junior, for example, told me that he left Beverly Hills with $2,100 of cash in his pocket, not $2,000, as I had initially written. Xavier corrected what I had written about the night Johnny was arrested on the gun charge. I had initially reported that the two were together when the police arrived. However, Xavier recalled that he had gone inside to change his shirt moments before the police arrived. He emerged to see Johnny wrestling with the officers. His absence during the police stop was part of what amplified his feelings of guilt, which he had conveyed to me during Johnny's court hearings. The most significant correction came from Junior, who filled me in on a detail that I would have missed even despite my best efforts. He told me that while the two of us were in Beverly Hills, Chad Campbell aggressively pressured him to sign a management contract. True to what I describe in chapter 6, Chad was indeed trying to build his own online persona by making music alongside Junior and the Corner Boys. However, Junior told me that when I wasn't in the room, Chad asked him to sign away the rights to his music. According to Junior, Chad suspected that I harbored similar plans, and that I would talk Junior out of a contractual relationship with Chad.

I employed all of these measures, and yet I know they're insufficient. Not because I could've done more, but because the recent critiques of ethnography may not be about accuracy and transparency at all. It's a peculiar thing: The loudest calls for verification are almost always leveled at scholars who expose injustice and give voice to the powerless. Why, for example, do critics always seem to require *extra* proof of abuse at the hands of police, border agents, and other state bureaucracies?[9] As we've seen, this verification is typically sought from the very parties doing the harm—as if an official position automatically makes someone's account more objective and reliable. But how an account becomes "official" is inseparable from existing structures of power and privilege. Society awards certain sources authority by denying it to others. I'm reminded of this point nearly every time I share my work with journalists and public audiences. Of all my findings, the one that receives the most skepticism is my observation that these young men *aren't* as violent as their videos, photos, and common stereotypes suggest. I'm repeatedly asked to provide additional evidence—including official police statistics—to somehow prove that urban black youth *aren't* trigger-happy superpredators willing to kill one another over the slightest insult on Twitter. I leave these interactions convinced that we need even *more* ethnographies highlighting the voices of marginalized communities, if for no other reason than to contest the often-erroneous narratives of police chiefs, politicians, and other traditional sources of expertise. At the same time, we can't simply take participants' statements at face value. The most careful ethnographers position themselves as a kind of skeptical intermediary, pointing out contradictions and questioning the political stakes in every account, whether official or not.

The second recent critique of ethnography originates closer to home, from those *within* the ethnographic community. There is a growing trend of vilifying fellow fieldworkers for engaging in what has become known as "cowboy ethnography."[10] This pejorative label refers to researchers who present their work in exoticized, self-aggrandizing, and moralizing ways. Cowboy ethnographers are criticized for capitalizing on middle-class curiosity to titillate their readers and sell additional copies of their books. In turn, they reify stereotypes, potentially doing more harm than good. According to the sociologist Victor Rios, this happens in the form of "jungle book tropes," which go something like this: "I got lost in the wild, the wild people took me in, they made me their king, and I lived to tell the tale."[11]

As close as I may have gotten to the Corner Boys, I wanted no part of a jungle book story. Besides, it would be an inaccurate depiction of my time in Taylor Park. I was never an insider, and certainly not a king. Throughout my two years with the Corner Boys, the social distance between us never fully faded from view. Whenever I thought it had, I was quickly disabused. At first, I imagined the Corner Boys and I would find deep commonalities, especially given my own background. My father is black, and I grew up in San Bernardino, California—a city known more for extreme poverty and gang violence than anything else. Incarceration, gun assaults, and demonization affected my family and friends as they do Taylor Park residents. To my frustration, however, none of this mattered to the Corner Boys. In fact, they didn't discover my racial identity and upbringing until about six months into my fieldwork. The group spent the next week marching me around the neighborhood, playfully sharing this information with their friends—"Did you know that Forrest is *black*!?" To them, I was a university professor whose job, dress, and way of speaking squarely marked me as a wealthy white adult. In a hyperseg-regated city like Chicago, this is about as much of an outsider as it gets. We were reminded of our differences every time we interacted with cops, security guards, and restaurant staff. These people routinely assumed I was the Corner Boys' probation officer or case manager. When I was around, patrol officers nodded as they drove past, rather than stopping and search-ing my companions. Virtually everyone treated the Corner Boys more respectfully when they were with me, revealing moral judgments that are inseparable from race and class.

By shaping my relationships in Taylor Park, my perceived identity di-rectly influenced the data I was able to collect. It affected what I was able (and not able) to analyze and, in turn, shaped the kinds of claims that I can make.[12] In some cases, it increased my exposure to certain kinds of data. For example, I easily witnessed and heard about the emotional re-wards of micro-celebrity. In addition to being a confidante and source of transportation for the Corner Boys, I brought out a fair share of their in-securities, posing a new and unexpected threat to the masculine authority they had worked so hard to build. Few days went by without them making barbed jokes about my car, job, income, and home—all things that, in their eyes, separated me from the streets, toughness, and "real" blackness.[13] In my first few weeks, when AJ and I spent long stretches of time together, the others routinely teased him for "talking white" or "acting school," as if I was somehow rubbing off on him. They also liked to remind me that despite my conventional measures of success, nobody ever recognized *me* in public. Yet, *they* were routinely stopped by fans hopeful for a selfie and a hug. Amid their one-upmanship, they made concerted efforts to expose me to interactions that proved their social value.

Meanwhile, my perceived identity limited access to other realms. This was nowhere more apparent than when I tried to spend more time with the women romantically involved with the Corner Boys. Time and time again, these young men deflected and refused my requests to interview and shadow these women. It seemed that the same insecurities that led the Corner Boys to continually remind me of their worthiness also fueled a paranoia that I might undermine their attractiveness in the eyes of their romantic interests. For weeks, I pestered AJ for Breanne's phone number and permission to contact her. I insisted that I only wanted to conduct an interview. From AJ's response, it was clear he feared I might ruin his arrangement, either by inadvertently undermining his online persona, or perhaps by redirecting Breanne's interest away from him and toward me. I suspect that he would have had a different response to a different researcher. It's likely that a younger graduate student or a woman ethnographer wouldn't have elicited such paranoia.

Reflecting on my own position in this way led me to take even more care as I wrote about the Corner Boys and their community. Following the lead of some of the most thoughtful ethnographers, I continually read back through the book and removed myself from the center of the story.[14] I stopped short of removing myself completely, however. For the sake of transparency, readers need to be able to assess my role and position as I gathered evidence for my claims.

It was a good start, but it wasn't enough. In the social media age, careless ethnographers aren't the only ones with the power to exoticize and typecast. Thanks to the democratization of digital production, some marginalized residents have taken the power to caricature into their own hands. In the case of drillers, the more delinquent and abnormal they can make themselves, their peers, and their neighborhoods appear, the more views and followers they attract, the more profit they make, and the greater their hope of upward mobility. It's a historical development that led me to revisit and rewrite much of this book. I came to realize that a responsible account required directing even *more* attention to the agency and ingenuity of these young people as they try to cash in on their stigma. It also forced me to continually remind readers that these online performances are often just that—*performances*. I repeatedly emphasize that not all utterances about criminality online are associated with criminal behavior offline. In fact, many displays of violence on social media are techniques for *avoiding* it in the streets.

I don't deny that these young men engage in violent, sometimes horrible, acts. They do. I don't sanitize their wrongdoing or excuse the pain they cause others.[15] But explaining *why* they (or anyone) might behave in these ways requires that we think about the broader structural and emotional contexts that surround them. To this end, my approach does what the media, the public, and even drillers themselves so often refuse to do—that is, publicly acknowledge that these are complex and contradictory young people. Despite the sticky, monolithic label of *gang member*, they move through the world inhabiting multiple roles that shape their decisions and experiences. They may sometimes be offenders, but they're also victims. They're enforcers of a violent street code, but they're also sons, fathers, friends, and lovers. They're drillers, but they're also teenagers trying to survive amid deplorable social conditions. These additional identities may not be as sexy or exciting, but they're equally, if not more, important if we're truly committed to reducing violence and improving neighborhood outcomes.

This is what distinguishes reflexive ethnography from voyeuristic slumming. The latter perpetuates reductionist stereotypes while the former highlights multidimensionality.[16] The latter extracts momentary thrills from socioeconomic disadvantage. The former problematizes that disadvantage, pinpointing its structural causes and consequences. Of course, representing marginalized communities more fully and accurately comes with its own complications. Given how invested the Corner Boys were in convincing the world of their violent criminality, I couldn't help but feel as though I was betraying them by presenting evidence to the contrary. Even though I wasn't exposing them directly or by name (yet another reason why their anonymity is so imperative), I've nonetheless revealed that the drill world—the world they actively create—is built on artifice and inauthenticity.

This leaves us with a new dilemma: What do we do when our efforts to disrupt stereotypes run counter to our participants' efforts to commodify them? In today's attention economy, as more and more people vie for micro-celebrity, it's a question that researchers won't be able to ignore much longer. I myself still struggle for a satisfying answer. On more than one occasion, I considered walking away from this project altogether. I'm glad I didn't. In the years since I left Taylor Park, the Corner Boys have become young adults. Now squarely in their twenties, most of them have stopped making music videos. Some have given up the pursuit of online infamy. They've turned to other concerns, like raising families, holding down jobs, and fighting criminal cases. But at each step of the way, they've been blocked and undermined by the videos, images, and other content they uploaded back when they were teenagers. Hearing about their struggles to move on in their lives has convinced me that it's more important than ever to develop multidimensional portraits, for the sake not only of these young men but also of the thousands of teens around the world following in their footsteps. Without these kinds of accounts, we'll never dismantle the stigma and structural violence that tarnish their communities and suffocate their futures.

Acknowledgments

■ ■ ■

This book would have been impossible without the Corner Boys and their families, who generously opened their lives to me for two full years. Words can't express how grateful I am for our time together. It's a debt that I will continue trying to repay for many years to come. I'm also grateful to my other Chicago collaborators, who helped coordinate and conceptualize this research from the very beginning: Jamie Kalven, Chaclyn Hunt, Ava Benezra, the Invisible Institute, Teny Gross, Eddie Bocanegra, William Pettis, Grant Buhr, Alicia Riley, and all the teens involved in the Youth/Police Project and the Story Squad program.

A small army of colleagues and friends helped me think through the research, read early versions of the book, and provided vital feedback. Early in the project, Jeff Lane pressed me to recognize the importance of social media and digital production in the lives of urban youth. Jeff introduced me to the new media literature and provided a model of digital urban ethnography. Across her dinner table, Laura Orrico was the very first to point out the changing role of gang violence and its commodification through social media. David Grazian, Andy Papachristos, and Robert Vargas generously flew to Chicago in the fall of 2017 to spend an entire day locked in a room with me and the first complete draft of the manuscript. Armed with their suggestions and comments, I spent the next year and half rewriting the book from start to finish. Audra Wolf, at the Outside Reader, waded through the book conference transcript to help me refocus the argument. Over quite a few dinners, drives, and cocktails, Harel Shapira offered sharp insights on a host of issues I was wrestling with, showing yet again why he's one of the most thoughtful (and generous) sociologists out there. Sarah Brayne and Issa Kohler-Hausmann— my amazing GJ ghoul crew—provided unmatched inspiration, feedback, and nourishment from the earliest days of this project. I'm so very lucky to have their brilliant minds on my team. Writing sessions and interstate check-ins with my dear friends Anthony Ocampo and Elena Shih kept the project moving forward, and kept me sane. One of my best friends, Rafeeq Hasan, constantly reminded me about the larger stakes of this project and checked me whenever I veered in unproductive directions. My regular Jamba Juice runs and campus walks with Tomás Jiménez have kept me grounded while opening my eyes to new ways of being a scholar, teacher, and father. During our transatlantic Skype meetings and daylong treks through Brixton and Chicago, Ciaran Thapar breathed new life into this project, underscoring the power of music, visibility, and dignity for marginalized young people.

The University of Chicago Sociology Department was my home throughout the majority of this project. The intense intellectualism of the place helped push me to think longer and harder about the work I was doing. I'm especially grateful to Kate Cagney, Kimberly Hoang, Chase Joynt, and Kristen Schilt for tempering the university's hunt for big ideas with real friendship. Stanford University has been the perfect place to think deeply about the ways social media and other technologies are transforming the dynamics of community life. The Department of Sociology is an especially warm and exciting home for me. I owe particular thanks to Michael Rosenfeld, Fred Turner, Angèle Christin, Jackie Hwang, David Grusky, David Pedulla, Matt Snipp, Robb Willer, Jennifer Brody, and Daniel Murray for their early and continued support. I benefited from the friendship and generosity of numerous others along the way: Elijah Anderson, Jacob Avery, Marie Berry, Chris Collichio, Charlie Collins, Mitch Duneier, Ellie Fishman, Anna Gibson, Alice Goffman, Jeff Guhin, Eric Klinenberg, Billy Kraemer, Alex Murphy, Benj Myers, John O'Brien, Josh Page, Mary Pattillo, Henri Peretz, Lorenzo Perillo, Steve Raudenbush, Iddo Tavory, John Tillman, Stefan Timmermans, Alex Wallash, and Fred Wherry. My life is immeasurably better because all of these people are in it.

Meagan Levinson, my editor at Princeton University Press, is an absolute gift. Every one of our meetings and phone calls, as we dove into line-by-line edits and ethical considerations, pushed me (and the book) in new directions and reignited my excitement for the project. I will be forever grateful.

I received generous funding for various stages of the fieldwork and writing. Without support from the Woodrow Wilson Foundation, the University of Chicago Urban Health Initiative, and the University of Chicago Women's Board, this research might never have happened. Some of the material found in chapter 5 previously appeared in Forrest Stuart, "Code of the Tweet: Urban Gang Violence in the Social Media Age," *Social Problems* (2019), Online First, https://academic-oup-com.stanford.idm.oclc.org/socpro/advance-article/doi/10.1093/socpro/spz010/5481058.

Last but certainly not least, I owe a major debt to my amazing family. My mom, Bobbi, my brothers, Matt and Nate, and my daughter, Farren, provided a safe haven and rays of hope during some incredibly difficult years. They continually remind me what really matters in life. And finally, I owe the most to Steph, my unbelievable wife. For so many reasons, this book is hers as much as it is mine. Our late-night conversations, after I returned from long days of fieldwork, completely reshaped this project and challenged everything I thought I knew about teens, trauma, and the young men I came to know throughout Chicago. Steph has an endless well of patience and compassion. I'm the luckiest man alive. Thank you.

Notes

■ ■ ■

PREFACE

1. Austen (2013).

2. The term *gang-associated* refers to someone who is "perceived as, self-reported as, or informally or formally labeled (typically by law enforcement or schools) as an actual gang member" (Rios 2017:20). As the sociologist Victor Rios (2017) argues, use of the term *gang-associated* (as opposed to *gang member*) encourages us to recognize the deep multidimensional complexity of these young people. This recognition is particularly important in the current social media age, as youth necessarily navigate multiple online and offline contexts that may or may not be related to gangs.

3. This area refers to the Chicago Police Department's District 7, which encompasses both Englewood and West Englewood. This estimate of gang factions and their activities is based on a combination of sources, including the Chicago Police Department's gang designations in District 7 (Englewood and West Englewood), and the 2012 and 2018 Chicago Crime Commission *Gang Book*. I compiled these numbers on drill music production by triangulating information from the 2012 and 2018 Chicago Crime Commission *Gang Book*, local gang violence prevention organizations, interviews with local gang-associated youth, and lengthy searches on YouTube by multiple research assistants.

4. Thapar (2017); Vice (2017); Beaumont-Thomas (2018); Thompson (2019).

5. Patton, Lane, et al. (2017); Lane (2019); Hancox (2019); Thompson (2019).

6. Throughout the book, I use pseudonyms for all individuals, groups, gangs, and neighborhoods that were directly involved in my fieldwork. Additional information on anonymization can be found in the Author's Note.

7. On the process and benefits of shadowing as a methodological approach, see Trouille and Tavory (2016).

8. Additional details on fieldwork methods and related concerns can be found in the Author's Note.

INTRODUCTION

1. For the uninitiated, drill music can be defined by its unique combination of sonic and social characteristics, both of which reflect the increasing democratization of the means of cultural production. Drill's grassroots character shapes its aesthetics, content, and ubiquitous role in community life. Sonically, drill sounds a lot like the "trap music" coming out of the American South in recent years. Unlike the hip-hop beats produced during the 1980s and 1990s, which drew heavily on loops sampled from feel-good funk and R&B music, both trap and drill enlist

electronic synthesizers and dissonant melodies to provide a dark, foreboding feeling. The growing accessibility of free and pirated software provides drill with an unmistakably "raw," homemade feel. In the early days of drill, volume levels were often mismatched and poorly mastered. Vocals were frequently off-beat and off-key. Sound effects, like sirens and gunshots, were pushed past the point of reason. With such a low barrier to entry, drillers have been capable of pumping out new songs and music videos via social media platforms and content-sharing services on a weekly, sometimes even *daily*, basis. The result is a kind of real-time narration of current affairs and exploits. Particularly for gang-associated youth, it provides a vehicle to boast about a recent drive-by, taunt specific individuals in rival gangs, or mourn the loss of a brother within a matter of hours. They do so while referring to specific friends and enemies by name, and referencing specific corners, buildings, and other locations, all while flashing firearms, money, and drug supplies.

2. Throughout the book, I use the term *driller* to broadly include those individuals who create and upload music videos and related content that display and emphasize violence, gang life, drugs, poverty, and other stigmatized images of urban ghettos. In Chicago, these individuals are most often referred to as "drill rappers." In London and Paris, it's "drillers." In other U.S. and international cities, they're often discussed under the vague title of "YouTube rappers" or "SoundCloud rappers," in reference to two of the most prominent music-sharing platforms. My use of the term *driller* is meant to encompass all of these, while drawing a distinction from other types of hip-hop artists, most notably "backpack rappers," "battle MCs," and other rappers who focus on more "socially conscious" topics or engage in nondigital modes of performance (see Harkness 2014; Lee 2016). Beginning around 2018, Chicago musicians began using additional terms to describe their genre, including *reality rap* and *pain music*.

3. For a more detailed definition and history of the digital, or "new," economy, see Amman et al. (2016); Neff (2012); Rosenblat (2018); Hyman (2018).

4. Perrin and Anderson (2019).

5. Suri and Gray (2016).

6. In 2009, Exxon Mobile had a market capitalization of $540 billion. In 2017, Apple had a $794 billion market capitalization (Galloway 2017; Taplin 2017).

7. For a discussion of the range of hopes projected onto technology firms, see Neff (2012); Marwick (2013); Rosenblat (2018).

8. Historically, this development coincides with the larger ideological and economic shift toward neoliberalism, in which economic risk shifted away from collective responsibility toward individual responsibility. As John Amman and colleagues wrote in 2016, "American workers now face a restructured labor market that asks individuals to bear more responsibility for their jobs, training, and benefits; a global labor market that pushes real wages down; and a broken social contract that replaces the promise of security with the hollow rhetoric of ownership" (Amman et al. 2016: 1). This drive to self-brand isn't wholly new. In his now-famous 1997 *Fast Company* article titled "The Brand Called You," Tom Peters insisted that we must now all brand ourselves because "we are all CEOs of our own companies: Me, Inc." The arrival of social media accelerated and intensified self-branding by offering new ways to make good on Peters's advice, thereby al-

lowing a range of users to curate and share their "profiles" with their intended audience.

9. https://www.youtube.com/yt/about/press/

10. See Tufekci (2013); Marwick (2013, 2015).

11. Baym (2018: 54–69).

12. The term *micro-celebrity* was first coined by Theresa Senft in her 2008 book *Camgirls: Celebrity and Community in the Age of Social Networks*. Since her original formulation, scholars have advanced the concept by theorizing micro-celebrity not as something one "is," but rather as something one "does," as a set of practices and mind-sets. As Marwick (2013: 114) writes, "Micro-celebrity is a state of being famous to a niche group of people, but it is also a behavior: the presentation of oneself as a celebrity regardless of who is paying attention." Outside of academic circles, micro-celebrities are also referred to as "influencers." *Influencers*, as defined by Abidin (2015), are "everyday, ordinary Internet users who accumulate a relatively large following on blogs and social media through the textual and visual narration of their personal lives and lifestyles, engage with their following in 'digital' and 'physical' spaces, and monetize their following by integrating 'advertorials' into their blog or social media posts and making physical appearances at events."

13. Senft (2008: 25).

14. Marwick and boyd (2011: 141).

15. Duffy (2017: 113).

16. Bourdieu (1996).

17. Bourdieu (1996) famously theorized that artists, like all cultural producers, are located within the "field of cultural production." Like a Russian nesting doll, the field of cultural production is located within the larger field of power. The field of power is, in turn, located within the even larger, all-encompassing field of social classes. Because these fields overlap, the location that any particular individual occupies in the field of cultural production corresponds to the location they occupy in the other fields. These positions fundamentally shape each artist's disposition and strategies—what Bourdieu refers to as "position-takings" (231–234). Stated more simply, artists' social and economic origins—their family wealth, where they went to school, or what neighborhood they grew up in, for example—shape how they think about, interact with, and compete against other artists (235–239). Although Bourdieu initially articulated this theory to analyze literature in the nineteenth century, scholars have successfully used this framework to examine a range of contemporary culture industries—from print journalism to television programming—within the larger political economic landscape (see Benson 1999; Hesmondhalgh 2002).

18. Throughout this book, I use Grazian's (2003: 10–11) definition of *authenticity* as "the credibility or sincerity of a performance and its ability to come off as effortless." Grazian and other sociologists forcefully remind us that authenticity is never an objective quality inherent in things; rather, it's a shared belief about which images, places, and products we perceive as "real." Authenticity, it turns out, is *always* a performance. "Like other kinds of stereotypes," Grazian (2003: 12) writes, "images of authenticity are idealized representations of reality, and are therefore little more than collectively produced fictions."

19. Grazian (2003: 6–7).

20. MacCannell (1999); Gottdiener (2000); Grazian (2003); Bernstein (2007); Wherry (2008).

21. This echoes Bourdieu's (1993: 70) finding that in their efforts to convey authenticity, novelists from disadvantaged backgrounds increasingly came to perform and embody the same stigmatized traits they depicted in their novels. As Bourdieu notes, they began to "accept themselves for what they are and . . . mark themselves positively with what is stigmatized—their provincial accent, dialect, 'proletarian' style, etc."

22. Consumers' desires for lurid tales of violent criminality are as old as popular culture. In *Savage Pastimes: A Cultural History of Violent Entertainment*, Harold Schechter (2005: 43) notes that "there is absolutely nothing new about the public's prurient interest in sensational crime." From gruesome dime novels in the 1800s to "murder ballads" of the 1930s and TV westerns of the mid-twentieth century, violence has always been one of the most profitable storylines. If anything, today's pop culture relies far more on sanitized simulations of violence. As social theorists like Michel Foucault (1977) and others graphically demonstrate, we continue moving further and further away from a society that once felt it was acceptable to treat executions and torture as legitimate forms of entertainment. This so-called civilizing process (Elias 1978) helps to explain why drillers' portrayal of seemingly "real" acts of gunplay and murder attract such attention. With so much simulated violence in popular media, consumers desperately desire a glimpse of the genuine article.

23. Wilson (1987, 1996).

24. A sample of those who have built on Wilson's work includes Duneier (1992, 1999); Pattillo (1999); Venkatesh (2006); Wacquant (2008).

25. Cohen et al. (2012); personal communication with Cathy Cohen, November 4, 2015.

26. See Selwyn (2004).

27. Rideout et al. (2011); Rideout (2015); Pew Research Center (2018).

28. As an extreme example, drillers make an ideal case for uncovering and theorizing digital disadvantage. As the sociologist Robert Zussman (2004: 362) reminds us, "Successful case studies look at extremes, unusual circumstances, and analytically clear examples, all of which are important not because they are representative but because they show a process or problem in particularly clear relief."

29. See Kubrin and Nielson (2014); Broussard (2015); Patton, Brunton, et al. (2017).

30. Kissinger and Raymond (2016).

31. Crane (2018).

32. See Mahtani (2017); Tarm (2018); Patton et al. (2013); Kapustin et al. (2017). Patton, Lane, et al. (2017: 1012), for example, assert that "gang members . . . use Twitter to threaten rival groups (including police), posture, and 'campaign for respect' through the incitement of violence. . . . [T]he same gang violence mechanisms . . . on the urban street unfold online." This scholarship advances a theory of "parallelism," in which online activity purportedly mirrors, or "parallels," offline activity. "Online identities and behaviors," write Pyrooz et al. (2015:

475), "are reflections of offline identities and behaviors, thus one is the analog of the other."

33. Urbanik and Haggerty (2018: 1355), emphasis mine.

34. Academic research on the connection between social media and gang behavior is overwhelmingly exploratory and speculative, relying on self-report surveys and/or content analyses of disembodied and decontextualized social media content. Most analyses take place several years after an initial upload, and often enlist people other than the actual content creators, and even non-gang-associated youth, to interpret the meanings and motivations behind the content (e.g., Johnson and Schell-Busey 2016; Patton et al. 2016; Patton, Lane, et al. 2017). With one notable exception (Lane 2019), researchers have yet to conduct direct, real-time observations alongside the actual producers of gang-related content and/or participants in ongoing gang conflicts.

35. Main (2018); Sweeney and Gorner (2018).

36. See Sharkey (2018).

37. Zimring (2008).

38. Federal Bureau of Investigation (2019); Statista (2019).

39. For a more detailed explanation of this historical process, see Sharkey (2018).

40. Sharkey (2018: 59).

41. As I detail further in chapter 3, the Corner Boys had surprising difficulty locating and acquiring reliable firearms when they felt they needed them most.

42. New research from the Northwestern sociologist Andrew Papachristos and colleagues lends additional support to this finding (Papachristos et al. 2015; Green et al. 2017; Papachristos et al. 2018). Across several innovative studies, they find that amid the great crime decline, violence stubbornly persists in poor black communities. There, the risk of victimization is exponentially higher than in more well-to-do communities. These disparities are even more pronounced when we think in terms of networks, rather than neighborhoods. Between 2006 and 2012, roughly 70 percent of nonfatal shootings in Chicago were concentrated among peer networks that make up a mere 6 percent of the city's total population. What's more, violence appears to spread, much like an infectious disease, within these networks. Accordingly, risk of exposure to violence increases with network embeddedness. My time with the Corner Boys strongly suggests that drillers and their closest peers make up some of these risky networks. As chapters 2 and 3 demonstrate, the larger a young man's micro-celebrity, the more embedded he becomes in the most violent networks. In fact, establishing ties with individuals who have been, or are anticipated to be, shot, arrested, or otherwise involved in noteworthy violence is a powerful method used by drillers to attract new fans and authenticate their violent personas.

43. I'm certainly not the first to make this point. I follow the lead of Fredrick Wherry (2011), Terry Clark (2004), Mary Pattillo (1999), David Grazian (2003), and Marcus Hunter and Zandria Robinson (2018), who have begun to consider how cultural production and consumption structure urban life and neighborhood outcomes.

44. To be clear, the long-standing focus on the material, economic realm has been important both sociologically and politically. For example, by unearthing the

economic functions of gang violence, and by arguing that gangs are essentially no different from other economic organizations in their efforts to control a local marketplace, economically focused gang scholars dealt a much-needed counterpunch to conservative pundits and their moralizing attacks on the urban poor (see Sanchez-Jankowski 1991: 126–127). As the anthropologist Philippe Bourgois (1996: 42) revealed, although gang violence "appears irrationally violent, 'barbaric,' and ultimately self-destructive to the outsider, [it] can be reinterpreted according to the logic of the underground economy as judicious public relations and long-term investment in one's 'human capital development.'" Gangs and gang violence cannot simply be dismissed as irrational behavior. These are not symptoms of pathology or manifestations of the so-called culture of poverty. Instead, gangs and their members are best understood as "innovators," to use Robert Merton's (1938) classic formulation. Denied the conventional pathways for achieving society's ideal goals and ends, they devise creative, though frequently violent, means for attaining American-style economic success (also see Contreras 2013).

45. Drillers present a particularly powerful example of symbolic violence—that is, the process whereby dispossessed groups unwittingly participate in their own dispossession despite (or perhaps as a result of) their dogged efforts to escape those conditions (Bourdieu and Wacquant 2004). Also see Willis (1981); MacLeod (1987).

CHAPTER 1: FROM THE DRUG ECONOMY
TO THE ATTENTION ECONOMY

1. Venkatesh (2005: 4) reports that in the 1990s, roughly 60 percent of poor black youth had "at least a passing involvement" with drug-selling gangs.

2. Venkatesh (1997: 84).

3. Davis (1990).

4. Jacobs and Wright (1999); Contreras (2013).

5. Venkatesh (2000); Ralph (2014); Vargas (2016).

6. See Kornblum and Janowitz (1974); Bensman and Lynch (1987).

7. Wacquant (2008: 58).

8. For a more detailed account of the international and domestic factors most responsible for deindustrialization, see Wolch and Dear (1993).

9. Wolch and Dear (1993: 4).

10. Wacquant and Wilson (1989).

11. Wacquant (2008: 58).

12. Wilson (1996).

13. Wacquant (2008: 57). The total population in the Grand Boulevard, Oakland, and Washington Park neighborhoods plummeted from 200,000 in 1950 to 102,000 in 1980 and eventually to 64,000 in 1990.

14. Wolch and Dear (1993); Bourgois (1996).

15. Wolch and Dear (1993).

16. Kasarda (1989).

17. Anderson (1990).

18. Anderson (1990: 242).

19. Anderson (1990: 4).

20. Levitt and Venkatesh (2000: 771).

21. Bourgois (1996: 85).

22. Levitt and Venkatesh (2000); Venkatesh (2005: 10).

23. Although I was not able to verify Rick's exact income during the 1990s, multiple longtime residents confirmed that he did in fact become one of Taylor Park's highest-ranking Black Count officers.

24. Anderson (1990); Venkatesh (2000); Venkatesh (2005); Harding (2010).

25. See Venkatesh (2006); Ralph (2014).

26. This distrust of the younger generation occurred despite the growing desire among shorties to join the gang and share in its profits. As Sudhir Venkatesh (2006) reports, some neighborhoods showed a 20 percent *increase* in active rank-and-file members between 1995 and 2000.

27. Jargowsky (2015).

28. These U.S. Census numbers underestimate the level of unemployment because they do not take into account community residents in jail or prison (see Western 2006).

29. Sharkey (2013); Chetty et al. (2018).

30. When Junior first told me the story, and when I fact-checked it with him years later, he struggled to provide me with an exact quantity. He continued to hold out his hand and draw a two-inch circle on his palm. I see his inability to describe the quantity in formal terms as yet more evidence of his inexperience dealing crack cocaine.

31. Padilla (1992).

32. Padilla (1992: 149).

33. For a more detailed discussion of the recent transition from drug dealing to stick-ups, see Contreras (2013).

34. In fact, whenever I attended local community-policing meetings, those in attendance tended to blame instances of theft on the infamous and equally mysterious Cinder Block.

35. See Bourgois (1996); Anderson (1999); Newman (1999); Rios (2011).

36. Bourgois (1996: 155).

37. See Hochschild (1983).

38. Bourgois (1996: 142); for a detailed discussion of the dynamics of the "teenage service class," see Ray (2017).

39. Stack (1974); Edin and Lein (1997).

40. It's difficult to pinpoint the music video's exact number of views. After reaching twenty-eight million views, the original video was removed from YouTube. Various versions have since been reposted by fans and other supporters of Chief Keef on numerous YouTube channels and pages. The later remixes and subsequent music videos created by more mainstream rappers such as Kanye West have pulled views away from Chief Keef's original video and its reposts.

41. Drake (2012).

42. Kongol (2013); Chicago Tribune (2017).

43. For an example of one such website, see Hey Jackass!, http://heyjackass.com/.

44. Diep et al. (2012).

45. Caramanica (2012).

46. Rose (1994); Baym (2018).

47. For a more detailed discussion of the "discovery" process, see Harkness (2014); Lee (2016).

48. It's worth noting that Keef did so from a place long regarded as a musical afterthought. If the chances of "getting discovered" were slim even in the entertainment capitals of Los Angeles and New York—where running into record execs by chance sustains the fantasy—the odds were even smaller for those based in Chicago. See Lee (2016) on how the physical proximity to the entertainment industry creates "momentous occasions" for aspiring rappers. These occasions lead them to (erroneously) believe that they are closer to "making it" than they really are, propelling them to sustain their pursuit of music careers in spite of unemployment, poverty, and lack of professional success.

49. In today's digital economy, this strategy is the new standard. Beyond Chicago, in places like Silicon Valley, this has become one of the most familiar and celebrated business models. Tech-savvy entrepreneurs continue to build smartphone applications, and launch one start-up businesses after another, in the explicit hope of being bought for millions of dollars by larger, more lucrative firms like Facebook and Apple.

50. Chicago Tribune (2017).

51. Rose (1994, 2008).

52. Main (2014).

53. Willis (1981); Gaines (1990); Pascoe (2007).

54. Lee (2016).

55. For a detailed description of freestyle rapping, see Lee (2016).

56. https://www.youtube.com/watch?v=vT6Ofz-IZN0.

57. In this respect, the attention economy attracts young participants for some of the same reasons the drug economy did in the 1990s. In the aptly titled article "'Are We a Family or a Business?'," Venkatesh and Levitt (2000) reveal that much of the allure of drug-selling gangs derived from their capacity to simultaneously provide employment and a close-knit social support system—a family. Selling crack on neighborhood corners not only offered teens higher pay and more personal dignity than mopping floors or busing tables; it also allowed them to work alongside their best friends. Corner crews built intense bonds of brotherhood as they collectively solved problems, divvied up profits, and generally hung out, fantasizing about the future.

58. A notable exception is Lane (2016, 2019).

59. Roderick et al. (2006).

CHAPTER 2: ALGORITHMS, ANALYTICS, AND AK-47S

1. Becker (1976, 1982); also see Peterson (1976, 1997).

2. For excellent applications of the art worlds approach, see Fine (2006); Mears (2011).

3. Arguably the most important pioneer in algorithmic curation is Google, with its PageRank program. This algorithm determines the importance, and thus

the "rank," of any given webpage on the internet by measuring its external links to other webpages (see Pasquinelli 2009; Bucher 2012).

4. See Alter (2017).

5. For more technical details on YouTube's video selection algorithm, see Davidson et al. (2010).

6. Tags are broad descriptions of a given video furnished by those who upload them. Drill music videos typically have tags like *Drill*, *Chicago*, *Chiraq*, and *Chief Keef*.

7. In the language of computer scientists, this behavior is said to "train" the YouTube algorithm to better recognize users' evolving tastes, thereby enabling the automated program to continue suggesting content that users will enjoy.

8. Roose (2019).

9. See especially Tufekci (2017); Noble (2018).

10. See Pariser (2011); Hallinan and Striphas (2016).

11. If anything, algorithmically curated content streams have been shown to grow more and more extreme over time. YouTube is currently under heavy scrutiny for nudging users toward increasingly radical, conspiratorial, white supremacist content (see Lewis 2018; Weill 2018; Roose 2019).

12. Bucher (2012); Wolf (2016).

13. In *Twitter and Tear Gas*, the sociologist and activist Zeynep Tufekci (2017) argues that Facebook's filtering algorithm diminished the initial impact of the Black Lives Matter (BLM) movement. According to Tufekci, in August 2014, following the police killing of eighteen-year-old Michael Brown, hundreds of BLM activists faced down militarized police forces in the streets of Ferguson, Missouri. Yet, "on Facebook's algorithmically controlled newsfeed," Tufekci writes, "it was as if nothing had happened" (2017: 155). According to Tufekci, Facebook's algorithm assigned lower priority to the news emerging from Ferguson. Instead, the algorithm provided users with content related to the "ice bucket challenge"—a worthy cause in which celebrities and ordinary users posted videos of themselves dumping buckets of ice on their heads and donating to an amyotrophic lateral sclerosis (ALS) charity. In order to overcome Facebook's automated filtering system, the BLM movement's content producers adapted and transformed their messages and uploads to be more "algorithm friendly."

14. As recently as 2015, Motahhare Eslami and colleagues found that 62.5 percent of users had no idea that the content they encountered on social media was controlled and curated by an algorithm (Eslami et al. 2015).

15. Social scientists are increasingly attuned to the growing number of cultural producers who are altering their production practices for the sake of generating additional web traffic, or "clicks." This is perhaps nowhere more apparent than in the field of journalism. The sociologist Angèle Christin (2018) finds that traffic is a constant topic of conversation in newsrooms, where journalists and editors evaluate headlines, stories, and newsworthiness in terms of clicks. As one newsroom staff member in the study confessed, "We know the recipes to get more traffic . . . kittens and sex, obviously" (Christin 2018: 1403). Hallinan and Striphas (2016) similarly report that Netflix relies on its algorithm and the viewing data it produces in order to vet potential acquisitions and design original content. This includes everything from decisions about casting to the pace of releases.

16. The remainder of the table indicates that about a quarter of viewers had actively searched for Junior or the title of this particular video in YouTube's internal search engine. A relatively smaller portion of these viewers had been directed to the video via an external website or by a video playlist created by other YouTube users.

17. By the time I wrapped up my time with the Corner Boys, titling a song or music video with the term *CBE* had become a taken-for-granted show of solidarity and support, precisely because the inclusion of this term directs the algorithm toward fellow Corner Boys' videos. The group saw the failure to include *CBE* in their titles as selfish, antagonistic, and grounds for informal sanctions. In fact, two members announced their disaffiliation from the Corner Boys with music videos that lacked the term in the title.

18. This technique is becoming increasingly common among "YouTubers" and other social media influencers across a range of cultural genres. Perhaps most strikingly, Becca Lewis (2018) recently discovered that this strategy is used by alt-right micro-celebrities. Lesser-known and upstart YouTubers "host" more popular names on their channels to expand their audience networks.

19. See Dyson (1996); Pattillo (1999); Kitwana (2006); Rose (2008); Jeffries (2011).

20. Pattillo (1999).

21. I devote more detailed attention to consumers' motivations and consumption practices in chapters 6 and 7.

22. See Jenkins (2006).

23. In 2018, Pro Tools retailed for roughly six hundred dollars.

24. I was not able to fully confirm Antoine's profits. After spending considerable time at his studio, watching cash change hands between him and a series of clients, however, I believe that the income he reported to me is accurate. In my conversations with the Corner Boys, they too felt that this was an accurate depiction of his income.

25. Lee (2016).

26. Harkness (2014: 119).

27. Lee (2016: 81–82).

28. This is in direct contrast to so-called bubblegum rappers, who sometimes make claims about gunplay and ghetto life despite biographies that include very little of either. Throughout my time with the Corner Boys, they pointed to Drake as one of the most blatant of such imposters. They know his biography well: Born Aubrey Graham, Drake found celebrity at a young age as a television actor, starring in eight seasons of the hit Canadian teen drama series *Degrassi*. As the son of a well-known rock drummer, Drake used professional connections and brand recognition to begin recording songs alongside some of the most celebrated names in the hip-hop and pop music industries. By age thirty-one, Drake had become the third-highest-grossing musician in the world, pulling in ninety-four million dollars in 2016 alone.

Despite his lifelong distance from the streets, Drake routinely capitalizes on the public's attraction to violent content. His song "Back to Back" is a case in point. Written as a "battle rap" challenging his music industry competitors, Drake raps the following lyrics:

Yeah, Twitter fingers turn to trigger fingers.
Yeah, you gettin' bodied by a singin' nigga.
I'm not the type of nigga that'll type to niggas.

In these lines, Drake unambiguously proclaims his preference for settling feuds through violent retribution ("trigger fingers"). He openly warns that although he may be known for making sultry love songs ("a singin' nigga"), he is still capable of murder ("gettin' bodied"), if necessary. Drake alleges that this is his favored method of responding to challenges, as opposed to feuding via Twitter and other social media platforms ("not the type of nigga that'll type to niggas"). Such claims of violence proved to be a winning formula for Drake, landing his song on Billboard's "Top 100 Songs of 2015."

29. The visual nature of this evidence is key. Across virtually every social situation, audiences overwhelmingly perceive visual displays as more credible, factual, and unmediated than nonvisual forms of proof. See Silbey (2008); German et al. (1982); Mnookin (1998); Stuart (2011).

30. Rose (2008: 136).

31. Auter and Davis (1991); Brown (2013).

32. The camera stabilizer in this case was the DJI Ronin-M, which retailed at the time for approximately one thousand dollars.

33. The need to create this slow-motion effect has increasingly compelled Chicago's top videographers to purchase even more expensive cameras. Top-of-the-line cameras record video in 60 and 120 frames per second, as opposed to the standard 24 frames per second found on entry-level cameras. This eliminates any stuttering or jerkiness when the footage is slowed down to half or one-quarter speed. This has put cash-strapped teens like Gio at an increasing disadvantage in terms of attracting clients. Even his friends and neighbors forgo his free services in favor of more pricey but high-quality video capabilities.

34. I wasn't surprised to learn that Junior hadn't cleared his plan with the rest of the drillers in the neighborhood. He had a general approach of asking forgiveness rather than permission. It was a constant source of contention between Junior and the rest of CBE, which led to more than a few disagreements and even fist fights.

35. Hunter et al. (2016).

36. A similar argument has been made by Pattillo (1999) and Rose (2008) in response to the popular notion that gangsta rappers are "just representing" the conditions of the ghetto. As Marcus Hunter and his colleagues (2016) point out, social scientific scholarship has tended to tilt toward this same focus on deficits and disorders. Although often done with the larger aim of improving deleterious conditions and reducing inequality, academic portrayals similarly run the risk of ignoring the full experiences of being black and being around black people in the city.

CHAPTER 3: KEEPIN' IT REAL

1. On this dilemma, and the perils of being seen as inauthentically "in the streets," see Rose (1994); Harkness (2014); Ralph (2014); Lee (2016).

2. Goffman (1956, 1967).

3. Meyrowitz (1985: 119).

4. Horton and Wohl (1956).

5. For example, among tech workers in Silicon Valley, building micro-celebrity requires posting photos and other content that convey an extraordinary level of entrepreneurial spirit, technical know-how, and business acumen (Marwick 2015). Similarly, middle-class teens aiming to build micro-celebrity upload graduation pictures, brag about their Friday night plans, and post videos of their musical talents (see boyd 2014). By doing so, they publicly convey their scholastic excellence and ease, social intelligence, and a diversity of talents—attributes that teachers, peers, and college admissions officers often reward. For additional examples of micro-celebrities, see Senft (2008); Marwick and boyd (2011); Tufekci (2013); Marwick (2013).

6. Marwick (2013).

7. boyd (2014)

8. The media researcher Alice Marwick (2013) illustrates these key dynamics by tracing the rise to fame of Cayla Friesz, a teenage girl Marwick describes as a "fairly ordinary Indiana high school sophomore" (Marwick 2015: 148). Over a very short time, Friesz amassed more than thirty thousand Instagram followers and a half dozen dedicated fan pages by simply uploading candid "selfie" photos of her daily life. Her uploads—which include her waking up, choosing an outfit, going to school, and hanging out on the weekends—provide a window into the private world of an "all-American" teen. Such "displays of inner life"—whether provided by Friesz or other micro-celebrities—are enhanced by the relatively permanent and searchable nature of digital social media. Social media uploads, notes danah boyd (2014: 33), "aren't just accessible to the audience who happens to be following the thread as it unfolds; they quickly become archived traces, accessible to viewers at a later time."

9. In Bourdieu's (1996) language, drillers' particular location in the larger "field of social classes" prompts these particular "position-takings" and strategies for distinguishing themselves from their competitors.

10. The new media scholar danah boyd (2014) writes extensively on the intergenerational misunderstandings and conflicts that occur between social-media-oriented teens and the adults in their lives who underestimate or misunderstand the importance and meanings of digital spaces in young people's lives. Although boyd focuses primarily on middle-class teens and their families, these dynamics similarly lead to alienation and mistrust between different generations of gang members.

11. Much of this attention focused on the collateral damage caused by Chicago's musical gang wars. In their attempt to flee the scene, Capo's murderers accidentally struck and killed a thirteen-month-old baby with their getaway car.

12. https://www.youtube.com/watch?v=LNzFQ4PNZXQ.

13. https://www.youtube.com/watch?v=vLSqCnwpSXU.

14. Tarm (2019).

15. Goffman (1956, 1967).

16. Throughout my time in Taylor Park, the local shooters maintained relatively low profiles on social media. They typically did not brag about violent acts they had recently committed, instead allowing drillers to brag about these incidents.

17. Collins (2008: 231).

18. The sociologist Fredric Thrasher (1927) was the first to observe that most gangs, regardless of their size or structure, are, at their core, a collection of close-knit pairs and trios—what Thrasher calls "two- and three-boy gangs." This pattern holds true in today's gangs, which are increasingly oriented toward collective tasks of cultural production.

19. See Desmond (2012); Desmond et al. (2015).

20. See Vargas (2016) for a more detailed discussion of the use of police scanners.

21. Drillers' various rewards and compensation are detailed in chapter 4.

22. The complex relationship between drillers and their fans, as well as the income and resources these fans provide drillers, is the topic of chapter 4.

23. The Chicago homicide rate dropped from its apex of 33 per 100,000 in the early 1990s to just over 20 per 100,000 in 2018.

24. For more comprehensive reviews of the potential mechanisms responsible for the "great crime decline," see Fagan et al. (1997); Sharkey (2018).

25. This notion is particularly prevalent in the fields of nonprofit violence prevention, intervention, and research. The scarcity of funding from both public and private sources, combined with the highly competitive grants landscape (Vargas 2019), provides an incentive to overstate violence. Ironically, anti-violence organizations and drillers rely on similar exaggerations of Chicago's gang violence problem to attract attention, acclaim, and steady income.

CHAPTER 4: CASHING IN ON CLOUT

1. See especially Marwick (2013); Duffy (2017).

2. Marwick (2013: 160).

3. Duffy (2017: x).

4. This definition of *hope labor* comes from Kuehn and Corrigan (2013). In calling our attention to digital dreams unfulfilled, sociologists and media scholars importantly remind us of the broader, unsettling implications of a digital economy that runs on hope labor. "Aspirational laborers," writes Duffy (2017: 183), "are often compelled to establish marketable personae—growing their metrics, cultivating skillsets, and unselfconsciously promoting their self-brand—all of which amount to immaterial labor in the service of consumer capitalism." Furthermore, the increasing willingness of job-seekers to engage in hope labor accelerates capital accumulation by empowering companies to continue lowering wages, reducing the number of full-time employees, and exploiting contingent workers. As Kuehn and Corrigan (2013: 20) argue, hope laborers "undermine the very labor market they aspire to enter by continually supplying it with individuals who are willing to work for nothing. Hope labor thus contributes to the precarity of contemporary work."

5. I am referring specifically to Duffy's discussions of Amber, Danielle, and Christina (2017: 58, 94, and 163, respectively).

6. Ehrenreich (2001: 27).

7. Marwick (2013: 115, emphasis mine).

8. Anderson (1978: 35).

9. As I always did on these trips, I booked an inexpensive hotel room for myself. From our first out-of-town trip together, the young men never stayed in my room. According to them, I simply wasn't much fun, which was completely fine with me. I didn't allow them to smoke weed or cigarettes in my room. I also didn't let them enter with women. That, combined with my desire to actually get a few hours of sleep each night rather than pull all-nighters alongside them, caused them to opt to stay elsewhere, usually in their own hotel rooms or in the homes of local fans.

10. Horowitz (1983); Anderson (1999); Garot (2010); Jones (2009); Harding (2010); Rios (2011); Stuart and Benezra (2018).

11. I detail these dangers in chapter 5.

12. Shaban (2018).

13. Terranova (2000).

CHAPTER 5: WHEN KEEPIN' IT REAL GOES WRONG

1. When I returned to Chicago in 2019 to share the book with Junior, he asked me to include this note, relaying his (forceful) statement that he never spoke with the detectives. He admitted that his mom had met with them, but only to pass along his message that he did not feel comfortable discussing the shooting.

2. boyd (2014).

3. Marwick (2013: 160).

4. Duffy (2017: 206).

5. Duffy (2017: 206).

6. Marwick (2013: 127–130).

7. By no means do I intend to discount the emotional and psychological pain caused by online ridicule, bullying, and hate speech encountered by the micro-celebrities profiled in existing accounts. My goal, rather, is to consider how an individual's structural position shapes the type and degree of consequences they encounter. Like the resources and symbolic capital individuals draw on to build micro-celebrity, its ramifications are not distributed evenly across society.

8. Anderson (1999: 72).

9. Jacobs and Wright (2006: 42).

10. Anderson (1999).

11. Jacobs and Wright (2006: 47).

12. Merry (1981).

13. An entire generation of urban ethnographic research has repeatedly revealed that even those who maintain the most violent reputations routinely take on passive, caring, and nonviolent roles behind closed doors, when their intended audiences include family, friends, and trustworthy associates. See Bourgois (1996); Rios (2011); Conteras (2013); Auyero and Berti (2015).

14. Garot (2010); Felstiner (1974).

15. Recently, this practice has gone viral in the form of the "No Lacking Challenge." In the challenge, people record themselves holding firearms as they approach and surprise unsuspecting friends. The goal is to reveal the friends as un-

prepared, or "lacking." Although the "No Lacking Challenge" has adherents across the United States and the world, this term and practice likely originated in Chicago. The "No Lacking Challenge" recently received elevated scrutiny and news coverage following a series of accidental shootings (see Roth 2018).

16. See Jacobs and Wright (2006); Collins (2008).

17. See Sanders (2017).

18. As defined by Andrejevic (2004: 488), lateral surveillance refers to "the use of surveillance tools by individuals, rather than by agents of institutions public or private, to keep track of one another."

19. Harcourt (2015).

20. Jones (2018: 32).

21. Gove (1985: 123).

22. Sampson and Laub (1992, 1995); Maruna (2001); Flores (2013); Hirschi and Gottfredson (1983); Farrington (1986).

23. Jones (2018).

24. Stuart (2016); Stuart and Benezra (2018); Kohler-Hausmann (2018); Brayne (2014); Goffman (2014).

25. Gelman et al. (2007).

26. Tonry (2001).

27. Clear (2007).

28. See Stuart et al. (2015) for a review of collateral consequences.

29. Broussard (2015); Buntin (2013).

30. Lexis Nexis (2014). In 2014, the New York Police Department boasted "the largest gang bust in history" when it arrested 103 alleged gang members following four years of monitoring their social media content (Patton, Brunton, et al. 2017).

31. Schimke (2016).

32. Lane (2019).

33. Lexis Nexis (2014).

34. See Rios (2011); Stuart and Benezra (2018).

35. Broussard (2015).

36. Rivlin-Nadler (2018); Tarm (2018).

37. Gross et al. (2017).

38. Eltagouri (2018).

CHAPTER 6: DIGITAL SLUMMING

1. Unfortunately, YouTube analytics don't provide more granular data than the state level. As a result, I'm unable to determine precisely what percentage of views originate in Chicago.

2. The question of why certain social groups consume certain cultural products is hotly debated. Cultural theorists generally agree that there is a tight correspondence, or "homology," between consumers' socioeconomic positions and their taste in cultural products (Bourdieu 1984). For a long time, we assumed that high-status groups distinguish themselves by gravitating primarily toward "highbrow" cultural products—think opera, abstract art, and literature—while shunning

all things considered "low-brow," such as folk music (see Beisel 1990; Murphy 1988; Levine 1990). Obviously, this notion falls apart when we consider someone like Chad's obsession with drill. More recently, however, consumer surveys have shown that high-status groups are increasingly "omnivorous." They're embracing, and even celebrating, certain "low-brow" cultural products (Peterson and Simkus 1992; Peterson and Kern 1996). We can count Chad among these cultural omnivores. But the question still remains: Why, exactly, are people like him so drawn to drill? What drives their "taste" for this cultural object? Most explanations point to large-scale societal changes, developments in the fine arts world, and generational shifts (for a review of these potential explanations, see Peterson and Kern 1996). More recently, scholars have sought answers at the individual level. As Benzecry (2011: 8) and others leading this approach reveal, "taste must be conceptualized as an activity, not as something that is 'already there,' but as something constituted and redefined in action by the many devices and practices implied by liking something. . . . Key here is the focus on how objects and interactions lend themselves to or *afford* uses."

3. This is the perspective and call to arms of the "music-in-action" approach, which I employ throughout this and the following chapter. For the theoretical premises and past research associated with this approach, see DeNora (2000, 2004); Hennion (2001); Benzecry (2011); Willis (2014); O'Brien (2017).

4. The sociologists David Snow and Leon Anderson (1987) refer to this process as "identity work"—defined as the process of creating, cementing, and sustaining aspirational identities. Identity work is usually most pronounced when people go through major life transitions or are attempting to justify new choices and behaviors. In her ethnography of hostess bars in Ho Chi Minh City, the sociologist Kimberly Hoang (2015) theorizes that desire (and thus desirability) is inseparable from the larger political economy. As she shows, hostess bar patrons draw on their divergent socioeconomic resources and available consumption practices to reimagine their own (and others') position within broader economic, social, and moral relations. As they consume the company and services of hostess bar employees, Western expatriates reassert their own masculinity, power, and desire, despite Western decline and Asian ascendancy in today's global economy.

5. Heap (2009: 191).

6. Grazian (2003).

7. hooks (1992).

8. hooks (1992: 25).

9. hooks (1992: 21).

10. Pattillo (1999: 133).

11. Smith (2017); Santa Cruz (2018a, 2018b).

12. Chiico x Cinco x Casper x Joker x Choo. 2017. *NH Anthem (Official Video)*, retrieved June 16, 2019 (https://www.youtube.com/watch?v=kwt0heJ5Bx4).

13. hooks (1992: 24).

14. Having been present when these exact photos were taken, I knew them to be exaggerations. In Junior's own words, he was just "flexing for the fans." The drugs usually belonged to someone else, the bills were often cheap counterfeits, and the guns were frequently missing bullets or even inoperable.

15. Heap (2009).
16. hooks (1992: 23).
17. For reviews of the field, see Brennan (2004); Parreñas (2011); Bernstein and Shih (2014); Hoang (2015); Shih (2016); Rivers-Moore (2016).
18. Pruitt and LaFont (1995); Brennan (2004); Bernstein (2007); Hoang (2015); Rivers-Moore (2016).
19. Hoang (2015).
20. Pruitt and LaFont (1995).
21. Hoang (2015).
22. Brennan (2004).
23. For the sake of transparency, I must note that I was never able to speak with any of the Corner Boys' out-of-town lovers privately—at least not for any prolonged amount of time. I had initially intended to conduct formal interviews with them. However, the Corner Boys did not permit me to contact these women on my own, even after my repeated assurances that my motives were purely academic. These young men were extremely fearful, paranoid even, that I might say something to ruin their arrangement. Recall that I nearly did this in Beverly Hills, when I accidentally disclosed to Chad that Junior was homeless. I sensed that some of the Corner Boys also worried that I might try to strike up my own romantic relationships with their lovers. Their paranoia wasn't directed at me personally. It was a general orientation. They routinely swore me to secrecy when I picked them up following their liaisons downtown, forbidding me to share their new relationships with fellow Corner Boys. Fortunately, they allowed me to occasionally tag along when they hung out with these women. I was disappointed at first. I was hoping to more fully analyze the unexpected form of sex work made possible through social media and digital production. My disappointment didn't last long, however. I'm convinced that interviews would have had their own issues and limitations. In this case, direct observations were likely the best option. Given how hesitant the Corner Boys were to outwardly frame these exchanges as sex work, it's likely that their lovers would have similarly avoided such characterizations. As my time in Taylor Park would continue to prove, there's often a wide gap between what people say (whether on social media or, in this case, in formal interviews) and what they actually do. For a more detailed discussion of this "attitude-behavior consistency" problem in fieldwork research, see Jerolmack and Khan (2014).
24. hooks (1992: 26).
25. Higginbotham (1993).
26. Pattillo (2007: 105). This practice is not, and has never been, exclusive to the black middle class. Chad Heap (2009) demonstrates that throughout American history, churchgoers, charity workers, and other social reformers have used their humanitarian contact with poor neighborhoods as part of a larger project of demonstrating their own elevated virtue. In fact, as Heap contends, these religious do-gooders are likely the originators of slumming.
27. Higginbotham (1993); also see McRoberts (2004).
28. Wilson (1987).
29. Wilson (1987: 56).
30. See also Anderson (1990) on the erosion of the "traditional old head."

CHAPTER 7: HOMETOWN HEROES OR LOCAL MENACE?

1. Pattillo (1999: 133).

2. DeNora (2000: 49).

3. In some contexts, getting "turnt" (or "turning up") can refer to getting wild, partying, or becoming intoxicated.

4. This ritual—of using music to build confidence and get into the appropriate mind-set for difficult tasks—is ubiquitous in society. Consider the iconic images of professional athletes, headphones cupping their ears, bobbing to "pump-up music" as they warm up prior to a contest.

5. For an example, see https://www.youtube.com/watch?v=8VfOOMUXlW8 (accessed April 12, 2016).

6. I was familiar with this song before hearing Allen sing it, as it contains my own first name.

7. In *Music in Everyday Life*, Tia DeNora (2000) describes how her respondents similarly "work through" bad moods by listening to aggressive, anti-establishment genres of music.

8. See Thrasher (1927); Sutherland (1937); Cloward and Ohlin (2013); Matsueda and Anderson (1998); Anderson (1999); Haynie and Osgoode (2005).

9. Harding (2010, chapter 3).

10. Drill music and its associated online content meet the sociologist Gary Alan Fine's (1979) criteria for determining whether a particular cultural item becomes part of group culture. Drill is "*known* to members of the interacting group, *usable* in the course of group interaction, *functional* in supporting group goals and individual needs, *appropriate* in supporting the status hierarchy of the group, and *triggered* by events which occur in group interaction" (Fine 1979: 733).

11. For other examples of competitive sociability in male-dominated settings, see Anderson (1978); Jerolmack (2009); Stuart (2016).

12. Watching these exchanges, I was reminded of the work of Clifford Geertz (1974: 74), who, in his classic study of Balinese cock fights, observes that Balinese men use fighting birds as "surrogates for their owners' personalities."

13. It's vital to note that these surrogate competitions closely mirror the competitive sociability found in most teenage peer groups, regardless of race, class, or neighborhood. Across the globe, young people pit their favorite athletes, celebrities, reality television stars, sports teams, and video game characters against those of their peers. The form of sociability observed among South Side teens is thus quite common. The specific *substance* of these particular interactions, however—the debate over who was killed, who was arrested, and who snitched—is particular to this social world.

14. See Bourdieu (1986); Carter (2005).

15. In this interaction, we can observe a momentary shifting of intragroup status. Antwan's lack of knowledge about recent rumors about Tay 600's betrayal results in temporary marginalization, while Devan's ability to quickly cue up evidence, and Kenyon's insider information moved these two teens into positions of authority and praise. Yet, as much as Antwan's momentary shifting within the group may sting, he has, nonetheless, fulfilled the minimum expectations of group membership.

16. Pattillo (1999: 145).

17. I wasn't able to fully confirm Antonio's story—he was traveling by himself on the train when the attack occurred. I collected other evidence, however, that leads me to believe Antonio's depiction. In formal interviews, multiple community center teens relayed that they, or someone they knew, had been approached and challenged on public transit for singing along to the "wrong" drill song.

18. Suttles (1972: 22). Also see Rymond-Richmond (2006).

19. Suttles (1972: 22).

20. Like other teens, Scotty frequently mentioned an online discussion board called TheHoodUp.com as a particularly helpful resource in building cognitive maps. The website lists notable Chicago gangs and the location of their gang turfs.

21. In 2013, the City of Chicago closed down fifty schools, predominantly located on the South and West Sides. As a result, even more students have been forced to traverse multiple gang turfs. For details on the policy decision and its results, see Ewing (2018); Shedd (2015).

22. Sharkey (2006).

23. This is one of the oldest and most consistent findings of gang research.

24. DeNora (2000: 61).

CONCLUSION

1. In the words of Richard Autry, founder of one of drill's most popular blogs, "If you see somebody that's living what they're talking about, it makes the music seem that much more realistic" (Coscarelli 2017).

2. Thapar (2017).

3. Thapar (2017).

4. See Steinbrink (2012); Frenzel et al. (2015).

5. Pulido et al. (2012).

6. Towns (2017); Magelsson (2012).

7. Zerva (2015).

8. Quoted in Zerva (2015: 521).

9. Towns (2017).

10. Bermudez (2015, 2017).

11. Wellman (1979); Wellman and Leighton (1979).

12. This solution to urban poverty has been most forcefully argued by William Julius Wilson (1987, 1996) and his students.

13. Anderson (2012).

14. Anderson (2012: 12).

15. See Bourdieu and Wacquant (2004) on "symbolic violence."

16. O'Connor (2009: 8).

17. See Stuart (2016) for a more systematic discussion of contemporary efforts to use police and social welfare policies to "cure" poor people of their supposed pathological decision making.

18. In previous research (see Stuart 2016), I've explored how caricatured representations of urban poverty have become powerful tools used by business interests

for luring mobile capital, wealthy residents, and customers to gentrifying down-town spaces. In Los Angeles, for example, new restaurants and bars have played on the proximity of the infamous Skid Row district and its associated images of comically drunken hobos "to more effectively market downtown as '*noir,* edgy, [and] frontier-like'" (Stuart 2016: 62).

19. Flores (2013); Decker et al. (2014).

20. Lee (2016).

21. Lane (2019).

22. O'Connor (1969); Cole (1983); Mutnick (2014); Griswold (2016); Gerber (2017).

AUTHOR'S NOTE

1. The sociologist Jack Katz (1997) refers to this as one of the most common and powerful "warrants" for ethnography.

2. Mills (1959).

3. The latest (and certainly most attention-grabbing) synthesis of these critiques comes from the Northwestern law professor and self-proclaimed "ethnography enthusiast" Steven Lubet (2018). In his 2018 book *Interrogating Ethnography*, Lubet combs through hundreds of ethnographies to point out what he sees as falsehoods, dramatizations, and factual errors related to these authors' inability or unwillingness to distinguish direct observations from participants' statements and local folklore. A mounting number of rebuttals have pushed back against Lubet for his "hatchet job" style of critique, hypocritical evidentiary standards, and call for ethnographers to behave more like adversarial trial lawyers, like him, in a quest for "objective truth." According to some of the most respected ethnographers, Lubet's critique stems from a fundamental misunderstanding of ethnography itself, from its epistemological commitments to how it refines existing theories and generates new ones. See Arthur (2019); Burawoy (2019); Hallett (2019); Sorensen et al. (2017); Timmermans (2019).

4. On the importance of analyzing the discrepancy between saying and doing, see Jerolmack and Khan (2014).

5. For others employing this approach, see Anderson (1978, 1990, 1999); Padilla (1992); Bourgois (1996); Pattillo (1999); Moskos (2008); Wacquant (2008); Rios (2011, 2017); Contreras (2013); Ralph (2014); Hoang (2015); Lane (2019).

6. Shklovski and Vertesi (2013); Lane (2019).

7. The strongest case against masking in ethnography was recently made by Jerolmack and Murphy (2017).

8. See Burawoy (2019).

9. Lubet (2018).

10. For more extensive discussions of "cowboy ethnography" and the dilemmas of researcher position and ethnographic representation, see Wacquant (2002); Gowan (2010); Rios (2011, 2017); Hoang (2015); Cobb and Hoang (2015); Small (2015).

11. I paraphrase Rios (2011: 14; 2017) here, whose model for avoiding the jungle book trope informs my own.

12. I've always felt that these kinds of statements—about the ways a researcher's position affected data collection—are incredibly difficult to substantiate. Like most ethnographers, I conducted my fieldwork alone. There were no other researchers in Taylor Park with me. This makes it difficult to offer strong causal claims about the ways data collection would have unfolded differently for someone with a different background or position. This is one advantage of collaborative ethnography, which allows researchers to compare and analyze their perceptions and impressions (see May and Pattillo-McCoy 2000). Nonetheless, I encountered multiple forms of evidence that strongly suggest many ways data collection was affected by my own personal attributes and biography.

13. This wasn't the first time I experienced this kind of teasing. Throughout my previous fieldwork in Los Angeles's Skid Row district, my blackness was similarly called into question on account of my graduate student status (see Stuart 2016).

14. Pattillo (1999); Contreras (2013); Shapira (2013); Hoang (2015); Small (2004, 2015); Ralph (2014); Lane (2019).

15. On the perils of such sanitized, "neoromantic" accounts, see Wacquant (2002); Gowan (2010).

16. Rios (2017).

References

■ ■ ■

Abidin, Crystal. 2015. "Micromicrocelebrity: Branding Babies on the Internet." *M/C Journal* 18 (5). (Retrieved November 2, 2018.) http://www.journal.media-culture.org.au/index.php/mcjournal/article/view/1022.

Alter, Adam. 2017. *Irresistible: The Rise of Addictive Technology and the Business of Keeping Us Hooked.* New York: Penguin.

Amman, John, Tris Carpenter, and Gina Neff. 2016. *Surviving the New Economy.* New York: Routledge.

Anderson, Elijah. 1978. *A Place on the Corner: A Study of Black Street Corner Men.* Chicago: University of Chicago Press.

Anderson, Elijah. 1990. *Streetwise: Race, Class, and Change in an Urban Community.* Chicago: University of Chicago Press.

Anderson, Elijah. 1999. *Code of the Street: Decency, Violence, and the Moral Life of the Inner City.* New York: W. W. Norton & Company.

Anderson, Elijah. 2012. "The Iconic Ghetto." *Annals of the American Academy of Political and Social Science* 642 (1):8–24. doi:10.1177/0002716212446299.

Andrejevic, Mark. 2004. "The Work of Watching One Another: Lateral Surveillance, Risk, and Governance." *Surveillance and Society* 2 (4):479–497.

Arthur, Mikaila Mariel Lemonik. 2019. "Ethnographers Are Not Lawyers, Ethnographies Are Not Trials: Standards of Evidence, Hearsay and the Making of Good Analogies." *Scatterplot: The Unruly Darlings of Public Sociology*, June 18. https://scatter.wordpress.com/2019/04/23/ethnographers-are-not-lawyers-ethnographies-are-not-trials-standards-of-evidence-hearsay-and-the-making-of-good-analogies/.

Austen, Ben. 2013. "Public Enemies: Social Media Is Fueling Gang Wars in Chicago." *Wired*, September 17. https://www.wired.com/2013/09/gangs-of-social-media/.

Auter, Philip J., and Donald M. Davis. 1991. "When Characters Speak Directly to Viewers: Breaking the Fourth Wall in Television." *Journalism Quarterly* 68 (1–2):165–171.

Auyero, Javier, and María Fernanda Berti. 2015. *In Harm's Way: The Dynamics of Urban Violence.* Princeton, NJ: Princeton University Press.

Baym, Nancy K. 2018. *Playing to the Crowd: Musicians, Audiences, and the Intimate Work of Connection.* New York: New York University Press.

Beaumont-Thomas, Ben. 2018. "Is UK Drill Music Really behind London's Wave of Violent Crime?" *The Guardian*, April 9, 8.

Becker, Howard S. 1976. "Art Worlds and Social Types." *American Behavioral Scientist* 19 (6):703–718.

Becker, Howard S. 1982. *Art Worlds.* Berkeley: University of California Press.

Beisel, Nicola. 1990. "Class, Culture, and Campaigns against Vice in Three American Cities, 1872–1892." *American Sociological Review* 55 (1):44–62.

Bensman, David, and Roberta Lynch. 1987. *Rusted Dreams: Hard Times in a Steel Community.* New York: McGraw-Hill.

Benson, Rodney. 1999. "Field Theory in Comparative Context: A New Paradigm for Media Studies." *Theory and Society* 28 (3):463–498.

Benzecry, Claudio E. 2011. *The Opera Fanatic: Ethnography of an Obsession.* Chicago: University of Chicago Press.

Bermudez, Esmeralda. 2015. "Salty, with No Sugarcoating: Foul-Mouthed Auntie Fee Is an Unlikely YouTube Cooking Sensation." *Los Angeles Times*, February 25, B1.

Bermudez, Esmeralda. 2017. "Internet Kitchen Sensation." *Los Angeles Times*, March 21, B5.

Bernstein, Elizabeth. 2007. *Temporarily Yours: Intimacy, Authenticity, and the Commerce of Sex*. Chicago: University of Chicago Press.

Bernstein, Elizabeth, and Elena Shih. 2014. "The Erotics of Authenticity: Sex Trafficking and 'Reality Tourism' in Thailand." *Social Politics* 21 (3):430–460.

Bourdieu, Pierre. 1984. *Distinction: A Social Critique of the Judgement of Taste*. Cambridge, MA: Harvard University Press.

Bourdieu, Pierre. 1986. "The Forms of Capital." In *Handbook of Theory and Research for the Sociology of Education*, edited by John G. Richardson. New York: Greenwood.

Bourdieu, Pierre. 1993. *The Field of Cultural Production: Essays on Art and Literature*. New York: Columbia University Press.

Bourdieu, Pierre. 1996. *The Rules of Art: Genesis and Structure of the Literary Field*. Palo Alto, CA: Stanford University Press.

Bourdieu, Pierre, and Loïc Wacquant. 2004. "Symbolic Violence." In *Violence in War and Peace*, edited by Nancy Scheper-Hughes and Philippe Bourgois. Malden, MA: Blackwell.

Bourgois, Philippe. 1996. *In Search of Respect: Selling Crack in El Barrio*. Cambridge: Cambridge University Press.

boyd, danah. 2014. *It's Complicated: The Social Lives of Networked Teens*. New Haven, CT: Yale University Press.

Brayne, Sarah. 2014. "Surveillance and System Avoidance: Criminal Justice Contact and Institutional Attachment." *American Sociological Review* 79 (3):367–391.

Brennan, Denise. 2004. *What's Love Got to Do with It?: Transnational Desires and Sex Tourism in the Dominican Republic*. Durham, NC: Duke University Press.

Broussard, Meredith. 2015. "When Cops Check Facebook: America's Police Are Using Social Media to Fight Crime, a Practice That Raises Troubling Questions." *The Atlantic*, April 19. http://www.theatlantic.com/politics/archive/2015/04/when-cops-check-facebook/390882/#disqus_thread.

Brown, Tom. 2013. *Breaking the Fourth Wall*. Edinburgh: Edinburgh University Press.

Bucher, Taina. 2012. "Want to Be on the Top? Algorithmic Power and the Threat of Invisibility on Facebook." *New Media and Society* 14 (7):1164–1180.

Buntin, John. 2013. "Social Media Transforms the Way Chicago Fights Gang Violence." *Governing Magazine*, September 30. http://www.govtech.com/public-safety/Social-Media-Transforms-the-Way-Chicago-Fights-Gang-Violence.html.

Burawoy, Michael. 2019. "Empiricism and Its Fallacies." *Contexts* 18 (1):47–53.

Caramanica, Jon. 2012. "Chicago Hip-Hop's Raw Burst of Change." *New York Times Online*, October 4. (Retrieved January 5, 2015.) http://www.nytimes.com /2012/10/07/arts/music/chicago-hip-hops-raw-burst-of-change.html.

Carter, Prudence L. 2005. *Keepin' It Real: School Success beyond Black and White.* New York: Oxford University Press.

Chetty, Raj, John N. Friedman, Nathaniel Hendren, Maggie R. Jones, and Sonya R. Porter. 2018. "The Opportunity Atlas: Mapping the Childhood Roots of Social Mobility." Working Papers 18-42, Center for Economic Studies, U.S. Census Bureau.

Chicago Tribune. 2017. "Timeline: Chief Keef's Milestones and Missteps." *Chicago Tribune Online*, April 13. (Retrieved April 14, 2017.) http://www.chicagotribune .com/entertainment/chi-chief-keef-timeline-20130621-htmlstory.html.

Christin, Angèle. 2018. "Counting Clicks: Quantification and Variation in Web Journalism in the United States and France." *American Journal of Sociology* 123 (5):1382–1415.

Clark, Terry Nichols, ed. 2004. *The City as an Entertainment Machine*. Amsterdam: Elsevier/JAI.

Clear, Todd R. 2007. *Imprisoning Communities: How Mass Incarceration Makes Disadvantaged Neighborhoods Worse.* New York: Oxford University Press.

Cloward, Richard A., and Lloyd E. Ohlin. 2013. *Delinquency and Opportunity: A Study of Delinquent Gangs.* New York: Routledge.

Cobb, Jessica Shannon, and Kimberly Kay Hoang. 2015. "Protagonist-Driven Urban Ethnography." *City and Community* 14 (4):348–351.

Cohen, Cathy, Joseph Kahne, Benjamin Bowyer, Ellen Middaugh, and Jon Rogowski. 2012. "Participatory Politics: New Media and Youth Political Action." *Youth and Participatory Politics Network.* https://www.civicsurvey.org /sites/default/files/publications/YPP_Survey_Report_FULL_0.pdf.

Cole, John Y. 1983. "Amassing American 'Stuff': The Library of Congress and the Federal Arts Projects of the 1930s." *Quarterly Journal of the Library of Congress* 40 (4):356–389.

Collins, Randall. 2008. *Violence: A Micro-Sociological Theory*. Princeton, NJ: Princeton University Press.

Contreras, Randol. 2013. *The Stickup Kids: Race, Drugs, Violence, and the American Dream.* Berkeley: University of California Press.

Coscarelli, Joe. 2017. "On the Run and Chasing Fame." *New York Times*, August 23, C1.

Crane, Emily. 2018. "Social Media Is Fanning Violence and Transforming Chicago's Gang Culture with Members Regularly Engaging in Taunts Online That Spiral into Deathly Street Violence, New Report Finds." *Daily Mail Online*, June 13. https://www.dailymail.co.uk/news/article-5840453/Social-media-fanning -violence-Chicagos-gang-culture.html.

Davidson, James, Benjamin Liebald, Junning Liu, Palash Nandy, Taylor Van Vleet, Ullas Gargi, Sujoy Gupta, Yu He, Mike Lambert, and Blake Livingston. 2010. "The YouTube Video Recommendation System." In *Proceedings of the Fourth ACM Conference on Recommender Systems.* New York: ACM.

Davis, Mike. 1990. *City of Quartz: Excavating the Future of Los Angeles*. London: Verso.

Decker, Scott H., David C. Pyrooz, and Richard K. Moule Jr. 2014. "Disengagement from Gangs as Role Transitions." *Journal of Research on Adolescence* 24 (2):268–283.

DeNora, Tia. 2000. *Music in Everyday Life*. Cambridge: Cambridge University Press.

DeNora, Tia. 2004. "Musical Practice and Social Structure: A Toolkit." In *Empirical Musicology: Aims, Methods, Prospects*, edited by Eric Clarke and Nicholas Cook. Oxford: Oxford University Press.

Desmond, Matthew. 2012. "Eviction and the Reproduction of Urban Poverty." *American Journal of Sociology* 118 (1):88–133.

Desmond, Matthew, Carl Gershenson, and Barbara Kiviat. 2015. "Forced Relocation and Residential Instability among Urban Renters." *Social Service Review* 89 (2):227–262.

Diep, Eric, Daniel Troisi, and Sam Weiss. 2012. "South Side Story: A Chief Keef Timeline." *Complex Online*, December 18. (Retrieved January 4, 2015.) http://www.complex.com/music/2012/12/chief-keef-timeline/chief-keefs-new-york-debut-at-sobs.

Drake, David. 2012. "Hip-Hop's Next Big Thing Is on House Arrest at His Grandma's: Meet Chief Keef." *Gawker*, March 12. https://web.archive.org/web/20150313192423/http://gawker.com:80/5892589/hip-hops-next-big-thing-is-on-house-arrest-at-his-grandmas-meet-chief-keef.

Duffy, Brooke Erin. 2017. *(Not) Getting Paid to Do What You Love: Gender, Social Media, and Aspirational Work*. New Haven, CT: Yale University Press.

Duneier, Mitchell. 1992. *Slim's Table: Race, Respectability, and Masculinity*. Chicago: University of Chicago Press.

Duneier, Mitchell. 1999. *Sidewalk*. New York: Farrar, Strauss, and Giroux.

Dyson, Michael Eric. 1996. *Between God and Gangsta Rap: Bearing Witness to Black Culture*. New York: Oxford University Press.

Edin, Kathryn, and Laura Lein. 1997. *Making Ends Meet: How Single Mothers Survive Welfare and Low-Wage Work*. New York: Russell Sage Foundation.

Ehrenreich, Barbara. 2001. *Nickel and Dimed: On (Not) Getting By in America*. New York: Metropolitan Books.

Elias, Norbert. 1978. *The Civilizing Process: The History of Manners*. New York: Urizen Books.

Eltagouri, Marwa. 2018. "The Story Behind the Viral Photo of a Kent State Graduate Posing with Her Cap—and a Rifle." *Washington Post Online*, May 17. https://www.washingtonpost.com/news/grade-point/wp/2018/05/16/the-story-behind-the-viral-photo-of-a-kent-state-graduate-posing-with-her-cap-and-a-rifle/?utm_term=.1901b3ef524f.

Eslami, Motahhare, Aimee Rickman, Kristen Vaccaro, Amirhossein Aleyasen, Andy Vuong, Karrie Karahalios, Kevin Hamilton, and Christian Sandvig. 2015. "I Always Assumed That I Wasn't Really That Close to [Her]: Reasoning about Invisible Algorithms in News Feeds." In *Proceedings of the 33rd Annual ACM Conference on Human Factors in Computing Systems*. New York: ACM.

Ewing, Eve L. 2018. *Ghosts in the Schoolyard: Racism and School Closings on Chicago's South Side*. Chicago: University of Chicago Press.

Fagan, Jeffrey, Franklin E. Zimring, and June Kim. 1997. "Declining Homicide in New York City: A Tale of Two Trends." *Journal of Criminal Law and Criminology* 88 (4):1277–1323.

Farrington, David P. 1986. "Age and Crime." *Crime and Justice* 7:189–250.

Federal Bureau of Investigation. 2019. "Table 1: Crime in the United States by Volume and Rate per 100,000 Inhabitants, 1998–2018." *Crime in the United States*. (Retrieved October 8, 2019.) https://ucr.fbi.gov/crime-in-the-u.s/2018/crime-in-the-u.s.-2018/tables/table-1.

Felstiner, William L. F. 1974. "Influences of Social Organization on Dispute Processing." *Law and Society Review* 9:63–94.

Fine, Gary Alan. 1979. "Small Groups and Culture Creation: The Idioculture of Little League Baseball Teams." *American Sociological Review* 44 (5):733–745.

Fine, Gary Alan. 2006. *Everyday Genius: Self-Taught Art and the Culture of Authenticity*. Chicago: University of Chicago Press.

Flores, Edward. 2013. *God's Gangs: Barrio Ministry, Masculinity, and Gang Recovery*. New York: New York University Press.

Foucault, Michel. 1977. *Discipline and Punish: The Birth of the Prison* New York: Vintage Books.

Frenzel, Fabian, Ko Koens, Malte Steinbrink, and Christian M. Rogerson. 2015. "Slum Tourism: State of the Art." *Tourism Review International* 18 (4):237–252.

Gaines, Donna. 1990. *Teenage Wasteland: Suburbia's Dead End Kids*. Chicago: University of Chicago Press.

Galloway, Scott. 2017. *The Four: The Hidden DNA of Amazon, Apple, Facebook, and Google*. New York: Portfolio/Penguin.

Garot, Robert. 2010. *Who You Claim: Performing Gang Identity in School and on the Streets*. New York: New York University Press.

Geertz, Clifford. 1974. "Deep Play: Notes on the Balinese Cockfight." *Daedalus* 134 (4):56–86.

Gelman, Andrew, Jeffrey Fagan, and Alex Kiss. 2007. "An Analysis of the New York City Police Department's 'Stop-and-Frisk' Policy in the Context of Claims of Racial Bias." *Journal of the American Statistical Association* 102 (479): 813–823.

Gerber, Alison. 2017. *The Work of Art: Value in Creative Careers*. Stanford, CA: Stanford University Press.

German, Charles W., Jerome L. Merin, and Robert M. Rolfe. 1982. "Videotape Evidence at Trial." *American Journal of Trial Advocacy* 6:209.

Goffman, Alice. 2014. *On the Run: Fugitive Life in an American City*. Chicago: University of Chicago Press.

Goffman, Erving. 1956. *The Presentation of Self in Everyday Life*. Garden City, NY: Anchor Doubleday.

Goffman, Erving. 1967. *Interaction Ritual: Essays on Face-to-Face Interaction*. Garden City, NY: Anchor Doubleday.

Gottdiener, Mark, ed. 2000. *New Forms of Consumption: Consumers, Culture, and Commodification*. Lanham, MD: Roman & Littlefield.

Gove, Walter R. 1985. "The Effect of Age and Gender on Deviant Behavior: A Biopsychosocial Perspective." *Gender and the Life Course*, edited by Alice S. Rossi. New York: Aldine Transaction.

Gowan, Teresa. 2010. *Hobos, Hustlers, and Backsliders: Homeless in San Francisco*. Minneapolis: University of Minnesota Press.

Grazian, David. 2003. *Blue Chicago: The Search for Authenticity in Urban Blues Clubs*. Chicago: University of Chicago Press.

Green, Ben, Thibaut Horel, and Andrew V. Papachristos. 2017. "Modeling Contagion through Social Networks to Explain and Predict Gunshot Violence in Chicago, 2006 to 2014." *JAMA Internal Medicine* 177 (3):326–333.

Griswold, Wendy. 2016. *American Guides: The Federal Writers' Project and the Casting of American Culture*. Chicago: University of Chicago Press.

Gross, Samuel R., Maurice Possley, and Kalara Stephens. 2017. "Race and Wrongful Convictions in the United States." National Registry of Exonerations, Newkirk Center for Science and Society, University of California–Irvine.

Hallett, Tim. 2019. "Bits and Pieces of Ethnographic Data on Trial." *Contemporary Sociology* 48 (3):255–261. doi:10.1177/0094306119841888.

Hallinan, Blake, and Ted Striphas. 2016. "Recommended for You: The Netflix Prize and the Production of Algorithmic Culture." *New Media and Society* 18 (1):117–137.

Hancox, Dan. 2019. "Skengdo and Am: The Drillers Sentenced for Playing Their Song." *The Guardian*, January 31, 6.

Harcourt, Bernard E. 2015. *Exposed: Desire and Disobedience in the Digital Age*. Cambridge, MA: Harvard University Press.

Harding, David J. 2010. *Living the Drama: Community, Conflict, and Culture among Inner-City Boys*. Chicago: University of Chicago Press.

Harkness, Geoff. 2014. *Chicago Hustle and Flow: Gangs, Gangsta Rap, and Social Class*. Minneapolis: University of Minnesota Press.

Haynie, Dana L., and D. Wayne Osgood. 2005. "Reconsidering Peers and Delinquency: How Do Peers Matter?" *Social Forces* 84 (2):1109–1130.

Heap, Chad. 2009. *Slumming: Sexual and Racial Encounters in American Nightlife, 1885–1940*. Chicago: University of Chicago Press.

Hennion, Antoine. 2001. "Music Lovers: Taste as Performance." *Theory, Culture and Society* 18 (5):1–22.

Hesmondhalgh, David. 2002. *The Cultural Industries*. London: Sage.

Higginbotham, Evelyn Brooks. 1993. *Righteous Discontent: The Women's Movement in the Black Baptist Church, 1880–1920*. Cambridge, MA: Harvard University Press.

Hirschi, Travis, and Michael Gottfredson. 1983. "Age and the Explanation of Crime." *American Journal of Sociology* 89 (3):552–584.

Hoang, Kimberly Kay. 2015. *Dealing in Desire: Asian Ascendancy, Western Decline, and the Hidden Currencies of Global Sex Work*. Berkeley: University of California Press.

Hochschild, Arlie. 1983. *The Managed Heart: Commercialization of Human Feeling*. Berkeley: University of California Press.

hooks, bell. 1992. "Eating the Other: Desire and Resistance." In *Black Looks: Race and Representation*. Boston: South End Press.

Horowitz, Ruth. 1983. *Honor and the American Dream: Culture and Identity in a Chicano Community*. New Brunswick, NJ: Rutgers University Press.

Horton, Donald, and R. Richard Wohl. 1956. "Mass Communication and Para-Social Interaction: Observations on Intimacy at a Distance." *Psychiatry* 19 (3):215–229.

Hunter, Marcus Anthony, Mary Pattillo, Zandria F. Robinson, and Keeanga-Yamahtta Taylor. 2016. "Black Placemaking: Celebration, Play, and Poetry." *Theory, Culture and Society* 33 (7–8):31–56.

Hunter, Marcus Anthony, and Zandria F. Robinson. 2018. *Chocolate Cities: The Black Map of American Life*. Oakland: University of California Press.

Hyman, Luis. 2018. *Temp: The Real Story of What Happened to Your Salary, Benefits, and Job Security*. New York: Penguin Books.

Jacobs, Bruce A., and Richard Wright. 1999. "Stick-Up, Street Culture, and Offender Motivation." *Criminology* 37 (1):149–174.

Jacobs, Bruce A., and Richard Wright. 2006. *Street Justice: Retaliation in the Criminal Underworld*. Cambridge: Cambridge University Press.

Jargowsky, Paul A. 2015. "Architecture of Segregation: Civil Unrest, the Concentration of Poverty, and Public Policy." *Century Foundation*. https://tcf.org/content/report/architecture-of-segregation/?agreed=1.

Jeffries, Michael P. 2011. *Thug Life: Race, Gender, and the Meaning of Hip-Hop*. Chicago: University of Chicago Press.

Jerolmack, Colin. 2009. "Primary Groups and Cosmopolitan Ties: The Rooftop Pigeon Flyers of New York City." *Ethnography* 10 (4):435–457.

Jerolmack, Colin, and Shamus Khan. 2014. "Talk Is Cheap: Ethnography and the Attitudinal Fallacy." *Sociological Methods and Research* 43 (2):178–209.

Jerolmack, Colin, and Alexandra K. Murphy. 2017. "The Ethical Dilemmas and Social Scientific Trade-Offs of Masking in Ethnography." *Sociological Methods and Research* 48 (4):801–827.

Johnson, Joseph D., and Natalie M. Schell-Busey. 2016. "Old Message in a New Bottle: Taking Gang Rivalries Online through Rap Battle Music Videos on YouTube." *Journal of Qualitative Criminal Justice and Criminology* 4(1): 42–81.

Jones, Nikki. 2009. *Between Good and Ghetto: African American Girls and Inner-City Violence*. New Brunswick, NJ: Rutgers University Press.

Jones, Nikki. 2018. *The Chosen Ones: Black Men and the Politics of Redemption*. Oakland: University of California Press.

Kapustin, Max, Jens Ludwig, Marc Punkay, Kimberley Smith, Lauren Speigel, and David Welgus. 2017. "Gun Violence in Chicago, 2016." University of Chicago Crime Lab.

Kasarda, John D. 1989. "Urban Industrial Transition and the Underclass." *Annals of the American Academy of Political and Social Science* 501 (1):26–47.

Katz, Jack. 1997. "Ethnography's Warrants." *Sociological Methods and Research* 25 (4):391–423.

Kissinger, Bill, and Marcella Raymond. 2016. "Social Media to Blame for Violent Start to 2016: Chicago Police." *WGN News Online*, January 13. https://wgntv.com/2016/01/13/chicago-police-make-shooting-arrests/.

Kitwana, Bakari. 2006. *Why White Kids Love Hip Hop*. New York: Basic Books.

Kohler-Hausmann, Issa. 2018. *Misdemeanorland: Criminal Courts and Social Control in an Age of Broken Windows Policing*. Princeton, NJ: Princeton University Press.

Kongol, Mark. 2013. "Police Shot at Chief Keef after Rapper Pointed Gun at Them." *DNAInfo*, January 14. (Retrieved November 2, 2018.) https://www.dnainfo.com/chicago/20130114/chicago/cops-shot-at-chief-keef-2011-after-teen-rapper-pointed-gun-police-say.

Kornblum, William, and Morris Janowitz. 1974. *Blue Collar Community*. Chicago: University of Chicago Press Chicago.

Kubrin, Charis E., and Erik Nielson. 2014. "Rap on Trial." *Race and Justice* 4 (3): 185–211.

Kuehn, Kathleen, and Thomas F. Corrigan. 2013. "Hope Labor: The Role of Employment Prospects in Online Social Production." *The Political Economy of Communication* 1 (1):9–25.

Lane, Jeffrey. 2016. "The Digital Street: An Ethnographic Study of Networked Street Life in Harlem." *American Behavioral Scientist* 60 (1):43–58.

Lane, Jeffrey. 2019. *The Digital Street*. New York: Oxford University Press.

Lee, Jooyoung. 2016. *Blowin' Up: Rap Dreams in South Central*. Chicago: University of Chicago Press.

Levine, Lawrence W. 1990. *Highbrow/Lowbrow: The Emergence of Cultural Hierarchy in America*. Cambridge, MA: Harvard University Press.

Levitt, Steven D., and Sudhir Alladi Venkatesh. 2000. "An Economic Analysis of a Drug-Selling Gang's Finances." *Quarterly Journal of Economics* 115 (3):755–789.

Lewis, Becca. 2018. "Alternative Influence: Broadcasting the Reactionary Right on YouTube." Data and Society Institute. https://datasociety.net/wp-content/uploads/2018/09/DS_Alternative_Influence.pdf.

Lexis Nexis. 2014. "Law Enforcement's Usage of Social Media for Investigations." *Lexis Nexis Risk Solutions*. https://risk.lexisnexis.com/insights-resources/white-paper/law-enforcement-usage-of-social-media-for-investigations.

Lubet, Steven. 2018. *Interrogating Ethnography: Why Evidence Matters*. New York: Oxford University Press.

MacCannell, Dean. 1999. *The Tourist: A New Theory of the Leisure Class*. Berkeley: University of California Press.

MacLeod, Jay. 1987. *Ain't No Makin' It: Aspirations and Attainment in a Low-Income Neighborhood*. Boulder, CO: Westview Press.

Magelssen, Scott. 2012. "You No Longer Need to Imagine." In *The Cultural Moment in Tourism*, edited by Laurajane Smith, Emma Waterton and Steve Watson. New York: Routledge.

Mahtani, Shibani. 2017. "Social Media Emerges as New Frontier in Fight against Violent Crime." *Wall Street Journal Online*, November 24. (Retrieved November 25, 2017.) https://www.wsj.com/articles/social-media-emerges-as-newfrontier-in-fight-against-violent-crime-1511528400.

Main, Frank. 2014. "The Most Dangerous Block in Chicago, Once Home to Michelle Obama." *Chicago Sun Times Online*, November 2. (Retrieved January 5, 2015.) https://chicago.suntimes.com/news/the-most-dangerous-block-in-chicago-o-block-once-home-to-michelle-obama/.

Main, Frank. 2018. "Murder 'Clearance' Rate in Chicago Hit a New Low in 2017." *Chicago Tribune Online*, February 9. https://chicago.suntimes.com/news /murder-clearance-rate-in-chicago-hit-new-low-in-2017/.

Maruna, Shadd. 2001. *Making Good: How Ex-Convicts Reform and Rebuild Their Lives*. Washington, DC: American Psychological Association.

Marwick, Alice E. 2013. *Status Update: Celebrity, Publicity, and Branding in the Social Media Age*. New Haven, CT: Yale University Press.

Marwick, Alice E. 2015. "Instafame: Luxury Selfies in the Attention Economy." *Public Culture* 27 (1 (75)):137–160.

Marwick, Alice E., and danah boyd. 2011. "To See and Be Seen: Celebrity Practice on Twitter." *Convergence: The International Journal of Research into New Media Technologies* 17 (2):139–158.

Matsueda, Ross L., and Kathleen Anderson. 1998. "The Dynamics of Delinquent Peers and Delinquent Behavior." *Criminology* 36 (2):269–308.

May, Reuben A. Buford, and Mary Pattillo-McCoy. 2000. "Do You See What I See? Examining a Collaborative Ethnography." *Qualitative Inquiry* 6 (1):65–87.

McRoberts, Omar M. 2004. *Streets of Glory: Church and Community in a Black Urban Neighborhood*. Chicago: University of Chicago Press.

Mears, Ashley. 2011. *Pricing Beauty: The Making of a Fashion Model*. Berkeley: University of California Press.

Merry, Sally Engle. 1981. *Urban Danger: Life in a Neighborhood of Strangers*. Philadelphia: Temple University Press.

Merton, Robert K. 1938. "Social Structure and Anomie." *American Sociological Review* 3 (5):672–682.

Meyrowitz, Joshua. 1985. *No Sense of Place: The Impact of Electronic Media on Social Behavior*. New York: Oxford University Press.

Mills, C. Wright. 1959. *The Sociological Imagination*. New York: Oxford University Press.

Mnookin, Jennifer L. 1998. "The Image of Truth: Photographic Evidence and the Power of Analogy." *Yale Journal of Law and Humanities* 10:1.

Moskos, Peter. 2008. *Cop in the Hood: My Year Policing Baltimore's Eastern District* Princeton, NJ: Princeton University Press.

Murphy, Raymond. 1988. *Social Closure: The Theory of Monopolization and Exclusion*. Oxford: Clarendon Press.

Mutnick, Deborah. 2014. "Toward a Twenty-First-Century Federal Writers' Project." *College English* 77 (2):124–145.

Neff, Gina. 2012. *Venture Labor: Work and the Burden of Risk in Innovative Industries*. Cambridge, MA: Massachusetts Institute of Technology Press.

Newman, Katherine. 1999. *No Shame in My Game: The Working Poor in the Inner City*. New York: Russell Sage Foundation.

Noble, Safiya Umoja. 2018. *Algorithms of Oppression: How Search Engines Reinforce Racism*. New York: New York University Press.

O'Brien, John. 2017. *Keeping It Halal: The Everyday Lives of Muslim American Teenage Boys*. Princeton, NJ: Princeton University Press.

O'Connor, Alice. 2009. *Poverty Knowledge: Social Science, Social Policy, and the Poor in Twentieth-Century US History*. Princeton, NJ: Princeton University Press.

O'Connor, Francis V. 1969. "The New Deal Art Projects in New York." *American Art Journal* 1 (2):58–79.

Padilla, Felix M. 1992. *The Gang as an American Enterprise*. New Brunswick, NJ: Rutgers University Press.

Papachristos, Andrew V., Christopher Wildeman, and Elizabeth Roberto. 2015. "Tragic, but Not Random: The Social Contagion of Nonfatal Gunshot Injuries." *Social Science and Medicine* 125 (1):139–150.

Papachristos, Andrew V., Noli Brazil, and Tony Cheng. 2018. "Understanding the Crime Gap: Violence and Inequality in an American City." *City and Community* 17 (4):1051–1074.

Pariser, Eli. 2011. *The Filter Bubble: How the New Personalized Web Is Changing What We Read and How We Think*. New York: Penguin.

Parreñas, Rhacel. 2011. *Illicit Flirtations: Labor, Migration, and Sex Trafficking in Tokyo*. Palo Alto, CA: Stanford University Press.

Pascoe, C. J. 2007. *Dude, You're a Fag: Masculinity and Sexuality in High School*. Berkeley: University of California Press.

Pasquinelli, Matteo. 2009. "Google's PageRank Algorithm: A Diagram of Cognitive Capitalism and the Rentier of the Common Intellect." In *Deep Search: The Politics of Search Beyond Google*, edited by Konrad Becker and Felix Stalder. London: Transaction Publishers.

Pattillo, Mary. 1999. *Black Picket Fences: Privilege and Peril among the Black Middle Class*. Chicago: University of Chicago Press.

Pattillo, Mary. 2007. *Black on the Block: The Politics of Race and Class in the City*. Chicago: University of Chicago Press.

Patton, Desmond Upton, Robert D. Eschmann, and Dirk A. Butler. 2013. "Internet Banging: New Trends in Social Media, Gang Violence, Masculinity and Hip Hop." *Computers in Human Behavior* 29 (5):A54-A59.

Patton, Desmond Upton, Robert D. Eschmann, Caitlin Elsaesser, and Eddie Bocanegra. 2016. "Sticks, Stones and Facebook Accounts: What Violence Outreach Workers Know about Social Media and Urban-Based Gang Violence in Chicago." *Computers in Human Behavior* 65:591–600.

Patton, Desmond Upton, Douglas-Wade Brunton, Andrea Dixon, Reuben Jonathan Miller, Patrick Leonard, and Rose Hackman. 2017. "Stop and Frisk Online: Theorizing Everyday Racism in Digital Policing in the Use of Social Media for Identification of Criminal Conduct and Associations." *Social Media and Society* 3 (3):1–10.

Patton, Desmond U., Jeffrey Lane, Patrick Leonard, Jamie Macbeth, and Jocelyn R. Smith Lee. 2017. "Gang Violence on the Digital Street: Case Study of a South Side Chicago Gang Member's Twitter Communication." *New Media and Society* 19 (7):1000–1018.

Perrin, Andrew, and Monica Anderson. 2019. "Share of U.S. Adults Using Social Media, including Facebook, Is Mostly Unchanged since 2018." Pew Research Center. https://www.pewresearch.org/fact-tank/2019/04/10/share-of-u -s-adults-using-social-media-including-facebook-is-mostly-unchanged-since -2018/.

Peters, Tom. 1997. "The Brand Called You." *Fast Company*, August 31, 83–90.

Peterson, Richard A. 1976. "The Production of Culture: A Prolegomenon." *American Behavioral Scientist* 19 (6):669–684.

Peterson, Richard A. 1997. *Creating Country Music: Fabricating Authenticity*. Chicago: University of Chicago Press.

Peterson, Richard A., and Roger M. Kern. 1996. "Changing Highbrow Taste: From Snob to Omnivore." *American Sociological Review* 61 (5):900–907.

Peterson, Richard A., and Albert Simkus. 1992. "How Musical Tastes Mark Occupational Status Groups." In *Cultivating Differences: Symbolic Boundaries and the Making of Inequality*, edited by Michèle Lamont and Marcel Fourier. Chicago: University of Chicago Press.

Pruitt, Deborah, and Suzanne LaFont. 1995. "For Love and Money: Romance Tourism in Jamaica." *Annals of Tourism Research* 22 (2):422–440.

Pulido, Laura, Laura R. Barraclough, and Wendy Cheng. 2012. *A People's Guide to Los Angeles*. Berkeley: University of California Press.

Pyrooz, David C., Scott H. Decker, and Richard K. Moule Jr. 2015. "Criminal and Routine Activities in Online Settings: Gangs, Offenders, and the Internet." *Justice Quarterly* 32 (3):471–499.

Ralph, Laurence. 2014. *Renegade Dreams: Living through Injury in Gangland Chicago*. Chicago: University of Chicago Press.

Ray, Ranita. 2017. *The Making of a Teenage Service Class: Poverty and Mobility in an American City*. Oakland: University of California Press.

Rideout, Vicky. 2015. "Common Sense Census: Media Use by Tweens and Teens." *Common Sense Media*. https://www.commonsensemedia.org/sites/default/files/uploads/research/census_researchreport.pdf.

Rideout, Victoria, Alexis Laricella, and Ellen Wartella. 2011. "Children, Media and Race: Media Use among White, Black, Hispanic and Asian American Children." Northwestern University Center on Media and Human Development. http://cmhd.northwestern.edu/wp-content/uploads/2011/06/SOCconfReportSingleFinal-1.pdf.

Rios, Victor. 2011. *Punished: Policing the Lives of Black and Latino Boys*. New York: New York University Press.

Rios, Victor M. 2017. *Human Targets: Schools, Police, and the Criminalization of Latino Youth*. Chicago: University of Chicago Press.

Rivers-Moore, Megan. 2016. *Gringo Gulch: Sex, Tourism, and Social Mobility in Costa Rica*. Chicago: University of Chicago Press.

Rivlin-Nadler, Max. 2018. "How Philadelphia's Social Media-Driven Gang Policing Is Stealing Years from Young People." *The Appeal*, January 19. https://theappeal.org/how-philadelphias-social-media-driven-gang-policing-is-stealing-years-from-young-people-fa6a8dacead9/.

Roderick, Melissa, Jenny Nagaoka, Elaine Allensworth, G. Stoker, Macarena Correa, and V. Coca. 2006. "From High School to the Future, a First Look at Chicago Public School Graduates: College Enrollment, College Preparation, and Graduation from Four-Year Colleges." *Consortium on Chicago School Research* https://consortium.uchicago.edu/publications/high-school-future-first-look-chicago-public-school-graduates-college-enrollment.

Roose, Kevin. 2019. "The Making of a YouTube Radical." *New York Times Online*, June 8. https://www.nytimes.com/interactive/2019/06/08/technology/youtube-radical.html.

Rose, Tricia. 1994. *Black Noise: Rap Music and Black Culture in Contemporary America*. Hanover, NH: University Press of New England.

Rose, Tricia. 2008. *The Hip Hop Wars: What We Talk About When We Talk About Hip Hop—and Why It Matters*. New York: Basic Books.

Rosenblat, Alex. 2018. *Uberland: How Algorithms Are Rewriting the Rules of Work*. Oakland: University of California Press.

Roth, Daniel. 2018. "Internet Craze the 'No Lackin Challenge' Where People Pull Guns on Each Other to Film Their Response Goes Horribly Wrong When a Memphis Boy, 17, Is Shot." *Daily Mail.com*, January 28. https://www.dailymail.co.uk/news/article-5321381/No-lackin-challenge-stunt-goes-horribly-wrong.html.

Rymond-Richmond, Wenona. 2006. "Transforming Communities: Formal and Informal Mechanisms of Social Control." In *The Many Colors of Crime: Inequalities of Race, Ethnicity, and Crime in America*, edited by Ruth D. Peterson, Lauren J. Krivo, and John Hagan. New York: New York University Press.

Sampson, Robert J., and John H. Laub. 1992. "Crime and Deviance in the Life Course." *Annual Review of Sociology* 18:63–84.

Sampson, Robert J., and John H. Laub. 1995. *Crime in the Making: Pathways and Turning Points through Life*. Cambridge, MA: Harvard University Press.

Sanchez-Jankowski, Martin. 1991. *Islands in the Street: Gangs and American Urban Society*. Berkeley: University of California Press.

Sanders, William. 2017. *Gangbangs and Drive-Bys: Grounded Culture and Juvenile Gang Violence*. New York: Routledge.

Santa Cruz, Nicole. 2018a. "Palos Verdes Estates Man Not Guilty in Suspected Shooting." *Los Angeles Times*, July 24, B1.

Santa Cruz, Nicole. 2018b. "Acquittal for Wealthy Teenager Is Scrutinized." *Los Angeles Times*, September 23, B1.

Schechter, Harold. 2005. *Savage Pastimes: A Cultural History of Violent Entertainment*. New York: St. Martin's Press.

Schimke, David. 2016. "Twin City Cops' Favorite Tool for Investigating Crimes These Days: Facebook." *Minneapolis Post*, August 15. https://www.minnpost.com/politics-policy/2016/08/twin-cities-cops-favorite-tool-investigating-crimes-these-days-facebook/.

Shklovski, Irina, and Janet Vertesi. 2013. "'Ungoogling' Publications: The Ethics and Problems of Anonymization." In *ACM Conference on Human Factors in Computing Systems*. New York: ACM.

Selwyn, Neil. 2004. "Reconsidering Political and Popular Understandings of the Digital Divide." *New Media and Society* 6 (3):341–362.

Senft, Theresa M. 2008. *Camgirls: Celebrity and Community in the Age of Social Networks*. New York: Peter Lang.

Shaban, Hamza. 2018. "Google Parent Alphabet Reports Soaring Ad Revenue Despite YouTube Backlash." *Washington Post Online*, February 1. https://www.washingtonpost.com/news/the-switch/wp/2018/02/01/google-parent-alphabet-reports-soaring-ad-revenue-despite-youtube-backlash/?utm_term=.524021068936.

Shapira, Harel. 2013. *Waiting for José: The Minutemen's Pursuit of America*. Princeton, NJ: Princeton University Press.

Sharkey, Patrick. 2006. "Navigating Dangerous Streets: The Sources and Consequences of Street Efficacy." *American Sociological Review* 71 (5):826–846.

Sharkey, Patrick. 2013. *Stuck in Place: Urban Neighborhoods and the End of Progress toward Racial Equality*. Chicago: University of Chicago Press.

Sharkey, Patrick. 2018. *Uneasy Peace: The Great Crime Decline, the Renewal of City Life, and the Next War on Violence.* New York: W. W. Norton & Company.

Shedd, Carla. 2015. *Unequal City: Race, Schools, and Perceptions of Injustice.* New York: Russell Sage Foundation.

Shih, Elena. 2016. "Not in My 'Backyard Abolitionism': Vigilante Rescue against American Sex Trafficking." *Sociological Perspectives* 59 (1):66–90.

Silbey, Jessica. 2008. "Cross-Examining Film." *University of Maryland Law Journal of Race, Religion, Gender and Class* 8:17.

Small, Mario Luis. 2004. *Villa Victoria: The Transformation of Social Capital in a Boston Barrio.* Chicago: University of Chicago Press.

Small, Mario L. 2015. "De-Exoticizing Ghetto Poverty: On the Ethics of Representation in Urban Ethnography." *City and Community* 14 (4):352–358.

Smith, Dakota. 2017. "Teen Accused of Murder Is Taken out of School." *Los Angeles Times*, November 14.

Snow, David A., and Leon Anderson. 1987. "Identity Work among the Homeless: The Verbal Construction and Avowal of Personal Identities." *American Journal of Sociology* 92 (6):1336–1371.

Sorensen, Juliet, Gary Alan Fine, Colin Jerolmack, Peter Moskos, and Robert L Nelson. 2017. "Ethnography, Ethics and Law." *Northwestern Journal of Law and Social Policy* 13:165.

Stack, Carol B. 1974. *All Our Kin: Strategies for Survival in a Black Community.* New York: Basic Books.

Statista. 2019. "Reported Violent Crime Rate in the United States from 1990 to 2018." *Statista Inc.*, September 27. (Accessed October 10, 2019.) https://www-statista-com.stanford.idm.oclc.org/statistics/191219/reported-violent-crime-rate-in-the-usa-since-1990/.

Steinbrink, Malte. 2012. "'We Did the Slum!'—Urban Poverty Tourism in Historical Perspective." *Tourism Geographies* 14 (2):213–234.

Stuart, Forrest. 2011. "Constructing Police Abuse after Rodney King: How Skid Row Residents and the Los Angeles Police Department Contest Video Evidence." *Law and Social Inquiry* 36 (2):327–353.

Stuart, Forrest. 2016. *Down, Out, and Under Arrest: Policing and Everyday Life in Skid Row.* Chicago: University of Chicago Press.

Stuart, Forrest, Amada Armenta, and Melissa Osborne. 2015. "Legal Control of Marginal Groups." *Annual Review of Law and Social Science* 11 (1): 235–254.

Stuart, Forrest, and Ava Benezra. 2018. "Criminalized Masculinities: How Policing Shapes the Construction of Gender and Sexuality in Poor Black Communities." *Social Problems* 65 (2):174–190. https://doi.org/10.1093/socpro/spx017.

Suri, Siddharth, and Mary L. Gray. 2016. "Spike in Online Gig Work: Flash in the Pan or Future of Employment?" Data and Society Research Institute. https://points.datasociety.net/spike-in-online-gig-work-c2e316016620.

Sutherland, Edwin H. 1937. "Editorial: The Professional Thief." *Journal of Criminal Law and Criminology* 28 (2):161–163.

Suttles, Gerald D. 1972. *The Social Construction of Communities.* Chicago: University of Chicago Press.

Sweeney, Annie, and Jeremy Gorner. 2018. "Chicago Police Solve One in 20 Shootings: Here Are Some of the Reasons Why That's So Low." *Chicago Tribune*,

August 8. (Retrieved October 8, 2019.) http://chicagotribune.com/news/breaking/ct-met-chicago-violence-clearance-rate-20180807-story.html/.

Taplin, Jonathan. 2017. *Move Fast and Break Things: How Facebook, Google, and Amazon Cornered Culture and Undermined Democracy*. New York: Little, Brown and Company.

Tarm, Michael. 2018. "Gangs Embrace Social Media with Often Deadly Results." *Associated Press*, June 11.

Tarm, Michael. 2019. "Telling Stories of Gang Life, While Risking Their Own." *WBEZ Chicago*, March 4.

Terranova, Tiziana. 2000. "Free Labor: Producing Culture for the Digital Economy." *Social Text* 18 (2):33–58.

Thapar, Ciaran. 2017. "From Chicago to Brixton: The Surprising Rise of UK Drill." *Fact Online*, April 27. https://www.factmag.com/2017/04/27/uk-drill-chicago-brixton/.

Thompson, Paul. 2019. "L.A.'s New Rap Stars Are Targets of the Justice System; They're Also Stylistic Innovators." *Fader Online*, March 19. https://www.thefader.com/2019/03/19/drakeo-the-ruler-bambino-03-greedo-lets-go-essay.

Thrasher, Frederic. 1927. *The Gang: A Study of 1,313 Gangs in Chicago*. Chicago: University of Chicago Press.

Timmermans, Stefan. 2019. "Hypocriticism." *Contemporary Sociology* 48 (3): 264–266.

Tonry, Michael. 2001. "Symbol, Substance, and Severity in Western Penal Policies." *Punishment and Society* 3 (4):517–536.

Towns, Armond R. 2017. "The 'Lumpenproletariat's Redemption': Black Radical Potentiality and LA Gang Tours." *Souls* 19 (1):39–58.

Trouille, David, and Iddo Tavory. 2016. "Shadowing: Warrants for Intersituational Variation in Ethnography." *Sociological Methods and Research* 48 (3):534–560. doi:10.1177/0049124115626171.

Tufekci, Zeynep. 2013. "'Not This One': Social Movements, the Attention Economy, and Microcelebrity Networked Activism." *American Behavioral Scientist* 57 (7):848–870.

Tufekci, Zeynep. 2017. *Twitter and Tear Gas: The Power and Fragility of Networked Protest*. New Haven, CT: Yale University Press.

Urbanik, Marta-Marika, and Kevin D. Haggerty. 2018. "'#It's Dangerous': The Online World of Drug Dealers, Rappers and the Street Code." *British Journal of Criminology* 58 (6):1343–1360.

Vargas, Robert. 2016. *Wounded City: Violent Turf Wars in a Chicago Barrio*. New York: Oxford University Press.

Vargas, Robert. 2019. "Gangstering Grants: Bringing Power to Collective Efficacy Theory." *City and Community* 18 (1):369–391.

Venkatesh, Sudhir Alladi. 1997. "The Social Organization of Street Gang Activity in an Urban Ghetto." *American Journal of Sociology* 103 (1):82–111.

Venkatesh, Sudhir Alladi. 2000. *American Project: The Rise and Fall of a Modern Ghetto*. Cambridge, MA: Harvard University Press.

Venkatesh, Sudhir Alladi. 2005. "Community Justice and the Gang: A Life Course Perspective." Working Paper.

Venkatesh, Sudhir Alladi. 2006. *Off the Books: The Underground Economy of the Urban Poor*. Cambridge, MA: Harvard University Press.

Venkatesh, Sudhir Alladi, and Steven D. Levitt. 2000. "'Are We a Family or a Business?': History and Disjuncture in the Urban American Street Gang." *Theory and Society* 29 (4): 427–462.

Vice. 2017. "La Vie Est Trill: A Guide to the French Rap Scene." *Vice Online*, January 23. https://www.vice.com/en_us/article/mggvwp/la-vie-est-trill-a-guide-to-the-french-hip-hop-scene.

Wacquant, Loïc. 2002. "Scrutinizing the Street: Poverty, Morality, and the Pitfalls of Urban Ethnography." *American Journal of Sociology* 107 (6):1468–1532.

Wacquant, Loïc. 2008. *Urban Outcasts: A Comparative Sociology of Advanced Marginality.* Cambridge: Polity Press.

Wacquant, Loïc, and William Julius Wilson. 1989. "The Cost of Racial and Class Exclusion in the Inner City." *Annals of the American Academy of Political and Social Science* 501 (1):8–25.

Weill, Kelly. 2018. "How YouTube Built a Radicalization Machine for the Far Right." *Daily Beast*, December 19. https://www.thedailybeast.com/how-youtube-pulled-these-men-down-a-vortex-of-far-right-hate?ref=scroll.

Wellman, Barry. 1979. "The Community Question: The Intimate Networks of East Yorkers." *American Journal of Sociology* 84 (5):1201–1231.

Wellman, Barry, and Barry Leighton. 1979. "Networks, Neighborhoods, and Communities: Approaches to the Study of the Community Question." *Urban Affairs Quarterly* 14 (3):363–390.

Western, Bruce. 2006. *Punishment and Inequality in America.* New York: Russell Sage Foundation.

Wherry, Fredrick F. 2008. *Global Markets and Local Crafts: Thailand and Costa Rica Compared.* Baltimore: Johns Hopkins University Press.

Wherry, Fredrick F. 2011. *The Philadelphia Barrio: The Arts, Branding, and Neighborhood Transformation.* Chicago: University of Chicago Press.

Willis, Paul E. 1981. *Learning to Labor: How Working Class Kids Get Working Class Jobs.* New York: Columbia University Press.

Willis, Paul E. 2014. *Profane Culture.* Princeton, NJ: Princeton University Press.

Wilson, William Julius. 1987. *The Truly Disadvantaged: The Inner City, the Underclass, and Public Policy.* Chicago: University of Chicago Press.

Wilson, William Julius. 1996. *When Work Disappears: The New World of the Urban Poor.* New York: Vintage.

Wolch, Jennifer R., and Michael J. Dear. 1993. *Malign Neglect: Homelessness in an American City.* San Francisco: Jossey-Bass.

Wolf, Christine T. 2016. "DIY Videos on YouTube: Identity and Possibility in the Age of Algorithms." *First Monday* 21 (6). https://firstmonday.org/ojs/index.php/fm/article/view/6787/5517.

Zerva, Konstantina. 2015. "Visiting Authenticity on Los Angeles Gang Tours: Tourists Backstage." *Tourism Management* 46:514–527.

Zimring, Franklin E. 2008. *The Great American Crime Decline.* New York: Oxford University Press.

Zussman, Robert. 2004. "People in Places." *Qualitative Sociology* 27 (4):351–363.

Index

■ ■ ■